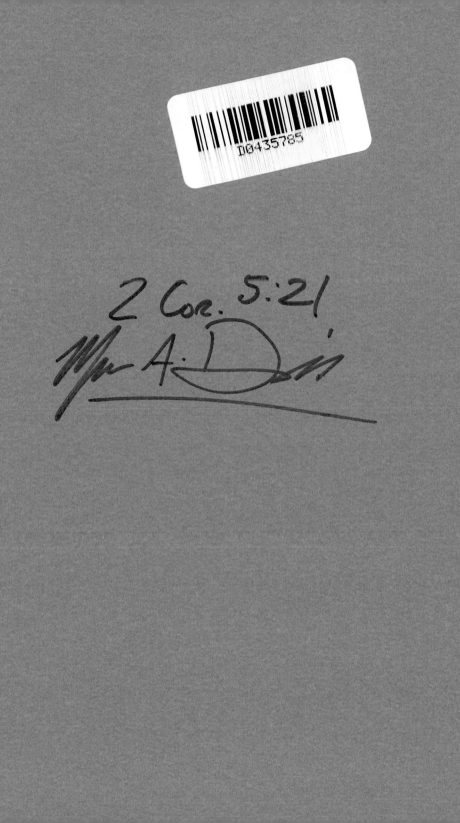

2 Cor. 5:21,

"This new book by Driscoll, one of the most promising young pastors I've met, and his theological partner Gerry Breshears, tell the old, old story in a contemporary, exciting, in-your-face manner. Though written to appeal to today's younger seekers, nothing of classic Christian theology is omitted. Those of my generation may bridle at some aspects of the book—but it's good if we do. This book is just what's needed for us to understand how to reach the postmoderns and a great tool to help all of us connect with young seekers. This is both bold and uncompromising. I can highly recommend it."
—CHUCK COLSON, founder, Prison Fellowship

"This book reveals Mark Driscoll as a highly powerful, colorful, down-to-earth catechist, targeting teens and twenty-somethings with the old, old story told in modern street-cred style. And Professor Breshears ballasts a sometimes lurid but consistently vivid presentation of basic truth about the Lord Jesus Christ."
—J. I. PACKER, Board of Governors' professor of theology, Regent College

"Mark and Gerry have packaged many of the deepest and sometimes hard-to-grasp theological truths about Jesus into an insightful (and at times, laugh-out-loud) book that brings the reader into close contact with the Jesus of both history and the Bible."
—LARRY OSBORNE, author; pastor, North Coast Church, Vista, California

"Mark Driscoll and Gerry Breshears combine profound understanding of modern culture with weighty Christian doctrine that is faithful to the Bible, and it's written in such an interesting style that it's hard to put down. I strongly recommend it!"
—WAYNE GRUDEM, author, *Systematic Theology*; research professor of
Bible and theology, Phoenix Seminary, Phoenix, Arizona

"*Vintage Jesus* offers a fresh, engaging, and insightful discussion of some of the oldest and most crucial truths about Jesus Christ that constitute the very core of the gospel itself. As I read, my heart leapt for joy for the wonder and brilliance of the truths being developed and also because Driscoll and Breshears uphold cherished realities that others in our day, sadly, despise and discard. If you think that you already know Jesus, think again. This book will open the eyes of many who have yet to see the radical nature of Jesus' life and teaching. For the spread of the gospel and the advancement of the kingdom, I can only hope many will read this book and embrace Jesus as the true Lord, God, Savior, and King that he is."
—BRUCE A. WARE, professor of Christian theology,
The Southern Baptist Theological Seminary

"In *Vintage Jesus,* Mark Driscoll and Gerry Breshears make biblical Christology accessible to readers of all ages and backgrounds, particularly those of the millennial generation, to which Driscoll also ministers effectively at Mars Hill Church in Seattle. The authors write with convictions, clarity, and humor, making effective use of cultural references and personal anecdotes to demonstrate the contemporary relevance of these timeless truths."
—ELLIOT MILLER, editor-in-chief, *Christian Research Journal*

"This is a great book about Jesus—yesterday, today, and forever relevant. The answers provided are right on and meaningful to everyone."
—ALLEN R. WEISS, president, Worldwide Operations Walt Disney Parks
and Resorts; chairman, Vision 360

"For thousands of years the debate about Jesus Christ has raged on. In recent times, the fire from this debate has grown hotter than ever. But in *Vintage Jesus,* Mark Driscoll and Gerry Breshears tear down the walls of doubt about who Jesus was. They lay a foundation of understanding about what he did. And they provide direction for what it all means to us today. By covering everything from who Jesus said he was to what will happen when he returns, Mark and Gerry direct the reader on a journey to the truth about the most influential and transcendent person ever to walk the earth—Jesus Christ."
>—ED YOUNG, senior pastor, Fellowship Church;
>author, *Outrageous, Contagious Joy*

"In a society where the Nicene Creed doesn't hold as much water as a tall Americano, Mark Driscoll and Gerry Breshears take an unabashed stance on biblical theology that comes as a refreshing yet timeless hyssop in response to a Christian sociological breakdown of truths. *Vintage Jesus* is the blueprint to a firm foundation for all Protestants, both young and old."
>—BRANDON EBEL, president, Tooth & Nail Records

"Vintage Jesus is engaging, hilarious, thoughtful, and an accurate portrayal of the authentic Jesus. Thanks to Driscoll and Breshears for introducing a new generation to the one who is King of Kings and Lord of Lords."
>—JOHN NEUFELD, senior pastor, Willingdon Church, Burnaby, B.C., Canada

"This is Driscoll's best and most important work so far. If you're hungry to know the Jesus of the Bible, *Vintage Jesus* can revolutionize your life. It speaks to today's generation with a prophetic sense of urgency. Get to know Jesus, now. Worship him, now. Follow him, now. Become his, now."
>—CRAIG GROESCHEL, senior pastor, LifeChurch.tv

"Wow! This is a powerful book. It's edgy, and, frankly, it made me uncomfortable at certain points . . . but for the right reasons. *Vintage Jesus* makes you realize that Jesus led an unvarnished life. Mark Driscoll and Gerry Breshears make sure that we understand that. We need light, not polish, over the story of Jesus, and that's exactly what this well-written and provocative work provides. It may make you squirm, but the strong biblical orientation and the crisp historic perspectives give you a context for that squirming! Like I said . . . wow!"
>—DAN WOLGEMUTH, president, Youth for Christ/USA, Inc.

"This book presents an honest view of Jesus without giving in to the pressure to soften him up. I had to grapple with the real vintage Jesus. This is a Savior worth fighting for."
>—MATT LINDLAND, 2000 Olympic silver medalist in wrestling;
>top-ranked middleweight mixed martial arts fighter

VIN†AGE JESUS

TIMELESS ANSWERS *to* TIMELY QUESTIONS

MARK DRISCOLL
& GERRY BRESHEARS

CROSSWAY BOOKS
WHEATON, ILLINOIS

Vintage Jesus: Timeless Answers to Timely Questions

Copyright © 2007 by Mark Driscoll and Gerry Breshears

Published by Crossway Books
    a publishing ministry of Good News Publishers
    1300 Crescent Street
    Wheaton, Illinois 60187

Art direction: Invisible Creature, Inc.

Design: Don Clark for Invisible Creature, Inc.

Photograph: Jerad Knudson

First printing 2008

Printed in the United States of America

Library of Congress Cataloging-in-Publication Data
Driscoll, Mark, 1970–
    Vintage Jesus : timeless answers to timely questions / Mark
Driscoll and Gerry Breshears.
        p. cm. (ReLit theology series)
    Includes index.
    ISBN 978-1-58134-975-7 (hc)
    1. Jesus Christ—Person and offices—Miscellanea. I. Breshears, Gerry,
1947–   . II. Title. III. Series.
BT203.D75   2007
232—dc22   2007032349

LB		18	17	16	15	14	13	12	11	10	09
15	14	13	12	11	10	9	8	7	6	5	4	3

*This book is dedicated to
anyone who takes Jesus seriously,
but not themselves.*

contents

Preface 9

1   Is Jesus the Only God? 11

2   How Human Was Jesus? 31

3   How Did People Know Jesus Was Coming? 55

4   Why Did Jesus Come to Earth? 73

5   Why Did Jesus' Mom Need to Be a Virgin? 89

6   What Did Jesus Accomplish on the Cross? 107

7   Did Jesus Rise from Death? 127

8   Where Is Jesus Today? 147

9   Why Should We Worship Jesus? 163

10   What Makes Jesus Superior to Other Saviors? 181

11   What Difference Has Jesus Made in History? 199

12   What Will Jesus Do upon His Return? 215

Notes 235

Subject Index 248

Scripture Index 250

PReFace

Resurgence Literature (Re:Lit) is a ministry of Resurgence (www.theresurgence.com). There you will find a growing repository of free theological resources, including audio and video downloads of the sermons on which this series is based, along with information on forthcoming conferences we host. The elders of Mars Hill Church (www.marshillchurch.org) have generously agreed to fund Resurgence along with the Acts 29 Church Planting Network (www.acts29network.org) so that our culture can be filled with a resurgence of timeless Christian truth that is expressed and embodied in timely cultural ways.

This book is a collaborative project between friends. As a young pastor, I desired to be as competent a Bible preacher as possible. This led to a close friendship with my professor Dr. Gerry Breshears, whose biblical insights have been invaluable to my understanding of the person and work of Jesus as revealed in Scripture. In the chapters of this book you will hear my voice since I crafted the words onto pages, but many of the concepts were shaped and formed by my good friend. I sent the manuscript to him for his insights and suggestions, and he also wrote the answers to common questions found at the end of each chapter. The many footnotes are provided by my incredibly helpful researcher, deacon Crystal Griffin. Our hope is that this book will be readable, practical, and biblical so that everyone from seminary professors and pastors to non-Christians would benefit from our work.

We also hope that this book will lead to many profitable discussions between you and your friends so that your friendships can grow around the person and work of Jesus as ours has through the discussions that led to this book. In addition, we intentionally introduce a number of

Christian doctrines in this book and thereby raise numerous questions about related theological issues (such as Scripture, the cross, the character of God, heaven and hell, and the church). Our friends at Crossway have kindly agreed to publish this book as the first in a series called *Vintage Jesus* that will build on the themes and doctrines introduced in this book.

CHAPTER ONE

IS JESUS THE ONLY GOD?

"You, being a man, make yourself God."

JESUS' ENEMIES (JOHN 10:33)

✝

Jesus Christ. No one is more loved and hated than Jesus Christ.

The name *Jesus* is derived from the Old Testament name *Joshua*, which means, "Yahweh God is salvation." The title *Christ* means one chosen and anointed by God to be the Messiah who delivers God's people.

Roughly two thousand years ago, Jesus was born in a dumpy, rural, hick town, not unlike those today where guys change their own oil, think pro wrestling is real, find women who chew tobacco sexy, and eat a lot of Hot Pockets with their uncle-daddy. Jesus' mom was a poor, unwed teenage girl who was mocked for claiming she conceived via the Holy Spirit. Most people thought she concocted a crazy story to cover the "fact" she was knocking boots with some guy in the backseat of a car at the prom. Jesus was adopted by a simple carpenter named Joseph and spent the first thirty years of his life in obscurity, swinging a hammer with his dad.

Around the age of thirty, Jesus began a public ministry that included preaching, healing the sick, feeding the hungry, and befriending social misfits such as perverts, drunks, and thieves. Jesus' ministry spanned only three short years before he was put to death for declaring himself to be God. He died by shameful crucifixion like tens of thousands of people before and after him.

At first glance, Jesus' résumé is rather simple. He never traveled more than a few hundred miles from his home. He never held a political office, never wrote a book, never married, never had sex, never attended college, never visited a big city, and never won a poker tournament. He died both homeless and poor.

Nonetheless, Jesus is the most famous person in all of human history. More songs have been sung to him, artwork created of him, and books written about him than anyone who has ever lived. In fact, Jesus looms so large over human history that we actually measure time by him; our calendar is divided into the years before and after his birth, noted as B.C. ("before Christ") and A.D. (*anno Domini*, meaning "in the year of the Lord"), respectively.

No army, nation, or person has changed human history to the degree that Jesus, the homeless man, has. Some two thousand years after he walked the earth, Jesus remains as hot as ever. In fact, as Paul promised in 2 Corinthians 11:3–4, the opinions about Jesus are countless in seemingly every area of culture.

JESUS OF POP CULTURE

On television, Jesus often appears on the long-running animation hits *The Simpsons* and *South Park*. Jesus also appears in the comedic sketches of vulgar comic Carlos Mencia's hit show *Mind of Mencia*, which explores everything from what it would have been like for Jesus to be married to his involvement in a royal religious wrestling rumble with the founders of other major world religions. Dog the Bounty Hunter, the famous Christian bail bondsman, prays to Jesus on almost every episode of his hit television show, gathering his wife in her clear heels and the rest of their chain-smoking, mace-shooting, criminal-pursuing, mullet-wearing posse to ask Jesus to bless each manhunt.

In the world of fashion, Jesus appears on numerous T-shirts, including the popular "Jesus is my homeboy" shirt, worn by everyone from Madonna to Ashton Kutcher, Ben Affleck, Brad Pitt, and Pamela Anderson.

Roughly one hundred films have been made about Jesus, including top-grossing movies like *The Passion of the Christ* and *The Da Vinci Code*, along with the bizarre Canadian kungfu/horror/musical/comedy *Jesus*

Christ Vampire Hunter (which pairs Jesus with Mexican wrestling hero El Santos to battle an army of vampires that can walk in the daylight). In the film *Talladega Nights: The Ballad of Ricky Bobby*, comedian Will Ferrell (as Ricky Bobby) prays to an "8-pound, 6-ounce, newborn infant Jesus" in "golden, fleece diapers."

There are even Jesus wrestling federations, such as Wrestling for Jesus, Ultimate Christian Wrestling, and The Christian Wrestling Foundation, with wrestlers named Zion and Satan and sponsors like auto parts stores and a tattoo parlor dedicated to redneck outreach. Jesus even appears on a 110-foot, 750-pound hot-air balloon, a monster truck, and innumerable tattoos. In the world of poker, Phil Gordon said, "Even Jesus wouldn't bet all of his chips on a Jack-three!"[1]

Musically, everyone from rapper Kanye West to rockers The Killers, punk rockers Green Day, American Idol country-crooner Carrie Underwood, and the world's top band, U2, are singing about Jesus. The Beatles' frontman John Lennon even once said, "We're more popular than Jesus now."

Even homosexuals have their own spin on Jesus. The homepage for the pro-gay Metropolitan Community Churches is www.Jesus.com. The portrayal of Jesus as a gay man also appears in the book *Jesus Acted Up* by Robert Goss and in the play *Corpus Christi* by Terrence McNally.

In the world of sports, it seems every time someone scores a touchdown, hits a shot at the buzzer, throws a no-hitter, or knocks someone out, they thank their Lord and Savior Jesus Christ, also affectionately referred to as "my Coach" and "The Big Guy Upstairs." Gigi Becali, owner of the Romanian soccer club Steaua, reportedly even commissioned a copy of da Vinci's *Last Supper* portrait, with himself as Jesus Christ.[2] It also seems that Jesus is a real baseball fan—there are twelve major league and sixty-two minor league baseball players with the name "Jesus" somewhere in their name.

Jesus is now even on the radio hosting a call-in show. The bald-headed, tattooed, thirty-seven-year-old Neil Saavedra pretends to be Jesus Christ on his Sunday morning *The Jesus Christ Show*.[3] The hit program is an exploration of what it would be like if Jesus lived in Los Angeles and hosted his own call-in advice show.

JESUS OF THE CULTS

It is fascinating how some people will boldly claim that all religions essentially teach the same thing. However, when it comes to Jesus, the cults and world religions in no way teach the same thing.

Liberal "Christians" and some of their Emergent offspring say Jesus was merely a good man, but they are not clear about his being the God-man. Jehovah's Witnesses say that Jesus was merely Michael the archangel, a created being that became a man.[4] Mormonism teaches that Jesus was not God but only a man who became one of many gods; it furthermore teaches that he was a polygamist and a half-brother of Lucifer. Unitarian Universalism teaches that Jesus was not God but rather essentially an incarnation of Mister Rogers, a great man to be respected solely for his teaching, love, justice, and healing. New Age guru Deepak Chopra told Larry King, "I see Christ as a state of consciousness we can all aspire to."[5] According to Scientology, Jesus is an "implant" forced upon a Thetan about a million years ago. I would explain that position more thoroughly but I have never smoked weed or done any drugs; subsequently, I apparently lack the imagination to understand a religion started by a science fiction writer that has unleashed Tom Crazy Cruise on the world as Billy Graham's evil *doppelgänger*. There is even a Canadian nudist-arsonist cult that thinks that the word "Jesus" in the Bible is a code word for hallucinogenic mushrooms that are to be eaten before getting naked and lighting things on fire.

JESUS OF THE OCCULT

Freemasonry, or the Masons, includes fourteen United States presidents, eighteen vice presidents, and five Supreme Court chief justices. Masonic lodge meetings include the reading of Scripture, but intentionally omit the name "Jesus."[6] Levi Dowling said Jesus underwent seven degrees of initiation (an occultic ceremony) in Egypt with the seventh degree making him the Christ.[7] Edgar Cayce said Jesus only became the Christ in his thirtieth incarnation after shedding his bad karma.[8]

JESUS OF THE RELIGIONS

Bahá'ís say that Jesus was a manifestation of God and a prophet but inferior to Muhammad and Bahá'u'lláh. Buddhism teaches that

Jesus was not God but rather an enlightened man like the Buddha. Hinduism, with its many views of Jesus, does not consider him to be the only God, but most likely a wise man or incarnation of God much like Krishna. Islam teaches that Jesus was merely a man and a prophet who is inferior to Muhammad. Speaking at an event hosted by the Muslim Student Association at the University of North Texas, Council on American-Islamic Relations vice president Eric Meek told students, "If Jesus were here, he'd be a Muslim."[9] The Dalai Lama said, "[Jesus] was either a fully enlightened being, or a *bodhisvatta* [a being who aids others to enlightenment] of a very high spiritual realization."[10] Indian Hindu leader Mahatma Gandhi said, "I cannot ascribe exclusive divinity to Jesus. He is as divine as Krishna or Rama or Muhammad or Zoroaster."[11]

JESUS OF THE FAMOUS AND INFAMOUS

The famous and infamous also have much to say about Jesus, including:

- President Thomas Jefferson: "Jesus did not mean to impose himself on mankind as the son of God ..."
- Prince Philip: "[Jesus] might be described as an underprivileged, working-class victim of political and religious persecution."
- Fidel Castro: "I never saw a contradiction between the ideas that sustain me and the ideas of that symbol, of that extraordinary figure [Jesus Christ]."
- Mikhail Gorbachev: "Jesus was the first socialist, the first to seek a better life for mankind."
- Malcolm X told *Playboy*: "Christ wasn't white. Christ was black. The poor, brainwashed Negro has been made to believe Christ was white to maneuver him into worshiping white men. . . . A white Jesus. A white Virgin. White angels. White everything. But a black Devil, of course."
- Martin Luther King Jr.: "Jesus Christ was an extremist for love, truth and goodness."
- Rollo May (American existential psychologist): "Christ is the therapist for all humanity."
- Lakota Native American tribe: Jesus is "the buffalo calf of God."

JESUS OF THE DEMONS

One of the more curious aspects of Jesus' earthly ministry is that people were often unable and/or unwilling to see him as God. Jesus used the word "dull" to refer to such people who were as discerning as the guys who drive for miles with their turn signal on. The exception to this rule, shockingly enough, was the demons. While many people said Jesus was demon-possessed and raving mad, the demons were more likely to get it right.[12]

The Gospel of Mark, the shortest gospel, gets right to the point. Jesus stirs up a ruckus when he comes to town. He calls, and tough men follow him. He teaches, and people are astonished. But it's the demons who know: "What have you to do with us, Jesus of Nazareth? Have you come to destroy us? I know who you are—the Holy One of God."[13]

In Mark 1:33–34 we read, "The whole city was gathered together at the door. And he healed many who were sick with various diseases, and cast out many demons. And he would not permit the demons to speak, because they knew him." In Luke 4:33–34 we read, "And in the synagogue there was a man who had the spirit of an unclean demon, and he cried out with a loud voice, 'Ha! What have you to do with us, Jesus of Nazareth? Have you come to destroy us? I know who you are—the Holy One of God.'" Again in Luke 4:40–41 we read, "Now when the sun was setting, all those who had any who were sick with various diseases brought them to him, and he laid his hands on every one of them and healed them. And demons also came out of many, crying, 'You are the Son of God!' But he rebuked them and would not allow them to speak, because they knew that he was the Christ."

Interestingly enough, the demons have some of the highest Christology in the gospels, though they themselves do not love Jesus or receive the gift of salvation from him. The demons even have a higher Christology than most present-day cults and world religions, which is, to say the least, tragic.

JESUS OF JESUS

Who exactly is Jesus? Is he a good man or God, the half-brother of Lucifer or a prophet, liar or truth-teller, therapist or communist, stand-up comic or just my uber-fly, holy homeboy? So much has been said about Jesus that it only seems appropriate to let Jesus speak for himself.

Therefore, we will examine ten ways by which Jesus flatly said he is the only God.

1) JESUS SAID HE CAME DOWN FROM HEAVEN.

On very rare occasions people will claim that they have been taken into heaven through something like a near-death experience (NDE). Examples include Betty Eadie's non-Christian book on the subject, *Embraced by the Light*, which was a bestseller some years back, along with the movie *Flatliners*.

Celebrities who have reported NDEs include Jayne Seymour, Peter Sellers, Elizabeth Taylor, Sharon Stone, Larry Hagman, Gary Busey, Tony Bennett, Burt Reynolds, Chevy Chase, George Lucas, and William Petersen. Ozzy Osborne also claimed to see "a white light shining through the darkness, but no ****ing angels, no one blowing trumpets and no man in a white beard."[14]

Dr. Melvin Morse wrote an entire book on NDEs called *Transformed by the Light*. Perhaps the most bizarre story in the book was about a forty-five-year-old Midwestern teacher who died and went to heaven to see the King—Elvis, not Jesus. Apparently so many people have had an NDE that resulted in their seeing Elvis instead of Jesus ruling over heaven that Raymond Moody has actually written a book about them called *Elvis After Life*.

The Muslim "prophet" Muhammad also claimed that on one occasion he was taken from earth to heaven. The Dome of the Rock standing on the site of the original Jewish temple in Jerusalem memorializing that alleged event is considered the third holiest Muslim monument in the world. It is said that from that place Muhammad ascended through the seven heavens on a strange heavenly beast called a Buraq into the presence of Allah, escorted by the angel Gabriel. There, he was reportedly met by various biblical figures such as Adam and Abraham along with many angels and even Moses with whom he chatted. It is said that during his visit to heaven Muhammad was ordered by Allah to have Muslims pray five times a day.

However, unlike a near-death experience or the purported heavenly glimpse of Muhammad, Jesus made an even more audacious claim. Jesus did not merely claim to have peeked into heaven to see King Elvis or Allah. Instead, Jesus boldly claimed to be God who lived in heaven but came down from his eternal home to visit the earth as a man: "For I have come down from heaven, not to do my own will but the will of him who sent me."[15] His audacious claim got him into trouble with those who heard him: "So the Jews grumbled about him, because he said, 'I am the bread that came down from heaven.' They said, 'Is not this Jesus, the son of Joseph, whose father and mother we know? How does he now say, "I have come down from heaven"?' . . . When many of his disciples heard it, they said, 'This is a hard saying; who can listen to it?' . . . After this many of his disciples turned back and no longer walked with him."[16]

His claim to be God incarnate has never been made by the founder of any other world religion. The closest anyone has come is the assertion by some Hindus that the Buddha is an avatar of Vishnu. But the Buddha himself never made such a claim. Conversely, Jesus clearly stated that he is God. God alone calls heaven his eternal home, and God alone could descend from heaven as opposed to ascending up to heaven.

Finally, the statement that he came down from heaven also indicates Jesus' eternality. Before his birth as a man, he lived with the Father in heaven. No mere human can say this.[17] Jesus also appears upon occasion in the Old Testament in christophanies, which are pre-incarnate cameos. For example, he wrestles with Jacob,[18] is worshiped by Joshua as the Lord of the army of heaven,[19] speaks to Isaiah in the temple,[20] and is the fourth man in the fiery furnace with Daniel and his friends.[21]

2) Jesus Said He Was More Than Just a Good Man.

Over the years I have had the privilege of talking about Jesus to literally thousands of non-Christians in conversations, e-mail correspondence, and radio interviews. Virtually no one I have ever spoken to thought Jesus was God or even a bad person. Instead, most everyone spouted the very common statements that "Jesus was a good man," "Jesus did a lot of nice things for people," and "Jesus never thought he was God but other people made that up about him." Perhaps lesbian Jewish actress Sandra Bernhard's sentiment, "I'm sure that Jesus was an incredible person," best sums up the majority mood.

Thich Nhat Hanh, author of *Living Buddha, Living Christ* and considered by many to be the most respected interpreter of Buddhism to the western world, after the Dalai Lama, said of Jesus, "Of course Christ is unique. But who is not unique? Socrates, Muhammad, the Buddha, you, and I are all unique."[22]

Apparently the idea that Jesus was merely a good guy but not God is nothing new. Mark 10:17–18 says, "And as he was setting out on his journey, a man ran up and knelt before him and asked him, 'Good Teacher, what must I do to inherit eternal life?' And Jesus said to him, 'Why do you call me good? No one is good except God alone.'" This man likely thought he was honoring Jesus by calling him a "good teacher." However, Jesus replied that since everyone is a sinner, there is no such thing as a good person—God is the only good person. In saying this, Jesus was revealing to the man that he was not merely a good person, but in fact God. Even Jesus' enemies were equally clear that Jesus refused to be considered merely a good man. They wanted to kill Jesus because he was "making himself equal with God."[23]

This fact of Jesus' uniqueness as more than just a good spiritual man is incredibly important. Perhaps the legendary Billy Graham said it best: "Jesus was not just another great religious teacher, nor was he only another in a long line of individuals seeking after spiritual truth. He was, instead, truth itself. He was God incarnate."[24]

3) JESUS SAID HE IS THE SON OF MAN.

When picking a title for himself, Jesus was apparently most fond of "Son of Man." He spoke of himself by this term roughly eighty total times among all four gospels. He lifted the title from the prophet Daniel, who penned it some six hundred years before Jesus' birth. In Daniel's vision, the Son of Man comes to the Ancient of Days, the Lord himself. But he comes from the clouds, from heaven, not from the earth. This indicates that he isn't a human. He is given messianic dominion and authority, something no angel can obtain. Only a divine person can receive this. Daniel is speaking of the same person as David speaks of in Psalm 110. The Old Testament sees this divine person sitting alongside the Lord as an equal. This second person of the Trinity was promised to receive the messianic mission to redeem the world, to trounce every enemy, and to rescue the trapped people. As God, he is exalted over all peoples, nations, cultures, and religions to be worshiped as the eternal King. Jesus is the one who claimed he would be the Son of Man coming with the clouds as God.[25]

4) JESUS PERFORMED MIRACLES.

Jesus was a great leader and teacher, but his ministry also included the miraculous—one line of evidence that he was in fact God and more than just another spiritually enlightened person. The acceptance of Jesus' miracles was perhaps most opposed during the modern era when scientific rationalism gave way to naturalism, whereby miracles were deemed philosophically impossible. Subsequently, cults that sprang up during modernity sought to ignore or deny Jesus' miracles. For example, the Unitarian Universalist book *A Chosen Faith* says, "Most of us would agree that the important thing about Jesus is not his supposed miraculous birth or the claim that he was resurrected from death, but rather how he *lived*. The power of his love, the penetrating simplicity of his teachings, and the force of his example of service on behalf of the disenfranchised and downtrodden are what is crucial."[26]

However, Jesus is emphatic that he did perform miracles and that they helped to prove his claims that he is God. In John 10:36b–39 Jesus said, "'Do you say of him whom the Father consecrated and sent into the world, "You are blaspheming," because I said, "I am the Son of God"? If I am not doing the works of my Father, then do not believe me; but if I do them, even though you do not believe me, believe the works, that you may know and understand that the Father is in me and I am in the Father.' Again they sought to arrest him, but he escaped from their hands."

There is ample evidence throughout the New Testament that Jesus performed many miracles. Nearly forty specific miracles are mentioned. In Mark's short Gospel alone, roughly one-third of the verses deal with miracles. Furthermore, even those who opposed Jesus acknowledged that he did perform miracles that needed to be accounted for.[27]

Opponents of Jesus outside of Scripture also testify to his miracles. The Jewish Talmud charged that Jesus "practiced magic."[28] Celsus, a strong opponent of Christianity, later repeated that claim.[29] The noted Jewish historian Josephus also reported that Jesus was "a doer of wonderful works."[30]

While some of the miracles Jesus performed are done by other humans, including driving out demons, healing diseases, and even raising someone from the dead,[31] other miracles are without human precedent. For example, the Gospel writers tell of the disciples, men who were seasoned fishermen, terrified by a raging storm and begging Jesus to rescue them. He rebuked the storm with one powerful command and there was immediately quiet calm. Creation obeyed the command of Jesus. Regarding the disciples, Mark 4:41 says, "They were filled with great fear and said to one another, 'Who then is this, that even the wind and the sea obey him?'" They knew their Bibles well. It is God who stills or raises storms with a word. Only God treats storms like this.[32]

Throughout his life, Jesus performed a great number of miracles; each demonstrated his rule over the physical world. In performing these miracles, we are told that his purpose was to prove he is God so that we would trust in him and receive salvation from him.[33] In this way, the miracles that Jesus performed were in fact signs pointing to his divinity.

5) JESUS SAID HE IS GOD.

Jesus clearly, emphatically, and repeatedly said he is God. If his statements were untrue, it would have been a blasphemous violation of the first commandment. The belief that Jesus is God is not something that Christians made up, but rather something that Christians believe because it was taught by Jesus himself. Many cults wrongly deny that Jesus is God or ever claimed to be God. For example, the Jehovah's Witnesses Watchtower Society says, "Jesus never claimed to be God."[34] Bahá'ís say that Jesus was a manifestation of God and a prophet but inferior to Muhammad and Bahá'u'lláh. Buddhism teaches that Jesus is not God but was rather an enlightened man like the Buddha. Christian Science founder Mary Baker Eddy flatly states, "Jesus Christ is not God."

Some key Scriptures illustrate how Jesus clearly said he is God and his hearers clearly understood his unparalleled claim. Mark 14:61–64 reports, "He remained silent and made no answer. Again the high priest asked him, 'Are you the Christ, the Son of the Blessed?' And Jesus said, 'I am, and you will see the Son of Man seated at the right hand of Power, and coming with the clouds of heaven.' And the high priest tore his garments and said, 'What further witnesses do we need? You have heard his blasphemy. What is your decision?'" John 8:58–59 reports that Jesus said, "'Truly, truly, I say to you, before Abraham was, I am.' So they picked up stones to throw at him, but Jesus hid himself and went out of the temple."

Jesus claimed eternality in saying that he existed before Abraham, who lived roughly two thousand years prior. Furthermore, in naming himself "I am," Jesus was declaring himself to be the same God who revealed himself by the title "I am" some fourteen hundred years prior when he spoke to Moses through the burning bush. As a result, those who heard Jesus rightly understood him as declaring himself to be the eternal God who saved Abraham and called Moses. Consequently, they called him a blasphemer for being a man who claimed to be God and sought to impose the death penalty on him for it.

In John 10:30–33 Jesus also said, "I and the Father are one." Then, "The Jews picked up stones again to stone him. Jesus answered them, 'I have shown you many good works from the Father; for which of them are you going to stone me?' The Jews answered him, 'It is not for a good work that we are going to stone you but for blasphemy, because you, being a man, make yourself God.'"

On this point, New York's Judge Gaynor once said of Jesus' trial at the end of his earthly life, "It is plain from each of the gospel narratives, that the alleged crime for which Jesus was tried and convicted was blasphemy."[35]

Throughout the history of the world, numerous people have claimed to speak for God. Yet there is a surprisingly short list of people who have actually claimed to be God. For example, such religious leaders as Buddha, Krishna, Muhammad, and Gandhi did not claim to be God. In fact, they assured their followers that they were not God. Jesus, in contrast, clearly and repeatedly said he is God. This is simply an astonishing claim that people kept seeking to kill Jesus for saying, because it would clearly be blasphemy if untrue. After all, could you even imagine someone walking up to you at a party wearing a nametag that simply said "God"? Nonetheless, Jesus repeatedly said he is God. He was not killed for his nice deeds or pithy parables, but for claiming to be God.

Today this claim is as controversial as ever. For example, while I was preaching the sermon on which this chapter is based, a man attending one of our evening services pulled out a machete and tried to get onto the stage, apparently to run me through for saying that Jesus alone is

God. He was screaming that Jesus is not God, until tackled and taken away from the premises by the police.

6) JESUS CONFIRMED TO OTHERS HE IS GOD.

Not only did Jesus repeatedly declare that he is God, but he also reiterated this fact when others doubted or opposed that claim. For example, Matthew 26:63–65 says: "But Jesus remained silent. And the high priest said to him, 'I adjure you by the living God, tell us if you are the Christ, the Son of God.' Jesus said to him, 'You have said so. But I tell you, from now on you will see the Son of Man seated at the right hand of Power and coming on the clouds of heaven.' Then the high priest tore his robes and said, 'He has uttered blasphemy. What further witnesses do we need? You have now heard his blasphemy.'"

As Matthew describes, religious leaders sought to condemn Jesus publicly for committing blasphemy (declaring himself to be God). The penalty for blasphemy was death; if Jesus were not convinced that he was God, then we would expect him to clarify the misunderstanding about himself in an effort to avoid a bloody death. Maybe he was just dyslexic and was only confessing he owned a "dog." But it was no mistake—Jesus declared he is God.

The fact that Jesus did not recant when challenged proves that everyone who has believed that Jesus claimed to be God has not misunderstood his words but has actually understood them clearly. Lastly, the Scriptures testify to additional occasions in which the religious leaders in Jesus' day recognized his claim to be God, for which Jesus never did apologize or recant.[36]

7) JESUS SAID HE WAS SINLESS.

Sin is both omission and commission. Sins of omission are when we fail to do something good, and sins of commission are when we do something wrong. Sin includes our thoughts, motives, words, and deeds, which are all seen objectively by our all-knowing God.

In the history of the world, no one has claimed with any credibility that they are without sin, because to do so is to declare that one's words, actions, thoughts, and motivations are continually perfect and pure. As the old adage goes, no one is perfect. To see if anyone has ever claimed to be sinless, I actually did a Google search for "sinless," only to find that there is a strip club by the same name. That pretty much sums up my point that the world is filled with sin.

Even those religious leaders who are widely commended as the most devout and morally upright (e.g., Mohammad, Gandhi, Mother Teresa, Billy Graham) have admitted that they are indeed sinners. As we read the Gospel accounts of Jesus' life, we often see him calling others to repent. We also see Jesus being tempted to sin.[37] Nevertheless, nowhere does Jesus sin or repent of any personal sin, because he was without sin. Jesus' enemies sought to bring up false charges of sin against Jesus, but their lies never agreed with one another and were found to be groundless.[38]

Tragically, some people do not believe that Jesus is sinless and therefore morally superior to everyone else. Fully 41 percent of adults believe that Jesus sinned when he was on the earth. Additionally, 43 percent of Hispanics, 43 percent of whites, and 32 percent of blacks agree with the statement "when He lived on earth, Jesus Christ was human and committed sins, like other people."[39] Even 40 percent of teenagers who claim to be born again and 52 percent of teenagers who attend a Protestant church likewise wrongly believe that Jesus committed sins like other people while on the earth.[40]

However, Jesus declared that he was not only morally superior to everyone who has ever lived, but in fact sinless. He further challenged anyone to prove him wrong: "Which one of you convicts me of sin? If I tell the truth, why do you not believe me?"[41]

The perfect, sinless life of Jesus makes him admittedly more holy and worthy of our devotion than anyone who has ever lived and helps to prove that he was and is God because God alone is without sin. This claim is unparalleled in history and is repeated by Jesus' disciples throughout the New Testament, most of whom suffered and died without recanting. Those who testify to the sinlessness of Jesus are those who knew him most intimately, such as his friends Peter[42] and John,[43] his brother James,[44] and even his former enemy Paul.[45] Additionally, even Judas who betrayed Jesus admitted that Jesus was without sin,[46] along with the ruler Pilate who oversaw the murder of Jesus,[47] a soldier who participated in the murder of Jesus,[48] and the guilty sinner who was crucified at Jesus' side.[49]

8) JESUS FORGAVE SIN.

While many of the resources in our world are spent on dealing with the effects of sin (e.g., war, illness, death, depression, crime, poverty), there is still no way for people to have their sins forgiven. At best, some religions try to teach their adherents what they can do to work hard at paying God back through such things as good works and reincarnation; they still lack any concept of forgiveness.

In light of this, Jesus' claims to forgive sin are simply astonishing. Speaking to a sinful but repentant woman in Luke 7:48 it is reported, "And [Jesus] said to her, 'Your sins are forgiven.'" Luke 5:20–21 also says, "And when [Jesus] saw their faith, he said, 'Man, your sins are forgiven you.' And the scribes and the Pharisees began to question, saying, 'Who is this who speaks blasphemies? Who can forgive sins but God alone?'"

Can you even imagine someone saying that he is God and has the authority to forgive your sin? Sin is the human problem. All sin is ultimately committed against God.[50] Subsequently, God alone has the power to forgive the sins of sinners.[51] Jesus could only forgive sin because he was and is God. In making this claim, Jesus is inviting us to confess our sins to him so that we may be forgiven through his substitutionary death and bodily resurrection. If he were not God, our sin simply could not be forgiven by him.

9) JESUS TAUGHT PEOPLE TO PRAY TO HIM AS GOD.

Prayer is how we mere mortals talk to God. But Jesus Christ actually told us to pray to him, and he did so repeatedly.[52] By doing so, Jesus was clearly stating that he is God. As a result of his teaching, both men like Stephen[53] and women like the Canaanite[54] did pray to Jesus as God. In Acts 7:59, we read that at the moment of his painful death by stoning, the early church deacon Stephen prayed, "Lord Jesus, receive my spirit." Many people throughout history and a few billion worshipers of Jesus on the earth today have, like Stephen, cried out to Jesus in prayer at their moments of most desperate need. If Jesus is not God who does not live forever and is not all-knowing or powerful enough to answer our prayers, then he is nothing more than a cruel sadist for asking us to pray to him in faith.

10) JESUS SAID HE IS THE ONLY WAY TO HEAVEN.

Not only did Jesus declare that he came down from heaven, but he also taught that he alone is the only way for anyone else to enter into heaven. While there are many religious and spiritual teachers who claim that they can point you to the path to heaven, they do not claim to be that path themselves. Jesus, in contrast, promised that he was the way to eternal life in heaven, saying in John 14:6, "I am the way, and the truth, and the life. No one comes to the Father except through me."

Jesus' words further prove that he was and is God. Because heaven belongs to God, it is God alone who determines who is granted access to it and who will live with him forever there. Some will protest that other religions provide additional paths to heaven, but Jesus debunked those myths by declaring that he alone is the sole, narrow path to eternal life and that all other paths are merely paths to eternal death in hell.[55] Sadly, in our day there are even pastors and Christian leaders who lack the courage to simply say what Jesus said and declare him to be the only way to heaven. For example, one female bishop for the Episcopalian church was asked by *Time* magazine, "Is belief in Jesus the only way to get to heaven?" Sadly, instead of using the opportunity to let Jesus speak for himself, she instead contradicted Jesus, saying, "We who practice the Christian tradition understand him as our vehicle to the divine. But for us to assume that God could not act in other ways is, I think, to put God in an awfully small box."[56]

The question remains to be answered, how should we respond to the incredible person, work, and claims of Jesus? We are left with only three possible responses: Jesus was a lunatic, Jesus was a liar, or Jesus is Lord. British author C. S. Lewis (1898–1963) wisely said:

> A man who was merely a man and said the sort of things Jesus said would not be a great moral teacher. He would either be a lunatic—on the level with the man who says he is a poached egg—or else he would be the Devil of Hell. You must make your choice. Either this man was, and is, the Son of God; or else a madman or something worse. You can shut Him up for a fool, you can spit at Him and kill Him as a demon; or you can fall at His feet and call Him Lord and God. But let us not come with any patronizing nonsense about His being a great human teacher. He has not left that open to us. He did not intend to.[57]

Liar?

Indeed, if untrue, Jesus' claims to be God would make him an evil cult leader much like David Koresh, who had a lengthy, televised standoff in 1993 with the Bureau of Alcohol, Tobacco and Firearms (BATF) and the FBI. Upwards of eighty-five of his followers died in their Waco compound, including approximately twenty-five children. Only nine members of the cult survived. Koresh proclaimed himself the "Son of God" and said he and not Jesus was the Lamb of Revelation.[58] Koresh was quoted as once saying, "Do you know who I am? God in the flesh ... stand in awe and know that I am God."[59] Simply, if Jesus is not God but claimed to be God and deceived others into dying for that claim, he is nothing more than a lying, demonized cult leader.

Lunatic?

While it is difficult to find anyone who claims to be God, I was able to find one guy on MySpace.com whose mom apparently told him he can become anything he wants if he just puts his mind to it and works hard. So he is hoping to become God at some point. But, it does not seem his quest for godhood will be achieved as he only has a few friends linked to his page. Why? Because he's nuttier than a Snickers bar, and if Jesus said he is God when in fact he were not, he would be a nut job, too.

Lord?

Jesus is not a liar or a lunatic, but rather God our Lord. Therefore, the appropriate response to Jesus is turning from sin to worship him alone as God. According to the first two commandments,[60] there is only one God, and that God alone is to be worshiped. The one God to be worshiped is Jesus.

In Scripture we see that Jesus is worshiped as the only God by the blind man,[61] the previously demonized man,[62] Thomas the doubter,[63] his best friend John,[64] all of the disciples,[65] a group of women,[66] the mother of James and John,[67] angels,[68] entire churches,[69] his own mother,[70] his own brothers,[71] little children,[72] and his former enemies like Paul.[73]

Having surveyed both what is said about Jesus by others and by Jesus himself, his own question to us is a fitting conclusion to this chapter: "Who do you say that I am?"[74]

ANSWERS TO COMMON QUESTIONS ABOUT JESUS' DIVINITY

DOES THE BIBLE CLEARLY SAY THAT JESUS IS GOD?

Yes, the Bible repeatedly and clearly declares that Jesus is God.[75]

Another way that the Bible speaks of Jesus as God is by applying to Jesus, in the New Testament, titles that are used of God in the Old Testament. Examples include:

- First and Last[76]
- Light[77]
- Rock[78]
- Husband or Bridegroom[79]
- Shepherd[80]
- Redeemer[81]
- Savior[82]
- Lord of Glory[83]

ISN'T JESUS REALLY AN ANGEL?

The Jehovah's Witnesses say that Jesus was not the creator God, but rather Michael the created archangel who became a man.[84] Speaking of Jesus, however, John 1:1 teaches that in the beginning (a reference to Genesis 1:1 when all created things were created), the Word was already in continuing existence. He was in face-to-face, personal relation with God when space-time, mass-energy, and the laws of nature were created. John 1:3 then tells us that the Word created all things. Paul says the same thing in Colossians 1:16–17. Throughout the Bible, it is clear that God is the one who creates. Passages like Isaiah 44:24 and Job 9:8 are very specific that it is only God who creates. So if the Word creates, as John says, he has to be God. He can't be anything less without violating foundational teachings of Scripture.

In the final phrase of John 1:1, it says "the Word was God." Now, a predicate nominative (noun + "linking verb" + noun) means the two nouns share characteristics. For example, when someone says, "The guy is a stud," it means he has studly characteristics. Likewise, when Scripture says "the Word was God," it means that the Word shares the same characteristics of God himself. Jehovah's Witnesses wrongly translate that phrase as "the Word was a god." But if this were correct, the Word would be one of several gods, something no Jew would ever say. Further, the Jehovah's Witnesses themselves do not believe that either. Simply, Jesus Christ the Word is God the Creator, not a created angel.

SINCE THE BIBLE SAYS GOD CANNOT DIE, YET JESUS DIED, DOES THAT NOT PROVE THAT JESUS CANNOT BE GOD?

It's true that God is immortal, which is simply a way of saying that he cannot die. Verses like 1 Timothy 1:17 say this plainly. It's equally clear that Jesus really died. That does not mean his existence ended. Rather it means his body and spirit were separated, just as ours are upon our death.

On this point, Philippians 2:6 says that before Jesus entered human history as a man, Christ had equality with God in every possible way. But he didn't think that was something to hang on to. Instead he emptied himself of that equality in humility to come "in the likeness of men."[85] Hebrews 2:17 says the same thing: "He had to be made like his brothers in every respect, so that he might become a merciful and faithful high priest in the service of God, to make propitiation for the sins of the people."

In conclusion, to identify with us and substitute himself for us, Jesus Christ humbled himself by becoming a human being to die like us so that we could have our sins forgiven. In this, Jesus remained God. Rather than refuting Jesus' divinity, his death reveals to us the love of God.

HOW COULD JESUS SAY "THE FATHER IS GREATER THAN I" (JOHN 14:28) IF HE IS IN FACT GOD?

Jesus absolutely did say that God the Father was greater than him. There will be no dodging what the Bible says by appealing to "textual corruption" or "later addition." Various critics of the Bible may do such a thing, but as followers of Jesus we must believe what God has spoken to us through his Word.

In saying this, Jesus was reminding the disciples that he was about to return to the Father from whom he had come.[86] In heaven, before his humble entrance into history as a human being, he enjoyed full glory and equality with the Father. But he humbled himself and gave up that equal status and position. So in his incarnate state, Jesus' status and position were under the Father.[87] This is all that was meant by Jesus' statement that the Father is greater than he.

ISN'T THE DEITY OF CHRIST AN IDEA THE CHURCH CREATED LATER?

Dan Brown and *The Da Vinci Code* have successfully repeated this tired idea. According to Brown, Constantine created the divine Jesus to cement his hold on power. But even a quick look at the Bible shows the deity of Jesus was the teaching from the earliest days of Christianity.

Everyone agrees that the book of Romans is authentically Pauline and was written around A.D. 60, two and a half centuries before Constantine. In Romans 9:5, Paul speaks of "the Christ who is God over all, blessed forever. Amen." Even earlier in 1 Corinthians 8:6, another unquestionably authentic Pauline book, Paul puts the Father and the Lord Jesus into a parallelism that clearly affirms the deity of Jesus.

There are many biblical references to the deity of Jesus. But there are also many references in the writings of the early church fathers. These lines of evidence are deftly defended by reliable scholars for those wanting to investigate these facts more thoroughly.[88] You can say that the fact of Jesus' deity is wrong, perhaps, but no person with even a passing knowledge of the early evidence can say that it was not affirmed from the beginning.

CHAPTER TWO

HOW HUMAN WAS JESUS?

**"'Behold, the virgin shall conceive and bear a son,
and they shall call his name Immanuel'
(which means, God with us)."**

MATTHEW 1:23

Jesus was a dude. Like my drywaller dad, he was a construction worker who swung a hammer for a living.[1] Because Jesus worked in a day when there were no power tools, he likely had calluses on his hands and muscles on his frame, and did not look like so many of the drag-queen Jesus images that portray him with long, flowing, feathered hair, perfect teeth, and soft skin, draped in a comfortable dress accessorized by matching open-toed sandals and handbag. Jesus did not have Elton John or the Spice Girls on his iPod, *The View* on his TiVo, or a lemon-yellow Volkswagen Beetle in his garage. No, Jesus was not the kind of person who, if walking by you on the street, would require you to look for an Adam's apple to determine the gender.

I'm not certain where the drag-queen Jesus myth originated, but it may be the result of confusing a Nazirite and a Nazarene. A man who took the Nazirite vow (like Samson) was not allowed to cut his hair or drink alcohol.[2] Because Jesus was from the town of Nazareth, some people have wrongly assumed that he took the Nazirite vow, which is something entirely different. We know from Scripture that Jesus drank wine and that men in his day did not think long hair was a cool rocker-dude statement, but rather a disgrace because no dude was supposed to look ladylike.[3]

The truth is that we have no idea how Jesus looked because there is simply no historical evidence. The Byzantines put a beard on Jesus as a symbol of power. The Victorians made Jesus blond. Out of the more than fifty mainstream films made about Jesus, he has never been played by an actor who is ethnically Jewish, which means those portrayals are also likely inaccurate.[4]

We can be sure that Jesus did not look like feminist Edwina Sandys' 1975 sculpture of a bare-breasted Jesus on the cross created to celebrate the United Nations' Decade of Women, which then went on display at the Cathedral of St. John the Divine in New York and the Yale Divinity School.[5] We can also safely assume that he did not look like the pictures of him that began appearing in Bibles as the number of illustrated Bibles soared from 16 percent to 59 percent of the market from 1810 to the 1870s.[6]

Perhaps the most famous picture of Jesus was made by Warner Sallman. His 1940 painting, *Head of Christ*, sold one hundred thousand copies in only two months in 1941 and went on to sell more than three million more copies in 1942. Commenting on the pictures of Jesus being cranked out in a previous generation, author Bruce Barton lamented that it seemed all the artists agreed to "make our Christ with a woman's face, and add a beard."[7]

The pursuit of the face of Jesus included "The Face of Christ in Art," an article that appeared in *The Outlook* in April 1899.[8] The typically staid magazine *Popular Mechanics* once even had the search for the face of Jesus as their cover story.[9] Thankfully, it showed Jesus as a regular-looking guy without supermodel, product-filled hair.

My point in all of this is that if we had seen Jesus as a man, we would have seen a normal guy carrying his lunch box in one hand and tool box in the other heading off to work. He did the normal things that actual people do, like farting, going to the bathroom, and blowing boogers from his nose. I say these things not to be sacrilegious or demeaning to Jesus in any way, but to point out that when entire books of the Bible (such as 1 John) are written in large part to defend that Jesus was fully human with a real physical body that functioned like our physical bodies, these are the practical implications.

In sum, Jesus looked like a normal, average dude. Or, in the words of the prophet Isaiah, "He had no form or majesty that we should look at him, and no beauty that we should desire him."[10] Indeed, when we examine the life of Jesus as told in Scripture, we see a man who does not appear at first glance to be God. Conversely, Jesus appears as a radically normal and average human being experiencing normal life events like the rest of us:

- Born of a woman[11]
- Had a normal body of flesh and bones[12]
- Grew up as a boy[13]
- Had a family[14]
- Obeyed his parents[15]
- Worshiped God[16] and prayed[17]
- Worked as a carpenter[18]
- Got hungry[19] and thirsty[20]
- Asked for information[21]
- Was stressed[22]
- Was astonished[23]
- Was happy[24]
- Told jokes[25]
- Had compassion[26]
- Had male and female friends he loved[27]
- Gave encouraging compliments[28]
- Loved children[29]
- Celebrated holidays[30]
- Went to parties[31]
- Loved his mom[32]

In the first chapter we examined the deity of Jesus by answering the question, "Is Jesus the only God?" Subsequently, in this chapter we will now examine the humanity of Jesus by answering the question, "How human was Jesus?" In doing so it is important to stress that while Jesus was fully human, he was not merely human.

The issue of Jesus' divinity and humanity has been one of the most controversial and confusing issues in all of Christian theology.[33] Many great Christian writers have commented on this point, including the following:

- ◉ Blaise Pascal: "The Church has had as much difficulty in showing that Jesus Christ was man, against those who denied it, as in showing that he was God; and the probabilities were equally great."
- ◉ G. K. Chesterton: People "are equally puzzled by His insane magnificence and His insane meekness. They have parted His garments among them, and for His vesture they have cast lots; though the coat was without seam woven from the top throughout."
- ◉ Madeleine L'Engle: "To be a Christian is to believe in the impossible. Jesus was God. Jesus was Human."
- ◉ Lord Byron (English poet): "If ever a man was God or God man, Jesus Christ was both."
- ◉ Puritan Phillip Brooks: "Jesus Christ, the condescension of divinity, and the exaltation of humanity."
- ◉ J. I. Packer: "The really staggering Christian claim is that Jesus of Nazareth was God made man. . . . The more you think about it, the more staggering it gets. Nothing in fiction is so fantastic as this truth of the Incarnation."
- ◉ Martin Luther: "You should point to the whole man Jesus and say, 'That is God.'"
- ◉ Saint Athanasius of Alexandria: "He became what we are that he might make us what he is."

There are two general ways in which various thinking has erred regarding the humanity and divinity of Jesus. The first is to deny the full divinity of Jesus in favor of his humanity; the second is to deny the full humanity of Jesus in favor of his divinity.

The denial of the full divinity of Jesus has been done by heretics such as the Ebionites, Dynamic Monarchianists, Nestorians, modalists, monarchianists, Sabellianists, Unitarians, Social Gospel proponents, "death of God" theologians, liberals, Arians, Jehovah's Witnesses, Mormons, functionalists, Adoptionists, Kenotics, Apollinarians, and more recently by the popular book and film *The Da Vinci Code*. According to the Jehovah's Witnesses cult, Jesus was created by God the Father billions of years ago as the archangel Michael and is not God equal to the Father.[34] The Mormon cult teaches that Jesus was born as the first and greatest spirit-child of the Heavenly Father and Heavenly Mother, and is also the spirit-brother of Lucifer who became a god but whose deity is no more unique than many people's. Some New Agers say Jesus was not fully God and fully man, but rather half man and half alien. Oneness Pentecostals falsely teach that there is no Trinity but rather that Jesus appears in the roles of Father, Son, and Spirit.

Furthermore, Creflo Dollar, who pastors the twenty-four-thousand-member World Changers Church International in College Park, Georgia, and whose sermons are aired worldwide by the Trinity Broadcasting Network (TBN), makes the bold declaration that "Jesus didn't come as God, He came as a man."[35] He goes on to insist that Jesus was *only* an anointed man: If Jesus came as God, then why did God have to anoint him? Jesus came as a man; that's why it was legal to anoint Him. God doesn't need *anointed*. He is anointing. Jesus came as a man and at age thirty, God is now getting ready to demonstrate to us and give us an example of what a man with the anointing can do."[36] If we follow the "logic" of his rhetorical questions, we would come to the conclusion that Jesus is not God. Later in the same sermon, Dollar says, "This ain't no heresy. I'm not some false prophet." But his lack of precision directs his listeners toward heresy. We must always affirm that Jesus is the God-man, Immanuel, God come in the flesh.

The denial of the full humanity of Jesus has been done by heretics such as Docetists, Gnostics, Modal Monarchianists, Apollinarian Paulicians, Monophysitists, New Agers, and Eutychians. Some Christian worship songs have also tended to lean toward a denial of the full humanity of Jesus. For example, there is a well-known hymn about Jesus as a baby that says, "no crying he makes," as if Jesus were not truly a human child that would cry to notify his mother when he was hungry, wet, or had an upset stomach. Also, the Orthodox and Catholic baby Jesus pictures are simply freakish, with him looking like a Mini-Me complete with a halo. Honestly, if I had a kid like that I would sleep with one eye open.

Perhaps the people who most commonly prefer Jesus' divinity over his humanity in our present age are hardcore Protestant Christian fundamentalists. They are so committed to preserving the divinity of Jesus that they tend to portray his humanity as essentially overwhelmed by his divinity so that he was largely not tempted to sin, if indeed tempted at all.

I first experienced this as a new Christian in a fundamentalist church where I asked the pastor a question about the temptation of Jesus mentioned throughout Scripture.[37] He immediately took me to James 1:13, which says, "God cannot be tempted with evil." He went on to say that because Jesus is God, when the Bible says he was tempted, he was not really tempted but basically faking it. His portrait of Jesus sounded eerily similar to Superman. He was saying that like Superman, Jesus only appeared to be a regular, tempted Galilean peasant; under the Clark Kent–like disguise there remained on Jesus' chest a big red "G" for God, which made him unable to really suffer from the same weaknesses as the rest of us mere mortals. The logical conclusion of this false teaching is that Jesus cannot be our mediator[38] because he is not fully human and therefore cannot represent us to God the Father.

In A.D. 451, the Council of Chalcedon met to wrestle with the confusion that surrounded the divinity and humanity of Jesus. They issued the Chalcedonian Creed, which cleared up many heresies that wrongly defined the humanity and divinity of Jesus. In sum, the creed declared that Jesus Christ is one person with two natures (human and divine) who is both fully God and fully man. Theologically, the term for the union of both natures in Jesus Christ is *hypostatic union*, which is taken from the Greek word *hypostasis* for "person." The renowned German pastor Dietrich Bonhoeffer said, "The Chalcedonian definition is an objective, but living, statement which bursts through all thought forms."[39] The Chalcedonian summary of the incarnation is the position held by all of Christendom, including Orthodox, Catholic, and Protestant Christians.

In keeping with the biblical position of Chalcedon, we must retain both the full divinity and full humanity of Jesus Christ. To accomplish this, we must conclude that when Jesus became a man, he did not change his identity as God but rather changed his role. According to the church father Augustine, "Christ added to himself which he was not, he did not lose what he was."[40]

Jesus, who was fully equal with God in every way, who was the very form of God, did not see that as something to keep in his grip, but emptied himself of that equal status and role to take the status and role of humanity. He who was and is God took the likeness of humanity. God became the "image of God" for the sake of our salvation.[41]

Theologians capture this laying aside of the divine equality, the divine lifestyle, with the phrase *he laid aside the independent exercise of his divine attributes*. What this means is that he didn't continually exhibit the so-called incommunicable attributes such as his immortality, omniscience, or omnipresence, except at the leading of the Holy Spirit.

Therefore, while Jesus remained fully man and fully God during his incarnation, he maintained all of his divine attributes and did avail himself of them upon occasion, such as to forgive human sin, which God alone can do.[42] The Bible is clear, however, that even when not availing himself of his divine attributes, he did in fact retain them. For example, in 1 Timothy 1:17, Jesus is the King who has the divine attributes of eternality, immortality, and invisibility and is called "the only God." According to other Scriptures, Jesus' other divine attributes possessed by him during his life on earth include omnipresence,[43] creator,[44] savior,[45] and deity as the only God.[46] In summary, Jesus did not in any way cease to be fully God while on the earth, but rather as Philippians 2:5–11 shows, he humbly chose not always to avail himself of his divine attributes.

Nonetheless, Jesus' life was lived as fully human in that he lived it by the power of the Holy Spirit. This point is perhaps best witnessed in the writings of Luke. The empowerment of Jesus through God the Holy Spirit is repeatedly stressed in his Gospel. There we find that Jesus was conceived by the Holy Spirit and given the title "Christ," which means anointed by the Holy Spirit.[47] Jesus baptized people with the Holy Spirit[48] and the Holy Spirit descended upon Jesus at his own baptism.[49] Furthermore, Jesus was "full of the Holy Spirit" and "led by the Spirit,"[50] came "in the power of the Spirit,"[51] and declared that "the Spirit of the Lord is upon me."[52] He also "rejoiced in the Holy Spirit."[53] Regarding the Holy Spirit's ministry to and through Christians, Jesus also promised that God the Father would "give the Holy Spirit to those who ask him"[54] and that the Holy Spirit would teach us once he was sent.[55]

In Luke's sequel, the book of Acts, Jesus told his disciples to wait to begin their ministry until the Holy Spirit came and empowered them.[56] Then the Holy Spirit descended upon the early Christians just as he had descended upon Jesus.[57] In this way, God revealed that through the power of the Holy Spirit, the followers of Jesus are given the ability to live a life like Jesus (though admittedly imperfectly since we remain sinners) by the same Holy Spirit that enabled Jesus. The result of the arrival of the Holy Spirit is that throughout the book of Acts, God's people are missionally engaged in culture, just as Jesus was. People are saved, churches are planted, cultures are redeemed, and God's kingdom is advanced by the power of God the Holy Spirit working through human beings.

Perhaps an admittedly imperfect analogy will help to clarify this difficult point. I am the father of five children, three young boys (Zachariah Blaise, Calvin Martin, Gideon Joseph) and two girls (Ashley Marisa, Alexie Grace). While my girls like to go out for tea and shoe-shopping on our daddy-dates, their brothers prefer to have wrestling matches with me to practice their Ultimate Fighting moves. In our matches, I remain in authority as their father and possess far superior strength that could be used to completely crush them. But, because I love them, want to identify with them, and be with them, I humble myself and lay aside some of my rights and strengths; I get down on the ground and take a beating from my boys. In a similar way, the teaching of Philippians and the repeated referrals to Jesus as a servant in Scripture (especially in Isaiah and the Gospels) denote the humility of Jesus to stoop to our level and dwell with us.

The Bible teaches that Jesus Christ is fully God who became a man and is "Immanuel," which means, "God with us."[58] It is important to note that this is the opposite of many religions that teach that men and women can become God or at least gods. This was Satan's first lie. Conversely, our God Jesus Christ humbled himself and entered into human history as a man to identify with us as our humble servant. As both God and man, Jesus alone can reconcile us to God as the only perfect God-man mediator. As theologian Donald Bloesch says, "Jesus therefore differs from other human beings in kind, not simply in degree."[59]

Furthermore, because Jesus' life is the perfect human life—the life that we are supposed to live by empowering grace through the Holy Spirit—it is important that we carefully examine the human life of Jesus. It is the life of Jesus that has generally been the subject of devotional study yet has been curiously omitted from some doctrinal statements. For example, the Apostles' Creed says that Jesus "was conceived of the Holy Spirit, born of the Virgin Mary, suffered under Pontius

Pilate, was crucified, died, and was buried." Curiously, this creed, which is second only to Scripture as fundamental and foundational Christian theological orthodoxy, essentially says nothing about Jesus' life as a man on the earth but quickly moves from his birth to his death. Thankfully, the Bible has much more to say about the life of Jesus, especially the humor, passion, and pain of Jesus.

JESUS WAS FUNNY

In the closing line of his book *Orthodoxy*, the popular writer G. K. Chesterton speaks of Jesus' lack of humor: "There was some one thing that was too great for God to show us when He walked upon our earth; and I have sometimes fancied that it was His mirth."[60] According to Chesterton, Jesus was probably not funny. Rather, he may have been one of those serious-looking religious types with furrowed brows who are too busy thinking through theological enormities and pointing out people's sins to tell a good joke, share a hearty laugh, or blow a few dollars and a few hours to go see a good stand-up comedian.

The apparent boring dourness of Jesus, the school wallflower who never got the punch line of any joke because he was too busy memorizing Lamentations while Herod's kids gave him wedgies, is precisely the cause of so many people thinking that going to church and going to the dentist are virtually synonymous. For example, the famous atheist philosopher Friedrich Nietzsche wrote about Jesus' earthly life saying, "Would that [Jesus] had remained in the wilderness and far from the good and just! Perhaps he would have learned to live and love the earth—and laughter too."[61]

This portrait of boring Jesus is far too popular, which explains why some Christians are theologically orthodox but comedically heretical. In reading the Gospels, you get the picture that Jesus was actually a pretty fun guy because he got invited to a lot of parties with some pretty wild people and crowds gathered around him because they enjoyed his company. Furthermore, how could Jesus be fully human and not occasionally tell a decent joke, when Ecclesiastes 3:4 says there is "a time to laugh"?

Vulgar comedian Carlos Mencia, in his "No Strings Attached" tour, claimed to be a Catholic Christian and said, "God wants you to laugh. God has a sense of humor. If you don't believe me, go to

Wal-Mart and look at people. God is funny." Self-described "feminist bisexual egomaniac" Camille Paglia said, "Jesus was a brilliant Jewish stand-up comedian, a phenomenal improviser. His parables are great one-liners."

My suspicion is that both Jesus and his comedic timing were perfect. For any guy reading this book, or any woman who has brothers or sons, can you even imagine Jesus and the ragtag bunch of twelve guys who hung with him for three years, without Jesus' ever making them double over in laughter, or Jesus himself at least once laughing so deeply that he snorted? That kind of stoicism is not sacred but rather Spock-like sin. Tragically, very little has been written on the humor of Jesus Christ, with the exception of a few recent books.[62]

As a preacher, I tend to use a lot of comedy in my sermons, which generally gets me into a lot of trouble. But when I read the Bible and examine my own life, I tend to see a lot of irony, sarcasm, and satire that is useful in a cutting and prophetic way. Elton Trueblood wisely says, "There are numerous passages . . . which are practically incomprehensible when regarded as sober prose, but which are luminous once we become liberated from the gratuitous assumption that Christ never joked. . . . Once we realize that Christ was not always engaged in pious talk, we have made an enormous step on the road to understanding."[63] Trueblood goes on to say, "Christ laughed, and . . . He expected others to laugh. . . . A misguided piety has made us fear that acceptance of His obvious wit and humor would somehow be mildly blasphemous or sacrilegious. Religion, we think, is serious business, and serious business is incompatible with banter."[64]

It is often the comedic exaggeration of Jesus that drives less-than-funny Bible commentators mad as they try to figure out such things as how a camel can fit through the eye of a needle.[65] In fact, one scholar argues that "the most characteristic form of Jesus' humor was the preposterous exaggeration."[66] Sadly, the Catholic Church in which I was raised and served as an altar boy missed the punch line when Jesus called Peter the Rock and, rather than a good laugh, ended up with the papacy.[67]

Jesus' humor was often biting and harsh, particularly when directed at the Pharisees. For example, he called them a bag of snakes,[68] said that their moms had shagged the Devil,[69] and mocked them for tithing out of their spice racks.[70]

Indeed, sometimes self-righteous religious folks take themselves way too seriously and the best response is to just make fun of them. This explains why Jesus also made fun of how some people pray[71] and fast.[72]

Sadly, because of the curse, we have far too many bad jokes and poor comedians whose delivery has been tragically compromised by the sin of their father Adam; comedy needs redemption too. Worse still is the occasional corny preacher joke that receives only the obligatory laugh—a sin that leads to comedic death.

JESUS WAS PASSIONATE

I'll never forget the day one of my childhood buddies told a group of us that his mother had threatened to give him a lobotomy if he did not calm down and stop jumping on their furniture, taunting their cat, and lighting off fireworks in their house. None of us boys knew what a lobotomy was until one of the boys in our pack explained that it was an operation where they scoop out part of your brain like the guts of a jack-o'-lantern so that you will calm down. At the time we did not know that his frustrated mom was just trying to scare him, but it worked. The young kid was terrified and became pretty compliant after we speculated about what kind of saw they would use to turn his head into a cookie jar with a lid and whether they would use a soup spoon or a wooden spoon to dig out part of his brain.

At this time I was also going to a Catholic church with my parents and in Sunday school they started telling us about Jesus. As they explained Jesus, I wondered if maybe his mom, Mary, had actually given Jesus a lobotomy. The Jesus I was told about could easily have passed for one of the kids in the ghetto daycares near my house who were pumped so full of NyQuil they would sit quietly and drool on themselves while watching cartoons until their moms came to pick them up after work. The Jesus I was introduced to was always mild mannered, endlessly patient, open, affirming, tolerant, only spoke in kind words, never got angry, and ran from conflict. Or, to butcher the prophet Isaiah, "a bruised reed of self-esteem he would not break."[73]

Worse still, this weird Jesus seemed to really like sheep. I never saw a picture of him with a baseball glove or with other kids, but I did see him with a lot of sheep. Sometimes they even made us glue cotton balls to construction paper in an effort to make our own sheep so that we could apparently be as weird as Jesus. In short, Jesus seemed downright freakish, definitely not the kind of guy you'd want on your baseball team because he'd never have the guts to slide hard into second to break up a double play or throw inside to a batter to back him off the plate. Rather, he'd prefer to pick flowers in the outfield and daydream about fluffy sheep while praying for his enemies and keeping his emotions under control.

The Bible says that God made us in his image, and it seems we like to return the favor.[74] For many years I wanted nothing to do with Jesus, not knowing that I did not really know anything about the Jesus of the Bible and was instead rejecting the lobotomized, flannel-graph, NyQuil Jesus of my Sunday school purgatory.[75] It seems like every generation seeks to give Jesus an extreme makeover.[76] Perhaps the most famous attempt was done by the early church leader Marcion. Marcion was embarrassed by the moody, angry, violent God of the Old Testament because he was apparently too much like an unpredictable junior high kid. Even portions of the Gospels made Marcion unhappy. So he launched a public relations campaign to get rid of the Old Testament and also put a few heavy coats of varnish on the Gospels so that Jesus looked more like the Lobotomized Lord. Marcion's approval ratings were fairly high until he was condemned as a heretic by the Bishop of Sinope, who happened to be his dad.

The traumatizing Lobotomized Lord of my childhood stuck with me until I actually read the Bible in college for myself. The evangelical kids on campus kept handing me tracts that told me that God loved me and had a wonderful plan for my life. As I read the Bible, though, they seemed to have gotten it wrong too--the Jesus I read about really seemed to jack with religious people a lot.

The Gospel of Mark, for example, revealed a Jesus who was antithetical to the "Gentle Jesus, meek and mild" sung about in Wesley's famous hymn. The portrait of Mark agrees more easily with that of former-major-league-baseball-player-turned-evangelist Billy Sunday who said, "Jesus was the greatest scrapper who ever lived."[77]

In the first chapter of Mark, Jesus starts off by yelling at complete strangers to repent of their sin, like the wingnuts with billboards who occasionally show up at shopping centers. Shortly thereafter, Jesus orders some guys to quit their jobs and follow him, and before long Jesus is telling a demon to shut up and healing a leper only to tell him to shut up too. In the second chapter, Jesus picks a fight with some well-mannered religious types and does the equivalent of breaking into a church on a Sunday morning to make a sandwich with the communion bread because he was hungry.

In the third chapter, Jesus gets angry and also grieves and apparently needs Paxil. Then he ignores his own mom, which threw Focus on the Hebrew Family into a tizzy, so they quickly issued a position paper renouncing his actions. In the fourth chapter, Jesus rebukes the wind, which caused an uproar with the local pantheists. In chapter 5, Jesus kills two thousand pigs, sending the animal rights activist blogosphere into a panic and creating a bacon famine only rivaled by the great Irish potato famine. In chapter 6, Jesus offends some people and apparently needs sensitivity training. In chapter 7, a few religious types have some questions for Jesus, and he cruelly calls them "hypocrites" and goes on a lengthy tirade about them, which seemed very intolerant of their alternative theological lifestyle.

In chapter 8, Jesus sighs in frustration, spits on a handicapped guy, and calls Peter "Satan," although thankfully no one sued for assault or slander. In chapter 9, Jesus gets sick of folks and asks them, "How long do I have to put up with you?" That's just before telling some other people to cut off their hands and feet and to gouge out their eyes—a statement which led to picketing from the local body dysmorphic disorder recovery group. In chapter 10, Jesus tells a rich guy to sell all his stuff and give the money to the poor, which put him in bad graces with the local prosperity-theology luncheon for pastors who were hoping for Bling Christ. In chapter 11, he has one of his guys take a donkey without asking like some kleptomaniac donkeylifter, proceeds to curse and kill a fig tree, which really upset the environmental activists who were promoting justification by recycling, and goes on to loot some small businesses and whip some small business leaders who were decent, tax-paying Republicans.

In chapter 12, Jesus tells people they are wrong and don't know their Bibles, which upset the postmoderns because Jesus was clearly using a narrow modernist epistemology. Jesus also tells some Sunday school teachers they are going to hell, which made the universalistic Emergent folks immediately engage in a conversation about the mythology of hell and fingerpaint about the emotional wounds caused by his words. In chapter 13, Jesus threatens to destroy the temple, which put the nation on heightened security alert that included taking off one's sandals before boarding a camel. In the fourteenth chapter, Jesus actually yells at his friends for taking a nap late at night after running them all over the place for about three years as an obvious workaholic who needed to start drinking decaf and listening to taped sounds of running water while doing aromatherapy so he could learn to relax. In chapter 15, the religious folk kill him for being like that, which seemed perfectly fine to everyone except a few women. The story ends in chapter 16 with him alive again and the trembling, astonished, and frightened disciples getting it and heading out to handle snakes while they go to offend the whole world with the gospel.

In summary, the Jesus of Mark's Gospel is not fitting for old ladies in hats and men in suits like those we see at church. Rather than handing out communion at church, if he were to show up, the men would need cups and the women boxes of tissue and flak jackets because the real Jesus is passionate and nothing like the Lobotomized Lord of the Thomas Kinkade paintings.

JESUS WAS BUMMED

Being fully human, Jesus experienced the entirety of human emotions, which means that he had some painful moments like the rest of us who suffer in a cursed and broken world. Predicting this hundreds of years before his birth, Isaiah 53:3 promised that Jesus would be "despised and rejected by men; a man of sorrows, and acquainted with grief."

One of the most astonishing things about Jesus is that as God he actually chose to come into our fallen, sick, twisted, unjust, evil, cruel, painful world and be with us to suffer like us and for us. Meanwhile, we spend most of our time trying to figure out how to avoid the pain and evil of this world while reading dumb books about the rapture just hoping to get out. Jesus truly lived a painful life that was fully human, as the following examples illustrate:

⊛ Jesus was tempted to sin by the Devil himself.[78]

- Jesus had money troubles that included being poor,[79] getting ripped off,[80] struggling to pay his taxes,[81] and being homeless.[82]
- People attacked Jesus by spreading vicious rumors,[83] physically abusing him,[84] and mocking and spitting on him.[85]
- Jesus was continually jacked with by religious neatniks.[86]
- Jesus had some bummer days marked by loneliness,[87] deep sorrow,[88] exhaustion,[89] and weeping.[90]
- Jesus' friends were a joke and no help in times of crisis;[91] they even betrayed him[92] and turned their backs on him.[93]
- Jesus' family thought he was a nut job.[94]
- Jesus turned to God the Father but did not have all his prayers answered as he requested.[95]
- Jesus bled.[96]
- Jesus died.[97]
- Jesus used his final breaths to forgive those who destroyed him.[98]

For those who are sick, abused, burned out, tired, bedridden, flat broke, tempted, weary, hated, lonely, and dying, the humanity of Jesus on his darkest days is encouraging. Without these insights into Jesus' life, it would be difficult for us to run to him in our time of need because we would be unaware of the similar experiences he had during his life on the earth. Those experiences make him a compassionate friend. Therefore, the humanity of Jesus is as important for our love of Jesus as his divinity.

The History Channel's two-hour documentary titled *The Passion: Religion and the Movies* explored the fascinating relationship between the divinity and humanity of Jesus and how that has played out in the cinema. The relationship between film and the church extends all the way back to Thomas Edison, who invented the first movie camera and tried to give its patent to his local church. They rejected it. The first cinema was apparently at the cathedral of Notre Dame until a cardinal had it removed.

The theological tension between Jesus' divinity and humanity has plagued filmmakers who have made films about Jesus. Such films are very important because they have helped influence how people perceive Jesus. The documentary even referenced the Council of Chalcedon and showed how the films done on Jesus have overly emphasized his divinity or humanity at the expense of the other. Essentially every film about

Jesus done prior to the days of the radical 1960s emphasized the deity of Jesus.

Seven of the first ten reel movies ever made were about Jesus and had the word "passion" in the title. The first feature-length movie of Jesus was made in 1912 and titled *From the Manger to the Cross, or Jesus of Nazareth*. That highly successful film was the first movie ever shot outside of a studio and was captured on location in Palestine and Egypt.

The legendary director and devout Christian Cecil B. DeMille literally transformed movie special effects with his 1923 film *The Ten Commandments*. In 1927, he also produced the life of Jesus in the movie *King of Kings*. In that film he was very careful to portray Jesus as very pious with little humanity; he even had a glowing aura around him, which made him appear like something an icon on the screen. Because the film was a silent movie, the printed dialogue was changed into various languages so that it could be shown to audiences around the world. In his biography, DeMille said that eight hundred million people in total were introduced to Jesus through his film and that only the Bible had done more for the cause of Jesus.[99] The film was so popular that churches began showing it and promoting it as a missionary tool, despite the fact that many churches were opposed to the immorality of Hollywood and the film industry and even preached from the pulpit against going to the cinema.

In 1932, Cecil B. DeMille directed the first "talkie" film based on the Bible. *The Sign of the Cross* explored the persecution of Christians under Nero and contained some very risqué scenes for that time. They included very revealing costumes on some women, barely concealing their full nudity, and the lucid images of a seductive lesbian dance. Eventually, he succumbed to the opposition of some Christians and rereleased the film with the objectionable scenes deleted.

In the 1950s, the film *The Robe* was released, based on the novel written by the minister Lloyd Douglas. The story centers on a Roman who helped oversee the crucifixion of Jesus and later converted to Christianity. It was a groundbreaking film that was the first to be filmed in CinemaScope and received four Academy Award nominations.

In the social upheaval of the 1960s, director George Stevens sought to retell the story of Jesus in a way that did not contain any subplot of anti-Semitism, where the Jews were portrayed as the murderers of Jesus.

Part of his motivation was his work in filming the horrors of the Nazi concentration camps and liberation of living captives. In 1965, Stevens produced *The Greatest Story Ever Told*, a three-hour film on the entire life of Jesus. To play Jesus, he chose an unknown Swedish actor named Max von Sydow, rather than actors such as James Dean, with whom he had previously worked. But the film proved to be out of touch with the mood of the times because it did not stress the humanity of Jesus.

In 1964, *The Gospel According to St. Matthew* was filmed, curiously, by gay, atheist, Marxist poet Pier Paolo Pasolini, who had previously been imprisoned for blasphemy in connection with another film he made. Many film critics consider this film to be the greatest ever made about Jesus because of the daring portrayal of his humanity. For dialogue, the film simply used every word from the Gospel of Matthew in the Bible. In the spirit of the 1960s, it portrayed Jesus as a revolutionary for the poor and a social activist rather than a passive teacher. To play Jesus, Pasolini chose a young student who came knocking on his door raising money for the Communist party. No one in the film, including the young man who played Jesus, had any acting experience. Everyone in the film was simply a regular person taken off the street, and the earthy film, with an emphasis on Jesus as a real human being, stood in contrast to the sweeping biblical epics of the previous era.

Pasolini's film paved the way for additional movies with an emphasis on Jesus' humanity. In the height of the 1970s' disco rage, the first film with a singing Jesus was made, *Godspell*. In 1973, the Norman Jewison film *Jesus Christ Superstar*, based on the Broadway play of the same name, was a rock opera complete with Jesus' band of hippie followers who sing and dance. Judas had an enormous Afro and flared pants as the film made every effort to update the humanity of Jesus for the culture of the day.

In 1977, one of the most respected films about the life of Jesus ever produced debuted on television as the miniseries *Jesus of Nazareth*. Dustin Hoffman and Al Pacino were considered for the role of Jesus, but ultimately the lesser-known actor Robert Powell was chosen, along with Michael York, who played the role of John the Baptizer. The miniseries was commissioned by the Pope, who used his 1977 Easter address to encourage people to go home and watch it. The show was incredibly popular and was used as a missionary tool by many

Christians and churches because it clearly showed both Jesus' humanity and his divinity.

1979 saw the making of a small film that has gone on to become the most watched film of all time. *The Jesus Film* was basically the telling of the Gospel of Luke. It was commissioned by the parachurch ministry Campus Crusade for Christ. Not funded by any Hollywood studio, the low-budget film had actor Brian Deacon playing the role of Jesus and was destined for a very limited release. But the film has since been shown as a missionary tool in so many nations of the earth that Crusade claims no less than two hundred million people have been converted to Christianity through the film. It seeks to strike a balance between the humanity and divinity of Jesus.

1979 also saw the making of one of the most controversial films about Jesus ever made, because of its overemphasis on Jesus' humanity at the expense of his deity. The very British Monty Python film with the working title *Jesus Christ: Lust for Glory* that was later changed to *Life of Brian* openly mocked Christians. In its most controversial scene, Jesus is shown in a jovial mood and singing about always looking on the bright side of life while hanging on the cross. Some critics said the film was blasphemous, churches came out in protest, outrage ensued, and the film was outlawed in parts of the Bible Belt along with some British cities.

Keeping with the theme of controversial films about Jesus, in 1988, director Martin Scorsese released *The Last Temptation of Christ*. The film was based on the 1961 novel of the same name, which the Vatican blacklisted for overemphasizing the humanity of Jesus and ignoring his divinity. In the film Jesus, who is played by Willem Dafoe, is not considered to be the Messiah but rather a man who avoids the cross and lives a normal human life that included marriage. The humanity of Jesus portrayed in the film went too far for Christians and a cultural battle ensued between the growing religious right and Hollywood. The subject of Jesus was so controversial that no other Bible film would be made in Hollywood for the next decade.

Then, Mel Gibson's film *The Passion of the Christ* exploded upon the world, grossing over $600 million at the box office alone. It is the highest-grossing R-rated movie ever. In its first week, it debuted at number one, despite its graphic violence. The success of the film is due, in part, to its ability to show the humanity of Jesus through the pain of his flogging and crucifixion without in any way negating his deity.

Having now established that Jesus is God who entered history as a man, and having explored the ways in which both theologians and filmmakers have erred in regard to the humanity and divinity of Jesus, we will now examine how people knew of his coming more than a thousand years in advance.

ANSWERS TO COMMON QUESTIONS ABOUT JESUS' HUMANITY

WHAT DOES INCARNATION MEAN?

The common jargon for the second member of the Trinity entering into history as a human being is *the incarnation* (from the Latin meaning "becoming flesh").[100] John 1:14 says the Word, the second person of the Trinity, became flesh. John's point is that the eternal, invisible God took on a totally physical body so that we could see him. The word "flesh" is like a slap in the face to the ethereally oriented Greeks and all Star Wars junkies who believe the perfect person is pure spirit like Yoda, Anakin Skywalker (a.k.a. Darth Vader), and Obi-Wan Kenobi. It says he became "meat." Much like "chili con carne" where *carne* means "meat," the incarnation teaches that Jesus took upon himself a literal human body. Subsequently, incarnation ("in" plus "carne") means "in flesh."

CAN WE CALL JESUS A PERSON INSTEAD OF A MAN?

Curiously, some people have started speaking of Jesus as if he were a she. For example, at her installation ceremony as head honchette, one new Episcopalian bishop spoke of "our mother Jesus."[101]

But Jesus was a man. He was anatomically male, a guy. Politically correct androgyny fans are particularly irked by the idea that God came to earth gendered, especially gendered male. But the Bible is exceedingly clear on this point. Even Dan Brown's ridiculous picture of Jesus in *The Da Vinci Code* got this point right, despite all the other nonsense he promotes.

On the other hand, Jesus *is* a person, a full person. The Chalcedonian Creed says he is truly God and truly man, with two natures coming together to form one person.

Jesus is not a myth, a legend, an idea, or a story, but a fully historical person who was born, lived, died, and rose again. Were we transported back in time to the days of Jesus we would have seen a man who ate food, got tired, enjoyed friends, and lived his life as a male person.

DID Jesus Have a Sin Nature?

This question has been a point of historical division between various Christian traditions. The Eastern church says yes. They focus on Romans 8:3, that the Father sent his own Son "in the likeness of sinful flesh and for sin," and Hebrews 4:15, which says he was one "who in every respect has been tempted as we are." They then argue that this could not be if he did not have any of the sinful thoughts or desires like the ones we wrestle with all the time. It is then argued that although Jesus had a sin nature, he overcame it and showed us the perfect obedience that we can follow to live holy lives.

The Western church says no. They focus on Hebrews 7:26–27: We "have such a high priest, holy, innocent, unstained, separated from sinners, and exalted above the heavens. He has no need, like those high priests, to offer sacrifices daily, first for his own sins." It is argued that if Jesus had a sin nature, he could not fit this description. Furthermore, if he had sinful character, then he would be a sinner.

We are inclined to go with the Western church and see the "likeness of sinful flesh" in Romans as a point of similarity rather than a point of character. Nonetheless, in the end it is probably a point on which Christians will need to agree to disagree while affirming the complete sinlessness of our Savior.

Was Jesus Perfect?

On one hand, the Bible insists that Jesus did not sin at all.[102] Even a hardened Roman centurion, akin to a Nazi Storm Trooper, said, "Certainly this man [Jesus] was innocent!"[103] Jesus was perfect in the sense that he never sinned, even when he was being tempted and tortured beyond imagination.

Jesus was the perfect man. He became like us in every way, except sinful, to be all that a human can be. In Hebrews 2:17, the writer says Jesus was made like us in every respect. Only then could he be a merciful and faithful high priest in the service of God, to make propitiation for the sins of the people.

On the other hand, it's shocking to find that Jesus had to become perfect! Ironically, the Bible insists that Jesus had to learn perfection. He learned it through his suffering, according to Hebrews 2:10. He was perfectly ready to suffer when he came to earth. But there's a different kind of perfection to learn in the reality of suffering. There is a learning by experience that no abstract lesson and no observation can match. He identified with us totally, through anguish and agony, so that he could be our sympathetic high priest.

Hebrews 5:8–9 says he learned obedience through his sufferings. He did not move from disobedience to obedience as children do once they are disciplined. There is no imperfection implied by moving to perfection of experience. Rather, Jesus learned obedience by obeying. He went from readiness to experience and proven virtue.

His obedience under trial, his perfection as he carried out his messianic mission, got him an A+ on his messianic report card, an "exceeds expectations" rating on every point of his messianic job evaluation. Simply, he was perfect.

In his learned perfection, he can make perfect forever those who are his brothers and sisters, set apart by grace through faith as members of his family, as Hebrews 10:14 teaches.

COULD JESUS HAVE SINNED?

While systematic theologians have spilled much ink on this point, the precise biblical answer is that we do not know. The Bible never addresses, much less answers, the question. Some will find this disturbing, but the Bible is clear that humility is the first requirement for a good theologian, so that we can be satisfied with what the God of the universe thinks we need to know.

In an effort to speak of this matter where Scripture is silent, some have turned to the logic of reason, such as the following syllogism:

God cannot sin.
Jesus is God.
Therefore, Jesus cannot sin.

But if we apply that same logical reasoning to the death of Jesus, we end up with a most unsatisfactory conclusion:

God cannot die.
Jesus is God.
Therefore, Jesus cannot die.

So what is wrong? Logic? Not at all. The problem is in the second line, the minor premise. Jesus is not *just* God. Rather he is God in the flesh, the God-man. He emptied himself of his equality with the Father and took on a fully human nature so that during his incarnation, while he remained fully God, he was also not merely God. As a result, to answer this question biblically requires the following syllogism:

God cannot sin.
Jesus is God-man.
Therefore, Jesus was tempted in every way as we, but absolutely without sin.[104]

Jesus was God in every way. But Hebrews 5:7–9 tells us it was necessary for him as the incarnate Son to learn obedience by learning to obey to an extent that no other human will ever experience. The temptations were horrific. The battle for victory was tougher than any Jack Bauer mission. But where Adam failed and fell, Jesus resisted and prevailed. Somehow in this, his humanity was completed, "made perfect" according to Hebrews 5:9. Thankfully, by this perfection "he became the source of eternal salvation."[105]

IF JESUS NEVER SINNED, WHY WERE SOME PEOPLE SO ANGRY WITH HIM?

While Jesus never broke any of God's laws as revealed in Scripture, he did not hold in high regard various social and religious customs (those that did not find their authority in Scripture). Subsequently, Jesus frequently felt free to break various social and religious customs when he felt it was necessary to further the work of God. Examples would include healing on the Sabbath,[106] throwing over tables in the temple,[107] eating with godless sinners,[108] and not washing his hands before eating.[109] Some people who were committed to defending their social and religious traditions despite the lack of biblical support were offended by Jesus' unwillingness to submit to their rules in addition to God's. Their tribe continues to this day among those who are prone to place the authority of cultural trend and religious tradition above Scripture.

IF JESUS HAD NO SIN NATURE, NO SINFUL DESIRES, HOW COULD HE REALLY BE TEMPTED?

Most people connect temptation with being "lured and enticed" by evil desires as spoken of in James 1:14. If that were the only form of temptation, then neither Jesus nor Adam and Eve could be truly tempted, since they had no sinful desires.

But there is another type of temptation: it is in my strength, my spiritual gift, or my virtue. That kind of temptation seeks to take a noble strength and use it in an ignoble way or for an ignoble end. This type of temptation is often under the guise of helping another person or doing a godly task.

Think of two men in the Darfur region of Sudan. Both are living in a squalid refugee camp. One is a self-centered pleasure seeker. The other is a godly father. They come into town and see a cart with fresh bread for sale. There is no one in sight.

The first man is tempted to satisfy his own selfish desire for good bread. That's normal temptation by evil desires.

But the second man sees the bread and immediately thinks of his two starving children back in the camp. His temptation is to do the fatherly thing and provide for his children. It's an even more powerful temptation. But there is no evil desire involved. His is only the noble desire to be a good dad exercised in the wrong way of stealing.

It seems most likely that Jesus' temptations were of this kind. Though they were very powerful he successfully resisted them, setting a pattern for us and preparing himself to be our great high priest.

CHAPTER THREE

HOW DID PEOPLE KNOW JESUS WAS COMING?

"Everything written about me in the Law of Moses and the Prophets and the Psalms must be fulfilled."

JESUS (LUKE 24:44)

✝

Usually a good story has a cliffhanger, but for this chapter we will spare the suspense and answer the question right up front. How did people know Jesus was coming? They read the Old Testament Bible. Jesus' entrance into history was eagerly awaited for over a millennium through prophecy. Those prophecies were fulfilled and give us the privilege of seeing God's Word proven true.

Roughly a quarter of the Bible was prophetic at the time it was written. Many of those prophecies specifically pointed to the coming of Jesus Christ as the Messiah, or the "anointed one."

Many notable Christian theologians have commented on how many of the prophetic promises of the Old Testament were fulfilled in Jesus' earthly ministry:

- Augustine: "The Old [Testament] is in the New revealed and the New is in the Old concealed."
- J. I. Packer: "The importance of this theme—the Old Testament pointing to Christ—is great."
- Graeme Goldsworthy: "The most compelling reason for Christians

to read and study the Old Testament lies in the New Testament. The New Testament witnesses to the fact that Jesus of Nazareth is the One in whom and through whom all the promises of God find their fulfillment."

⊕ Lesslie Newbigin: "The theme of promise and fulfillment runs like a thread throughout the whole Bible."

⊕ Walter Kaiser: "A straightforward understanding and application of the text leads one straight to the Messiah and to Jesus of Nazareth, who has fulfilled everything these texts said about his first coming."

⊕ Martin J. Selman: "Jesus both fulfilled and expanded the messianic ideas of the Old Testament."

⊕ Kim Riddlebarger: "Jesus Christ [is] the sum and substance of biblical prophecy."

⊕ Edmund P. Clowney: ". . . we may see the Lord of the Word in the Word of the Lord."

⊕ Puritan Thomas Manton: "Christ is the living Bible."

Jesus' own words on this point are even more important. Jesus himself repeatedly said that he was the thread that wove together the entire Old Testament. Practically, this means that Scripture is not rightly understood or taught unless the person and work of Jesus are the central truth being revealed.

Jesus summarized the purpose of his entire ministry as fulfilling every aspect of the Old Testament laws and prophecies.[1] In an argument with some of the most devoutly religious and biblically literate people who have ever lived, Jesus made some astonishing claims.[2] He accused Bible scholars who had given their life to memorizing entire books of the Old Testament of not knowing their Bibles at all. In all of their studies, they had failed to see that he alone was the central theme of Scripture and they refused to trust in him alone for salvation. Specifically, their hopes rested on the Laws of Moses; they trusted that, through their own pious obedience to God's commands, they could obtain their own salvation through their own righteousness. Yet Jesus said that Moses, who penned the first five books of the Old Testament, was writing about him.[3] By saying this, Jesus was showing that even the commands of the Old Testament served to reveal how sinful we are because we continually fail to obey both the spirit and the letter of the law. They also reveal that the sinless Jesus is our only hope. Sadly, as religious people often do, they read the Bible looking for ways to be the hero of their own life rather than reading it to see themselves as villains and Jesus as their hero.

Jesus also models for us a proper use of the Old Testament, by which he alone is the hero and theme. Following his resurrection from death, Jesus showed how all that was written by Moses, the prophets, and the Psalms was ultimately fulfilled in him alone.[4] Therefore, in this chapter we will follow both the instruction and example of Jesus by examining twenty-five Old Testament prophetic promises given hundreds and thousands of years before their fulfillment in Jesus.

Each prophecy reveals how God clearly prepared his people for the coming of Jesus. By comparing each Old Testament promise to its corresponding New Testament fulfillment, we can see that the New Testament is built upon the Old Testament. Further evidence is the fact that there are more than three hundred quotes and thousands of references and inferences to the Old Testament in the New Testament.

Most of this chapter will simply be the reading of Scripture. We are trusting God the Holy Spirit who inspired the writing of Scripture to also illuminate your understanding so that your trust in both Scripture and Jesus are increased. One final note: the authors listed are those the Bible credits. The dates are approximate but accurate according to timelines taught by scholars who honor God's Word.

1) 4000 B.C.: Adam and Eve receive the prophecy that the Messiah (Jesus) would be born of a woman.

PROMISE: "'I will put enmity between you and the woman, and between your offspring and her offspring; he shall bruise your head, and you shall bruise his heel'" (Gen. 3:15).

FULFILLMENT: "But when the fullness of time had come, God sent forth his Son, born of woman, born under the law . . ." (Gal. 4:4).

2) 2000 B.C.: Abraham receives the promise that the Messiah (Jesus) would descend from Abraham, through his son Isaac (not Ishmael), Isaac's son Jacob (not Esau), and Jacob's son Judah (not any of the other eleven brothers).

PROMISE: "'In you [Abraham] all the families of the earth shall be blessed'" (Gen. 12:3); "God said, 'No, but Sarah your wife shall bear you a son, and you shall call his name Isaac. I will establish my covenant with him as an everlasting covenant for his offspring after him'" (Gen. 17:19); "'I see him, but not now; I behold him, but not near: a star shall come out of Jacob, and a scepter shall rise out of Israel ...'" (Num. 24:17); "'The scepter shall not depart from Judah, nor the ruler's staff from between his feet, until tribute comes to him; and to him shall be the obedience of the peoples'" (Gen. 49:10).

FULFILLMENT: "The book of the genealogy of Jesus Christ, the son of David, the son of Abraham. Abraham was the father of Isaac, and Isaac the father of Jacob, and Jacob the father of Judah and his brothers ..." (Matt. 1:1–2).

3) 700 B.C.: Isaiah prophesies that Jesus' mother would be a virgin who conceived by a miracle and that Jesus would be God who became a man.

PROMISE: "'Therefore the Lord himself will give you a sign. Behold, the virgin shall conceive and bear a son, and shall call his name Immanuel'" (Isa. 7:14).

FULFILLMENT: "Now the birth of Jesus Christ took place in this way. When his mother Mary had been betrothed to Joseph, before they came together she was found to be with child from the Holy Spirit. And her husband Joseph, being a just man and unwilling to put her to shame, resolved to divorce her quietly. But as he considered these things, behold, an angel of the Lord appeared to him in a dream, saying, 'Joseph, son of David, do not fear to take Mary as your wife, for that which is conceived in her is from the Holy Spirit. She will bear a son, and you shall call his name Jesus, for he will save his people from their sins.' All this took place to fulfill what the Lord had spoken by the prophet: 'Behold, the virgin shall conceive and bear a son, and they shall call his name Immanuel' (which means, God with us)" (Matt. 1:18–23).

4) 700 B.C.: Micah prophesies that Jesus would be born in the town of Bethlehem.

PROMISE: "But you, O Bethlehem Ephrathah, who are too little to be among the clans of Judah, from you shall come forth for me one who is to be ruler in Israel, whose coming forth is from of old, from ancient days [eternity]" (Mic. 5:2).

FULFILLMENT: "In those days a decree went out from Caesar Augustus that all the world should be registered. This was the first registration when Quirinius was governor of Syria.... And Joseph also went up from Galilee, from the town of Nazareth, to Judea, to the city of David, which is called Bethlehem, because he was of the house and lineage of David, to be registered with Mary, his betrothed, who was with child. And while they were there, the time came for her to give birth. And she gave birth to her firstborn son and wrapped him in swaddling cloths and laid him in a manger, because there was no place for them in the inn" (Luke 2:1–7).

5) 700 B.C.: Isaiah prophesies that Jesus would live his life without committing any sins.

PROMISE: "He had done no violence, and there was no deceit in his mouth" (Isa. 53:9).

FULFILLMENT: "For to this you have been called, because Christ also suffered for you, leaving you an example, so that you might follow in his steps. He committed no sin, neither was deceit found in his mouth" (1 Pet. 2:21–22).

6) 700 B.C.: Hosea prophesies that Jesus' family would flee as refugees to Egypt to save his young life.

PROMISE: "When Israel was a child, I loved him, and out of Egypt I called my son" (Hos. 11:1).

FULFILLMENT: "Now when they had departed, behold, an angel of the Lord appeared to Joseph in a dream and said, 'Rise, take the child and his mother, and flee to Egypt, and remain there until I tell you, for Herod is about to search for the child, to destroy him.' And he rose and took the child and his mother by night and departed to Egypt and remained there until the death of Herod. This was to fulfill what the Lord had spoken by the prophet, 'Out of Egypt I called my son'" (Matt. 2:13–15).

7) 400 B.C.: Malachi prophesies that Jesus would enter the temple. This is important because the temple was destroyed in A.D. 70 and no longer exists; subsequently, the prophecy could not have been fulfilled anytime after A.D. 70.

PROMISE: "Behold, I send my messenger, and he will prepare the way before me. And the Lord whom you seek will suddenly come to his temple; and the messenger of the covenant in whom you delight, behold, he is coming, says the LORD of hosts" (Mal. 3:1).

FULFILLMENT: "Now there was a man in Jerusalem, whose name was Simeon, and this man was righteous and devout, waiting for the consolation of Israel, and the Holy Spirit was upon him. And it had been revealed to him by the Holy Spirit that he would not see death before he had seen the Lord's Christ. And he came in the Spirit into the temple, and when the parents brought in the child Jesus, to do for him according to the custom of the Law . . ." (Luke 2:25–27).

8) 700 B.C.: Isaiah prophesies that John the Baptizer would prepare the way for Jesus.

PROMISE: "A voice cries: 'In the wilderness prepare the way of the LORD; make straight in the desert a highway for our God'" (Isa. 40:3).

FULFILLMENT: "In those days John the Baptist came preaching in the wilderness of Judea, 'Repent, for the kingdom of heaven is at hand.' For this is he who was spoken of by the prophet Isaiah when he said, 'The voice of one crying in the wilderness: "Prepare the way of the Lord; make his paths straight"'" (Matt. 3:1–3).

9) 700 B.C.: Isaiah prophesies that Jesus would perform many miracles.

PROMISE: "Then the eyes of the blind shall be opened, and the ears of the deaf unstopped; then shall the lame man leap like a deer, and the tongue of the mute sing for joy" (Isa. 35:5–6).

FULFILLMENT: "Now when John heard in prison about the deeds of the Christ, he sent word by his disciples and said to him, 'Are you the one who is to come, or shall we look for another?' And Jesus answered them, 'Go and tell John what you hear and see: the blind receive their sight and the lame walk, lepers are cleansed and the deaf hear, and the dead are raised up, and the poor have good news preached to them'" (Matt. 11:2–5).

10) 500 B.C.: Zechariah prophesies that Jesus would ride into Jerusalem on a donkey.

PROMISE: "Rejoice greatly, O daughter of Zion! Shout aloud, O daughter of Jerusalem! Behold, your king is coming to you; righteous and having salvation is he, humble and mounted on a donkey, on a colt, the foal of a donkey" (Zech. 9:9).

FULFILLMENT: "And when he had said these things, he went on ahead, going up to Jerusalem. . . . And they brought it [the colt] to Jesus, and throwing their cloaks on the colt, they set Jesus on it. And as he rode along, they spread their cloaks on the road. As he was drawing near—already on the way down the Mount of Olives—the whole multitude of his disciples began to rejoice and praise God with a loud voice for all the mighty works that they had seen, saying, 'Blessed is the King who comes in the name of the Lord! Peace in heaven and glory in the highest!'" (Luke 19:28, 35–38).

11) 1000 B.C.: David prophesies that Jesus would be betrayed by a friend.

PROMISE: "Even my close friend in whom I trusted, who ate my bread, has lifted his heel against me" (Ps. 41:9).

FULFILLMENT: "And [Judas] came up to Jesus at once and said, 'Greetings, Rabbi!' And he kissed him. Jesus said to him, 'Friend, do what you came to do'" (Matt. 26:49–50).

12) 500 B.C.: Zechariah prophesies that Jesus' betraying friend would be paid thirty pieces of silver for handing him over to the authorities and that the payment would be thrown in the temple in disgust (again, the temple was destroyed in A.D. 70, so this prophecy could not have been fulfilled after that time).

PROMISE: "Then I said to them, 'If it seems good to you, give me my wages; but if not, keep them.' And they weighed out as my wages thirty pieces of silver. Then the LORD said to me, 'Throw it to the potter'—the lordly price at which I was priced by them. So I took the thirty pieces of silver and threw them into the house of the LORD, to the potter" (Zech. 11:12–13).

FULFILLMENT: "Then one of the twelve, whose name was Judas Iscariot, went to the chief priests and said, 'What will you give me if I deliver him over to you?' And they paid him thirty pieces of silver" (Matt. 26:14–15); "And throwing down the pieces of silver into the temple, he departed, and he went and hanged himself. But the chief priests, taking the pieces of silver, said, 'It is not lawful to put them into the treasury, since it is blood money.' So they took counsel and bought with them the potter's field as a burial place for strangers" (Matt. 27:5–7).

13) 700 B.C.: Isaiah prophesies that Jesus would be beaten, would have his beard plucked out, and would be mocked and spit on.

PROMISE: "I gave my back to those who strike, and my cheeks to those who pull out the beard; I hid not my face from disgrace and spitting" (Isa. 50:6).

FULFILLMENT: "Then they spit in his face and struck him. And some slapped him . . ." (Matt. 26:67).

14) 1000 B.C.: David prophesies that lots would be cast for Jesus' clothing.

PROMISE: ". . . they divide my garments among them, and for my clothing they cast lots" (Ps. 22:18).

FULFILLMENT: "When the soldiers had crucified Jesus, they took his garments and divided them into four parts, one part for each soldier; also his tunic. But the tunic was seamless, woven in one piece from top to bottom, so they said to one another, 'Let us not tear it, but cast lots for it to see whose it shall be.' This was to fulfill the Scripture which says, 'They divided my garments among them, and for my clothing they cast lots.' So the soldiers did these things" (John 19:23–24).

15) 700 B.C.: Isaiah prophesies that Jesus would be hated and rejected.

PROMISE: "He was despised and rejected by men; a man of sorrows, and acquainted with grief; and as one from whom men hide their faces he was despised, and we esteemed him not" (Isa. 53:3).

FULFILLMENT: "And those who passed by derided him. . . . So also the chief priests, with the scribes and elders, mocked him. . . . And the robbers who were crucified with him also reviled him in the same way" (Matt. 27:39–44).

16) 700 B.C.: Isaiah prophesies that, though hated and rejected, Jesus would not defend himself.

PROMISE: "He was oppressed, and he was afflicted, yet he opened not his mouth; like a lamb that is led to the slaughter, and like a sheep that before its shearers is silent, so he opened not his mouth" (Isa. 53:7).

FULFILLMENT: "But when he was accused by the chief priests and elders, he gave no answer" (Matt. 27:12).

17) 1000 B.C.: David prophesies that Jesus would be crucified (hundreds of years before the invention of crucifixion).

PROMISE: "For dogs encompass me; a company of evildoers encircles me; they have pierced my hands and feet" (Ps. 22:16).

FULFILLMENT: "And when they came to the place that is called The Skull, there they crucified him, and the criminals, one on his right and one on his left" (Luke 23:33).

18) 700 B.C.: Isaiah prophesies that Jesus would be killed with sinners.

PROMISE: "Therefore I will divide him a portion with the many, and he shall divide the spoil with the strong, because he poured out his soul to death, and was numbered with the transgressors" (Isa. 53:12).

FULFILLMENT: "Then two robbers were crucified with him, one on the right and one on the left" (Matt. 27:38).

19) 1400 B.C.: Moses prophesies that none of Jesus' bones would be broken.

1000 B.C.: David prophesies the same.

PROMISE: "You shall not break any of its [the Passover lamb's] bones" (Ex. 12:46); "He keeps all his bones; not one of them is broken" (Ps. 34:20).

FULFILLMENT: "So the soldiers came and broke the legs of the first, and of the other who had been crucified with him. But when they came to Jesus and saw that he was already dead, they did not break his legs. But one of the soldiers pierced his side with a spear, and at once there came out blood and water. He who saw it has borne witness—his testimony is true, and he knows that he is telling the truth—that you also may believe. For these things took place that the Scripture might be fulfilled: 'Not one of his bones will be broken'" (John 19:32–36).

20) 1000 B.C.: David prophesies that Jesus would be forsaken by God.

PROMISE: "My God, my God, why have you forsaken me? Why are you so far from saving me, from the words of my groaning?" (Ps. 22:1).

FULFILLMENT: "And about the ninth hour Jesus cried out with a loud voice, saying, 'Eli, Eli, lema sabachthani?' that is, 'My God, my God, why have you forsaken me?'" (Matt. 27:46).

21) 700 B.C.: Isaiah prophesies that Jesus would die.

PROMISE: "He was cut off out of the land of the living, stricken for the transgression of my people" (Isa. 53:8b).

FULFILLMENT: "Then Jesus, calling out with a loud voice, said, 'Father, into your hands I commit my spirit!' And having said this he breathed his last" (Luke 23:46).

22) 700 B.C.: Isaiah prophesies that Jesus would be buried in a tomb given to him by a rich man.

PROMISE: "And they made his grave with the wicked and with a rich man in his death, although he had done no violence, and there was no deceit in his mouth" (Isa. 53:9).

FULFILLMENT: "When it was evening, there came a rich man from Arimathea, named Joseph, who also was a disciple of Jesus. He went to Pilate and asked for the body of Jesus. Then Pilate ordered it to be given to him. And Joseph took the body and wrapped it in a clean linen shroud and laid it in his own new tomb, which he had cut in the rock. And he rolled a great stone to the entrance of the tomb and went away" (Matt. 27:57–60).

23) 1000 B.C.: David prophesies that Jesus would resurrect from death.

700 B.C.: Isaiah prophesies the same.

PROMISE: "For you will not abandon my soul to Sheol, or let your holy one see corruption" (Ps. 16:10); "Yet it was the will of the LORD to crush him; he has put him to grief; when his soul makes an offering for guilt, he shall see his offspring; he shall prolong his days; the will of the LORD shall proper in his hand. Out of the anguish of his soul he shall see and be satisfied; by his knowledge shall the righteous one, my servant, make many to be accounted righteous, and he shall bear their iniquities" (Isa. 53:10–11).

FULFILLMENT: "For David says concerning him, 'I saw the Lord always before me, for he is at my right hand that I may not be shaken; therefore my heart was glad, and my tongue rejoiced; my flesh also will dwell in hope. For you will not abandon my soul to Hades, or let your Holy One see corruption. You have made known to me the paths of life; you will make me full of gladness with your presence.' Brothers, I may say to you with confidence about the patriarch David that he both died and was buried, and his tomb is with us to this day. Being therefore a prophet, and knowing that God had sworn with an oath to him that he would set one of his descendants on his throne, he foresaw and spoke about the resurrection of the Christ, that he was not abandoned to Hades, nor did his flesh see corruption. This Jesus God raised up, and of that we all are witnesses" (Acts 2:25–32).

24) 1000 B.C.: David prophesies that Jesus would ascend into heaven and take the souls of departed Christians with him.

PROMISE: "You ascended on high, leading a host of captives in your train" (Ps. 68:18).

FULFILLMENT: "But grace was given to each one of us according to the measure of Christ's gift. Therefore it says, 'When he ascended on high he led a host of captives, and he gave gifts to men.' . . . He who descended is the one who also ascended far above all the heavens, that he might fill all things" (Eph. 4:7–10).

25) 1000 B.C.: David prophesies that Jesus would sit at the right hand of God.

PROMISE: "The LORD says to my Lord: 'Sit at my right hand, until I make your enemies your footstool'" (Ps. 110:1).

FULFILLMENT: "He is the radiance of the glory of God and the exact imprint of his nature, and he upholds the universe by the word of his power. After making purification for sins, he sat down at the right hand of the Majesty on high." (Heb. 1:3).

In summary, God's people knew their Savior Messiah Jesus was coming because they carefully and prayerfully read the Old Testament Scriptures. Because those Scriptures were divinely inspired, they revealed future events surrounding the life, death, resurrection, and ascension of Jesus Christ in amazing detail. God alone is both knowledgeable of and sovereign over the details of future events. God himself throws down the gauntlet on this issue. For example, in Isaiah 41:21–24, he invites the false gods of the earth to step into the ring with him:

> Set forth your case, says the LORD; bring your proofs, says the King of Jacob. Let them bring them, and tell us what is to happen. Tell us the former things, what they are, that we may consider them, that we may know their outcome; or declare to us the things to come. Tell us what is to come hereafter, that we may know that you are gods; do good, or do harm, that we may be dismayed and terrified. Behold, you are nothing, and your work is less than nothing; an abomination is he who chooses you.

Furthermore, Jesus is the centerpiece of both history and Scripture and, without being hyperbolic, everything is ultimately about Jesus. This point may seem obvious to many but is sadly overlooked by many Bible teachers. To illustrate this point, perhaps three examples would be helpful.

First, I am not a frequent listener of Bible preachers on the radio, but occasionally I do tune in to hear what is being said. The last few occasions I was driving on road trips in my Jeep and listened for a few hours at a time to various well-known Bible preachers without hearing them say the name of Jesus at all.

Second, in our area it is common for many of the churches that are politically active to align with people of various faiths (e.g., Jews, Muslims) on issues and legislation where there is common interest, such as the free practice of religion or sanctity of human life. While this is not problematic, I was saddened to hear about various evangelical Christian churches in our area going one step further. They invited

Jewish rabbis in to teach classes on the Old Testament to Christians, blindly assuming that teaching the Bible without believing in Jesus as the Messiah could somehow be faithful to the entire purpose of Scripture, which is the revelation of Jesus Christ.

Third, while visiting a major American city, a young pastor who is a friend and part of our church planting network attended one of the most prominent churches in America, hoping to learn from what they were doing. He sat through an entire sermon and reported that at no time in the entire service, including the singing and sermon, was the name of Jesus ever mentioned. Apparently, the sermon ended with an altar call invitation for people to go to heaven when they died, but the name of Jesus or an explanation of what he did through the cross and empty tomb was not mentioned even in passing.

Sadly, it is too common for churches not to speak of Jesus, which is a tragedy akin to a wife rarely uttering the name of her own husband. In our day when there are innumerable contradictory beliefs about who God is, Christians must be clear that their God is Jesus Christ alone so as to communicate the same central truth that Scripture does. No matter how many verses are used, the Bible has not been rightly understood or proclaimed unless Jesus is the central focus and hero.

Furthermore, the presence of clear prophetic promises is one of the unique characteristics of Christianity and distinguishes it from every other world religion and cult. On this point, one scholar has said of the Bible:

> It is the only volume ever produced . . . in which is to be found a large body of prophecies relating to . . . the coming of One who was to be the Messiah. The ancient world had many different devices for determining the future, known as divination, but not in the entire gamut of Greek and Latin literature, even though they use the words prophet and prophecy, can we find any real specific prophecy of a great historic event to come in the distant future, nor any prophecy of a Savior to arise in the human race. . . . [Islam] cannot point to any prophecies of the coming of Mohammed uttered hundreds of years before his birth. Nether can the founder of any cult . . . rightly identify any ancient text specifically foretelling their appearance.[5]

Regarding the importance of prophetic biblical prophecy about Jesus, Bible scholar J. Dwight Pentecost says:

> Some people have given such intensive study to the subject of prophecy that they have completely missed seeing the Lord Jesus Christ in their study of the Word. The Scripture was given to us to reveal Him. He is its Theme. He is the Center about which all the Scripture revolves. . . . The first great result of the study of prophecy is that the prophetic Scriptures prove to us the authority of the entire Word of God. The Bible is different from every other religious book. There is no other book upon which a religion has been founded which includes prophecy within it. . . . There is no greater test or proof of the inspiration, validity, authority, and trustworthiness of the Bible than the proof of fulfilled prophecy.[6]

Dr. Pentecost wisely connects the nature of fulfilled prophecy with the trustworthiness of Scripture because it is nothing less than God's revelation of history to us in advance. There is simply no way to explain the specificity and variety of fulfilled prophecy in Scripture apart from the miraculous hand of God at work in the writing of Scripture. Josh McDowell says, "The Old Testament, written over a 1,000-year period, contains several hundred references to the coming Messiah. All of these were fulfilled in Jesus Christ."[7] Furthermore, the remaining unfulfilled prophecies about Jesus Christ the Messiah will be fulfilled upon his second coming.

For a moment, think about how specific many of the prophecies are (e.g., born in the tiny town of Bethlehem, born before A.D. 70, pierced side) and the astounding nature of others (e.g., virgin birth, bodily resurrection). The renowned seventeenth-century philosopher Blaise Pascal did just that and concluded, "If a single man had written a book foretelling the time and manner of Jesus's [*sic*] coming and Jesus had come in conformity with these prophecies, this would carry infinite weight. But there is much more here. There is a succession of men over a period of 4,000 years, coming consistently and invariably one after the other, to foretell the same coming; there is an entire people proclaiming it, existing for 4,000 years to testify in a body to the certainty they feel about it, from which they cannot be deflected by whatever threats and persecutions they may suffer. This is of a quite different order of importance."[8] The bottom line is that Jesus' fulfill-ment of specific Old Testament messianic prophecies is far beyond any coincidence.

After surveying less than half of the Old Testament prophecies regarding Jesus, it is shocking to consider that some people flatly deny that there is even one Old Testament prophecy regarding Jesus to be found anywhere in Scripture. For example, deist revolutionary Thomas Paine said, "I have examined all the passages in the New Testament quoted from the Old, and so-called prophecies concerning Jesus Christ, and I find no such thing as a prophecy of any such person, and I deny there are any."[9] Until I became a Christian at the age of nineteen, I sadly agreed in principle with Thomas Paine. I too would have denied that Scripture included prophetic revelation of the future from God. I would have been highly skeptical that the coming of Jesus into human history was in any way revealed in advance.

Yet God in his patient kindness brought me to a Bible study led by a man who had a PhD in the Old Testament language of Hebrew and also a kind, pastoral disposition that was willing to endure the arrogant assumptions of people like me. I can still remember the day I was holding a copy of a Bible that had been given to me as a high school graduation present and asked him why he thought I should believe it to be truth from God.

His grinning face and dancing eyes that peered out from behind his glasses gave me the sense that I was about to take my first trip to a theological woodshed with a seasoned veteran. I was not disap-pointed. He took me through perhaps every prophecy that I have included for your examination in this chapter with the deft precision of a K-1 fighter landing one blow after another to systematically dis-mantle his opponent.

When he finished, he then wisely shifted the burden of proof to me, asking, "What other explanation besides God can you give me to account for the fulfillment of these prophecies given by many authors over the course of many years, each revealing specific details about the person and work of Jesus?" I had absolutely no answer and realized that I would be a fool to remain hard-hearted and reject so much clear and compelling evidence.

That man remains a dear friend to this day because God opened the gifts of Jesus and Scripture to me through him. Since that day, my entire life has been transformed through my time in Scripture with Jesus. In sharing with you this gift that was given to me, it is my sincere hope and prayer that God would either grant you faith or grow your faith in the Jesus of Scripture.

ANSWERS TO COMMON QUESTIONS ABOUT PROPHECIES REGARDING JESUS' COMING

ISN'T THE 4000 B.C. DATE FOR ADAM AND EVE PRETTY NAÏVE WHEN MANY BIBLICAL SCHOLARS AND SCIENTISTS HAVE PRETTY MUCH DEMOLISHED THE CREDIBILITY OF THAT DATE?

Actually, no. There is an admitted ton of debate about the date. But I [Gerry] simply took the easy way out: I just started with Abraham at about 2000 B.C. and then went with what the Bible records, adding up the ages in Genesis 5 and 11 to get back to the time of Adam and Eve.

You'll often hear that these two genealogies skip generations. That is true for the genealogies of Jesus in Matthew 1 and Luke 3, where the intention is to show the family line, not every generation. So there are no numbers there. But Genesis 5 and 11 give each father's age when the son was born. You just can't say they are approximate unless you mess with the text of Scripture.

Furthermore, while there is great debate about the age of the earth, there is much more agreement between the biblical and the scientific data on the age of the first true *Homo sapiens,* that is, true humans who lived in villages and practiced agriculture. Scientists pretty consistently agree that humans began living in farming villages about 7,000 years ago. Considering these people are usually committed to naturalistic evolution and old earth, the closeness of this date and the biblical date is amazing. Their studies are now concluding that there was a first human female ("mitochrondial Eve") and a first human male ("Y-chromosomal Adam"). These two original humans are genetically unconnected to other *Homo* species such as *Homo neanderthalensis* and *Homo erectus.* To me, that sounds like a couple of created human beings.

You can check it out for yourself. One good book is *Who Was Adam?: A Creation Model Approach to the Origin of Man* by Fazale Rana and Hugh

Ross. Do some web searches on "first farming villages" or "origin *Homo sapiens*" or "mitochrondial Eve." It will be a bit confusing at first, but read carefully. Just remember that most studies cite the date of the origin of the first man-like creature, so-called "anatomically modern humans," at a couple of hundred thousand years ago. This is not true *Homo sapiens* with agriculture and villages of which the Bible is speaking. Also remember that these anthropological genetic studies are usually tainted by philosophical pre-commitments. Furthermore, this whole discipline is in its early stages and many facts are yet to be discovered.

WHAT DOES IT MEAN THAT AN OLD TESTAMENT PROPHECY IS FULFILLED IN JESUS CHRIST?

Many times we limit the meaning of the word *fulfill* inappropriately. The term can have several meanings—as most words do (e.g., ask yourself how many meanings there are for the word *pig*). In some cases, *fulfill* means the Old Testament has made a specific prediction of an event in Jesus' life. We see this in the virgin birth.

In other cases, *fulfill* means the Old Testament gives stories or accounts that set patterns that correspond to the life of the Messiah. Many of these Old Testament passages leave us expectant for more. One example is the sacrifice of Isaac, which leaves us looking for another sacrificed son on Mount Zion. In another case, Hosea speaks of God faithfully bringing his son, Israel, out of Egypt after they fled there for protection. Since the whole Old Testament is looking forward to the Messiah, it is not surprising that his greater Son will also come out of Egypt after he fled there for protection. As another example, Matthew makes a parallel between the murder of children by cruel oppressors in the days of Israel's exile[10] and the murder in Bethlehem by equally cruel oppressors.

The unstated but clear point of parallel is God's word of comfort for the uncomforted. That promise, which was given in the Old Testament, is now being fulfilled in Jesus. What is being fulfilled is God's larger purpose of a new covenant promise that surrounds the specific stories in the Old Testament.

HOW CAN WE SAY JESUS FULFILLED OLD TESTAMENT PROPHECIES WHEN THERE ARE MANY THAT HE DID NOT FULFILL?

This potent question is the excuse that many Jewish people use to support their contention that Jesus is not the promised Messiah. Their hope is that the Messiah will kick out the oppressors and then establish the Jewish people in Israel under his perfect reign. We see this in Ezekiel 36:24–38, one of the many new covenant prophecies.

Bible-believing Christians respond as Jesus did: the work of the Messiah comes in two parts, servant and king, lamb and lion. You can see Jesus' explanation of this distinction in passages such as Luke 19:11–27. Yet another can be found in the beginning of Acts. Jesus told the apostles that the promised Holy Spirit would soon come upon them.[11] They immediately thought of the new covenant promises in passages like Ezekiel 36. They connected the coming of the Spirit to the restoration of Israel. They very understandably asked, "Lord, will you at this time restore the kingdom to Israel?" Jesus explained to them that the kingdom promise was still to be fulfilled in the future. Their job was the same as ours: by the power of the Spirit, give everyone the good news that the Messiah Jesus has come as Lamb; believe and repent in his death and resurrection so we can have forgiveness of sin and new life in Christ and his community. But it also foretells the certain promise. Jesus the lion will come again and judge the world with righteousness, just as the prophets foretold.

These prophecies are not unfilled in the sense that they've failed. Rather they are yet to be fulfilled. The exact fulfillment of the lamb prophecies of Jesus' first coming makes us even more confident in the fulfillment of the lion prophecies of Jesus' second coming.

CHAPTER FOUR

WHY DID JESUS COME TO EARTH?

"For I have come down from heaven, not to do my own will but the will of him who sent me."

JESUS (JOHN 6:38)

✝

Not only are human history and our calendar divided around the coming of Jesus, each year the world's biggest holiday, Christmas, is devoted to celebrating Jesus' entrance into human history. As the eminent theologian Bart Simpson once said, "Christmas is a time when people of all religions come together to worship Jesus Christ." The question to be answered, then, is why did Jesus come to earth?

There are a seemingly endless number of ways that the question can be answered, depending on whom you ask. Thankfully, Jesus himself answers this question and clears up the confusion. Jesus repeatedly (no less than some thirty-nine times in the Gospel of John alone) said that he was God who was sent from heaven to the earth on a mission by God the Father.[1] Jesus described this mission as fulfilling the entirety of the Old Testament promises. In Matthew 5:17–18, Jesus said, "Do not think that I have come to abolish the Law or the Prophets; I have not come to abolish them but to fulfill them. For truly, I say to you, until heaven and earth pass away, not an iota, not a dot, will pass from the Law until all is accomplished."

Therefore, Jesus' mission on the earth was not to diminish, disregard, or disavow the Old Testament. Rather, he came to fulfill all that was anticipated of him in the Scriptures. One helpful way of seeing this glorious truth is to recognize that three primary offices are woven throughout the Old Testament: prophet, priest, and king. Each of these Old Testament offices is ultimately fulfilled in Jesus. His mission on the earth was to reveal himself to us in each of these three ways.

JESUS THE PROPHET

In the Old Testament, the prophet revealed God by speaking God's Word. The prophet was courageously bold and willing to stand up against an entire nation, if needed, to confront sin, command repentance, and cry out the truth of God. Subsequently, the prophet received strong reactions from people who either loved or hated him. This was because the prophet's words would bring the repentant to brokenness and the unrepentant to hard-heartedness. As the Puritans used to say, "The same sun that melts the ice hardens the clay."

The prototypical and greatest of the Old Testament prophets was Moses. Moses promised that one day a greater prophet than he was coming as the fulfillment of prophetic ministry.[2] The prophecy of Moses was fulfilled when Jesus the prophet arrived as promised.[3]

The prophet is inextricably connected to the word of God because the prophet's ministry was to proclaim God's word. According to the Old Testament scholar Gerhard von Rad, the phrase "the word of Yahweh" appears 241 times in the Old Testament. Of those occurrences, 221 were on the lips of prophets as their declaration that they were speaking revelation by no less than God's authority.

Jesus the prophet is superior even to the great prophets of the Old Testament. Unlike the prophets who spoke by God's authority, because Jesus was God, he spoke by his own authority as the source, center, and sum of truth. Consequently, rather than appealing to God's authority, Jesus simply said, "I say to you . . ."[4]

Those who heard Jesus teach were keenly aware of the fact that he did not speak as any other religious leader but rather spoke by his own authority. His hearers "were astonished at his teaching, for he taught them as one who had authority, and not as the scribes."[5] Furthermore,

Jesus says, "I tell you the truth" at least fifty times in John's Gospel alone. He is emphatic that he is the truth-telling prophet.

Jesus' superiority to the Old Testament prophets also extends to his relationship with the Word of God. Scripture reveals that Jesus did not only proclaim the written Word of God, but was literally the incarnate living Word of God. John says, "In the beginning was the Word, and the Word was with God, and the Word was God. . . . And the Word became flesh and dwelt among us, and we have seen his glory, glory as of the only Son from the Father, full of grace and truth."[6] The written Word of God, or Scripture, exists to reveal the incarnate Word of God, the Lord Jesus Christ.

Furthermore, as a prophet, Jesus came to preach and is the greatest preacher who ever has or ever will preach. Jesus himself said that one of the reasons he came to earth was to preach: "And Simon and those who were with him searched for [Jesus], and they found him and said to him, 'Everyone is looking for you.' And he said to them, 'Let us go on to the next towns, that I may preach there also, for that is why I came out.' And he went throughout all Galilee, preaching."[7] As a prophet, Jesus is to be understood as the truth-telling, boldly confrontational preacher who attacks our sin, folly, and rebellion by rebuking us and commanding us to repent.

For some, the role of Jesus as prophet can be misunderstood. For example, I once had a curious conversation with a new Christian in our church. He had begun reading the Bible and when I asked him how it was going, he despairingly said that it was not working. Uncertain of what he meant, I asked him to explain himself. He said that he had been reading the Bible but that the more he read it, the more depressed he became; the more he read, the more he realized how much sin was in his life. I explained to him that Jesus remains a prophet today and was speaking to him through Scripture by truthfully pointing out sin in his life. Rather than being depressed, he was experiencing conviction that, if accompanied by repentance, would lead to joy. As we spoke further, his countenance changed as he came to understand Jesus' loving role of prophet in his life. Jesus was putting a finger on his chest, looking him in the eye, naming his sin, and telling him to go and sin no more. For that to actually occur, I also explained how he would need to understand Jesus' ministry to him as priest.

JESUS THE PRIEST

In the Old Testament, the priest would humbly stand between God and people as a mediator of sorts. He would bring the hopes, dreams, fears, and sins of the people before God as their advocate and intercessor. He would hear their confession of sin and pray for them. Furthermore, central to his role was the offering of sacrifices to show that sin was very real and deserved death, while asking God for gracious forgiveness. Then he would speak God's blessing on them. All of the functions of a priest are ultimately fulfilled in Jesus.

The book of the Bible that deals most thoroughly with the priestly role of Jesus is Hebrews. In Hebrews, we are told that Jesus is our "high priest."[8] In humility, although God, Jesus became a human being so as to identify with us. As fully God and fully man, Jesus alone is able to be the mediator between us and God.[9]

As our priest, Jesus has also offered a sacrifice to pay the penalty for our sin. Not only is Jesus a priest who is superior to the Old Testament priests, his sacrifice is also superior to theirs—he gave his own life and shed his own blood for our sin.[10]

Hebrews reveals that Jesus' ministry as our priest did not end with his return to heaven. Rather, Jesus is alive today and ministers to us as our high priest who intercedes for us before God the Father.[11] Practically, this means that Jesus actually knows us, loves us, pays attention to our lives, and cares for us. He does this not because we are great, but rather because he is our great high priest. It is Jesus our priest who knows every hair on our head, day of our life, longing of our heart, and thought in our mind. At this very moment, Jesus is bringing our hurts, suffering, needs, and sins to the Father in a prayerful and loving way as our priest.

Jesus' priestly intercession makes both our prayer and worship possible. We pray to and worship the Father through Jesus our priest by the indwelling power of God the Holy Spirit, who has made our bodies the new temples in which he lives on the earth.

When we understand Jesus as our priest, we are able to know that he loves us affectionately, tenderly, and personally. Furthermore, Jesus' desire for us is nothing but good, and his ministry results in nothing less than life-changing intimacy with God the Father. This is all made possible by Jesus who as our prophet not only tells us what to do but also makes new life and obedience possible by his loving, compassionate, patient service to us as a faithful priest.

In his role as priest, Jesus is different from all other man-made religions and their false portraits of God. Virtually every religion sees God in a harsh, cutting, prophetic way. Jesus is the only God who gets off his throne to humbly serve us and give us grace and mercy.

The theme of the humble priestly service of Jesus is a thread woven throughout the New Testament. In Luke 19:10, Jesus says, "For the Son of Man came to seek and to save the lost." In this wonderful statement, Jesus, our loving and concerned priest, sees us sinners as utterly lost, not unlike foolish children who have run from the home of their father and are utterly without hope of ever finding their way home. Yet Jesus humbly, kindly, patiently, graciously, and continually pursues us, out of his great love for us.

An example of Jesus' priestly work in the life of one person is found in Matthew 9:9–13. We meet a man named Matthew, a crooked thief and tax collector who is despised by everyone. While sitting at his tax booth extorting people one day, none other than Jesus walks by. Rather than confronting Matthew as the prophet, Jesus surprisingly extends a hand of friendship to him by inviting himself to Matthew's house for dinner. Joining them later at the party at Matthew's house was nothing short of a very bad hip-hop video, complete with women in clear heels, dudes with their pants around their ankles and handguns in their underwear strap, lots of gold teeth, bling, spinners on camels, cheap liquor, and grinding to really loud music with a lot of bass. When word got out to the religious folks, they were perplexed as to how Jesus could roll with such a jacked-up posse. Jesus' answer was purely priestly. Jesus said that they were sick and needed mercy.

The religious people in Jesus' day, as well as every day since, stood at a distance to point out the sin in people's lives in a prophetic way. But they failed to take the next priestly step of pursuing friendship with sick sinners in an effort to expose them to the patient, loving mercy of God, which alone can heal our sickness and sin.

On another occasion, Jesus spoke of his priestly role in terms of humbly serving us: "the Son of Man came not to be served but to serve, and to give his life as a ransom for many."[12] We live in a world where everyone wants to be served and hardly anyone wants to serve. Anyone

who questions this should simply pay attention to how service industry workers such as baristas, bank tellers, and grocery store clerks are
bossed around by people who think they are little gods and mocha
lords who are free to give freakishly detailed orders to their minions.
Unlike the average person who only wants to be served, Jesus is our
great and humble priest who serves us. Jesus has served us by giving
his own life in exchange for ours and continues serving us to this very
day.

Perhaps the most insightful text of Scripture on the importance
of the priestly ministry of Jesus is Hebrews 4:15–16, which says, "For
we do not have a high priest who is unable to sympathize with our
weaknesses, but one who in every respect has been tempted as we are,
yet without sin. Let us then with confidence draw near to the throne
of grace, that we may receive mercy and find grace to help in time of
need." Because he has been where we are, Jesus not only preaches to
us as our prophet, but also sympathizes with us as our priest. Jesus
is sympathetic to our temptations, weakness, suffering, sickness,
disappointment, pain, confusion, loneliness, betrayal, brokenness,
mourning, and sadness. Jesus does not refrain from entering our
sick, fallen, and crooked world. Instead, he humbly came into this
world to feel what we feel and face what we face while remaining sinless. Subsequently, Jesus can both sympathize with and deliver us.
Practically, this means that in our time of need, we can run to Jesus our
sympathetic priest who lives to serve us and give us grace and mercy
for anything that life brings.

As our prophet, Jesus speaks to us boldly. As our priest, Jesus serves
us humbly. Because he is also our king, his speaking and serving extend
to every aspect of our lives.

JESUS AS KING

When the Bible speaks of Jesus as "Lord," it is saying in shorthand
that Jesus is the king of all kings who rules over all of creation. In
John 18:36–37, Jesus has a discussion with a king and reveals that he
is indeed the King who rules over all kings with a kingdom that rules
over all of creation. Echoing Jesus, theologian and politician Abraham
Kuyper once said, "There is not a square inch in the whole domain of

our human existence over which Christ, who is Sovereign over all, does not cry, 'Mine!'"[13]

Jesus taught that his kingdom includes ruling over both the material and immaterial worlds, that which is visible and physical and that which is invisible and spiritual.[14] This means that Jesus rules over angels and demons, Christians and non-Christians, moderns and post-moderns, men and women, young and old, rich and poor, healthy and sick, Republicans and Democrats, simple and wise, and the living and the dead.

Furthermore, Jesus rules over every single aspect of our lives individually. There is not one part of our life that does not belong to Jesus or exist under his sovereign rule. Jesus is not just the King who rules over nations on the earth and principalities and powers in the heavens, but he also rules over our pants, web browser, refrigerator, debit card, cubicle, and car horn. As our king, Jesus demands and deserves obedient loyalty to his commands over every aspect of our life. Subsequently, there is no such thing as a personal life for the Christian.

This point was made painfully obvious to me in a conversation I once had with a guy who admitted he was addicted to alcohol and pornography but also claimed to be a Christian husband and father. When I put my finger in his life in a prophetic way, he responded that he did not want to talk about his "personal life" because it was no one's business but his. In a priestly way I tried to explain to the guy that you cannot call Jesus Lord and stand before him drunk and tell him that it is none of his business. The failure to see Jesus as king over all of creation in general and all of our life in particular leads to nothing but hypocrisy, secrecy, and shameful privacy as we continue to live in darkness.

JESUS IN TRI-PERSPECTIVE

Jesus came to reveal to us this tri-perspectival understanding of who he is and what he has done. As prophet, Jesus confronts us and calls us to repentance of sin. As priest, Jesus comforts us and comes to us to save us from sin and enable new life. As king, Jesus commands us to relinquish authority of our life so that every facet of our life is under constant sanctifying transformation.

Theologically, there is really little if any debate about these matters among Bible-believing Christians. Yet the same people who believe these things can still fail to live according to them. This point was made clear to me while on a date night with my wife, Grace. As we were sitting at a coffee shop playing Scrabble and chatting, she asked me why this tri-perspectival view of Jesus mattered practically. I answered her question with a story from my own life that I pray is helpful to you.

I grew up in a working-class, Irish-Catholic family, and the closest thing I had to a Trinitarian God was baseball, girls, and being left alone. While many Catholics are Christians, I was not one of them. I was basically a moral guy who stopped going to church in his teens but avoided drinking, drugs, and other things in an effort to be a good person.

Upon high school graduation I entered college and decided that it would be fun to reinvent myself and do all the things I had not done. So I joined a frat thinking it would be fun to drink, chase women, and basically try and break the Ten Commandments as often as possible. During the first week of class our frat hosted the first party of the year and I was excited to begin my collegiate imbecility. The basement of our frat was set up with loud music, cheap beer, and darkness broken only by black light scattered throughout the room. When I asked what the black light was for, one of the frat brothers explained that women would be showing up wearing nothing but white T-shirts and that we were supposed to write on those shirts with highlighter pens while they drank beer, thereby enabling us to grope them as public foreplay. As a lost frat guy, the entire plan seemed both depraved and brilliant.

Shortly thereafter, dozens of beautiful young women began pouring into the frat basement all wearing white T-shirts as advertised. They drank heavily, danced wildly, and wanted to be groped and written on. I got dressed in something decent and stood at the doorway into the party, ready to literally walk into a whole new world, when Jesus came to me as my prophet. Though I was not a Christian, I was literally stopped by God at the threshold of the party and was deeply aware that I could not enter the room because it was the gateway to a new life that was not for me. Uncertain of what was going on, I did not attend my first frat party or even hold my first beer. Instead, I went to the library since it was the only thing open, and sat there most of the night wondering what I should do with the rest of my life while guys pursuing real degrees sat nearby actually studying.

I returned to the frat later that night and simply climbed into bed to get some sleep. I awoke early the next morning while everyone else was sleeping off their hangovers. I entered the living room to find a freshman woman sitting on the couch, naked and huddled up under a blanket crying. I asked her what was wrong, and she told me that she had woken up naked and sore with someone she did not know and wanted to go home but could not find her clothes.

I felt sick to my stomach and as she cried, Jesus again came to me as a prophet and showed me the damage I would be doing to women if I did not repent by leaving the frat and pursuing a new life. I gave the young woman one of my sweat outfits and walked her home because it was still dark out and I wanted to make sure she got home safe.

I returned to the frat to pack up my things, resign my membership, and move into a dorm. I had no friends and did not know anyone and felt incredibly lonely and confused about what I was supposed to be doing with my life. It was then that Jesus came to me as a priest. I was compelled to start reading the Bible, and as I did, I learned about Jesus and his love for me and service to me through the cross to take away my sin and change my sinful desires. One day while reading Romans in my dorm room, Jesus saved me and made me a Christian. It was around that time that my pledge class from the frat was arrested for stealing items from local businesses for a party. They spent the weekends of their freshman year in jail and their evenings doing community service. Had I stepped into the party, I would have literally entered a new life that included time in jail as a convicted criminal.

As I read the Bible, I felt compelled to also join Bible studies and attend church to learn more about Jesus. Through friends I met in church and Bible studies, I began to learn about the role of Jesus as my king. Subsequently, I began to see that everything in my life was now about Jesus, which meant that everything—my major, work ethic, future, finances, schedule, sexuality, and relationships—had to be subject to the rule of Jesus. To live apart from the King's loving wisdom would be sheer folly.

As prophet, Jesus was actively pointing out sin in my life through Scripture and the Holy Spirit. As king, Jesus was revealing to me the implications of his rule over my entire life. As priest, Jesus was kindly and patiently forgiving my sin and changing my life through his Word, his Spirit, and the people whom he had brought alongside of me as friends. Early in my Christian life, I was blessed to see Jesus in each of his three roles and experience the difference it makes to see how they work together in a perfect way.

Without being overly critical, I do believe that most Christians and Christian traditions have a propensity to underemphasize one aspect of Jesus' ministry, which can have very tragic effects. Personally, I have an easy time understanding the priestly role of Jesus for the victims of sin, but I can sometimes be overly harsh with a sinner. When someone sins, I more easily see them needing Jesus as prophet rather than priest, which is not always the case. Sometimes, as Paul says, it is the kindness of God that brings about our repentance. Practically, this means that I am prone toward fundamentalism.

PROPHET + KING - PRIEST = JESUS OF FUNDAMENTALISM

Fundamentalist Christians who are prone to legalism, moralism, and a general lack of love, grace, mercy, or patience are often the product of a deficient understanding of Jesus as priest. The strength of fundamentalism is its keen awareness of Jesus' prophetic role as bold truth-teller and commander of repentance, along with his role as king who rules and reigns in all authority. However, they are also prone not to appreciate fully the priestly role of Jesus. As a result, God seems primarily cold, distant, stern, harsh, and even cruel. Their Jesus sits on a throne far away and yells at us but never gets off that throne to help. He's just sitting there, disappointed, waiting for us to mess up. In short, this is a God that we are more prone to run away from than toward in our time of need. The result of this error is either despair or pride, but not worship, humility, or joy. Because God is a boss who yells at us, this form of religion traps us into a cycle where if we think we're doing well, we get proud, and if we think we're doing poorly, we get depressed. At no point do we receive loving help because Jesus is not fully valued as a priest.

PROPHET + PRIEST - KING = JESUS OF EVANGELICALISM

The curious fact of modern evangelicalism is that there is both a general assent to basic Christian truths, and a moral life that is virtually indistinguishable from the average non-Christian in areas such as sexual sin.

Researchers such as George Barna have built entire ministries quantifying these facts statistically. Why does this happen? Because the role of Jesus as king is apparently diminished or dismissed.

In this form of religion, people know that Jesus speaks the truth as their prophet and loves them as their priest. So when they sin, they know that Jesus will forgive them and still love them. But they still rule over their own life. When they need help, they read the Bible or ask Jesus to serve them. Practically, they don't see Jesus ruling over them, but rather coming alongside them to help them to achieve their objectives. He is only allowed to do so when he is invited. The result is a double-life of hypocrisy in which we call Jesus Lord, call his Word true, and then do whatever we want in some areas of our life because the pants are mine, the money is mine, the web browser is mine, the food is mine, the alcohol is mine, the schedule is mine, the life is mine, and the glory is mine, and I will rule as king over aspects of my own life with Jesus as little more than my trusty assistant.

PRIEST + KING - PROPHET = JESUS OF LIBERALISM

Liberal Christianity is prone to understand Jesus as our priest, who is filled with grace, love, mercy, and tolerant patience, as well as our king, who rules over all peoples and seeks to extend to them grace, love, and mercy. However, the weakness of typical liberal Christianity is that it fails to fully appreciate the hard-edged role of Jesus as prophet. The sad result is that Jesus is seen as someone who would never offend us, raise his voice, hurt our feelings, speak harshly, or command individuals to repent with a sense of urgency because he is only infinitely patient, tolerant, and understanding.

By way of illustration, I recall a conversation I once had with a liberal Christian pastor who was president of a large network of liberal churches. He told me that a pastor should never say anything that would offend anyone because the only way we offend someone is when we speak out of a place of pride. I asked him if Jesus was therefore guilty of the sin of pride because many people were furious with him to the degree that they shouted, "Crucify him!" Seeing he was on the horns of a dilemma, he agreed that Jesus was both the most humble person who has ever lived and did say some things that his hearers considered harsh because of their prophetic edge. Jesus sometimes spoke tenderly as a priest, but he also spoke tersely as a prophet to ensure that the sword of truth was removed from its scabbard and wielded with full force.

When Jesus is not seen as prophet, sinful beliefs and behaviors are blessed because to speak the truth and command repentance would require a prophetic voice. Subsequently, liberal Christianity is mired in such things as homosexuality and universalism, as if every sexual practice and every religious belief were acceptable in the eyes of Jesus.

Jesus came to the earth to reveal himself to us as our prophet who speaks to us, priest who walks with us, and king who rules over us. Jesus' ministry continues today and his roles are the same yesterday, today, and forever. For the three offices of Jesus to be of the greatest benefit to us, we must humbly ask God to reveal to us which aspect of Jesus' ministry we are most likely to misunderstand or even ignore and read Scripture with a humble heart seeking to see Jesus in the fullness of his glory. Having understood why Jesus came, we can now explore how Jesus came through the Virgin Mary.

ANSWERS TO COMMON QUESTIONS ABOUT JESUS' MISSION

HOW CAN JESUS REALLY SYMPATHIZE WITH ME AS MY PRIEST IF HE IS SINLESS AND THEREFORE HAS NOT EXPERIENCED THE DEVASTATION OF SIN LIKE I HAVE?

While it is true that Jesus has not sinned in any way, it is also true that he has taken our sin to himself completely. In a haunting phrase, Isaiah tells us, "Surely he has borne our griefs and carried our sorrows."[15] According to David, the Messiah declares, "I am a worm and not a man, scorned by mankind and despised by the people."[16] Jesus himself said, "How is it written of the Son of Man that he should suffer many things and be treated with contempt?"[17] We see this in the horrors of the Garden of Gethsemane, where Jesus was incredibly distressed at the thought of taking sin upon himself and being punished for our sins. Paul explains that "for our sake he [the Father] made him [the Son] to be sin who knew no sin."[18]

This likely means that Jesus took on the weight of sin as he progressed through his life. Rather than some sort of covenantal bookkeeping action that took place on the cross, Jesus actually carried the reality of sin, felt its weight, and was troubled by its real impact on him during his life.[19] By way of modern analogy, he is a little like Frodo on the way to Mount Doom. The closer he gets, the heavier the ring becomes. Finally he cannot go on, and Sam has to carry him to the completion of his mission. Jesus was on a similar mission, a quest, really. The closer he got to Calvary, the heavier the mission weighed upon him. Finally, in the Garden of Gethsemane he was nearly overwhelmed, when Luke tells us that an angel came to strengthen him. Nonetheless, Jesus went on alone.

In all this horror, however, Jesus never gave in to sin. The holiness of

Jesus the prophet is still very real. But Jesus also did learn to help us as priest by personally experiencing the devastating weight of our sin.

IF I HAVE TO OBEY JESUS AS KING, ISN'T THAT SALVATION BY GOOD WORKS?

It depends on what you mean by salvation. If you mean being accepted as God's child (what we call justification or acceptance), there are no works involved at all. Offering God good works to pay for our invitation to be his child would be the worst kind of insult. By way of analogy, imagine being a wildly disobedient teenager trapped in the foster care system because no one wanted to adopt you. Then imagine being invited to have dinner with the president himself. As you come into his home, he has carefully ensured that everything is perfect for the evening. He seats you next to him in a place of honor so that you can talk personally. He ensures that you get the very best food. Then, at the end of the evening, he walks you to your very own bedroom and he explains that he has chosen to love you, adopt you, and devote himself to being the kind of father that transforms your life. Imagine at that moment taking the $1.89 you have in your pocket and handing it to him to pay him back for everything and expecting him to be thrilled with your response.

Likewise, God needs nothing from us, and nothing we can do for God or give to God obligates him to us in any way. There is absolutely nothing we can do to make God want us as his children. God is a father who adopts and loves us by pure grace alone.

But once we are his kids, God our Father does not want us to stay in our wretchedness. He does not save us to be miserable. This part of salvation is called sanctification, our growth in Christlikeness. He knows we can't do it on our own, so he sends the Holy Spirit to help us be all we really can and want to be. Similarly, God the Spirit works totally without charge in pure grace.

Paul explains: "For by grace you have been saved through faith. And this is not your own doing; it is the gift of God, not a result of works, so that no one may boast."[20] That is the justification piece, the full acceptance by the Lord of the universe. No works of any kind are commingled with God's grace, period. Then, speaking about accepted, Spirit-empowered people, Paul says, "For we are his workmanship, created in Christ Jesus for good works, which God prepared beforehand, that we should walk in them."[21] That is the sanctification piece, the growth to Christian adulthood as a member of God's family.

This life of new good works is not something we have to do so that God will love us. Rather, it is something we get to do because our Father already does love us. Deep down, as members of God's family, what we really want to do is live new lives as fully satisfied children of the King. Although we are not saved by our good works, we are most certainly saved to our good works.

CHAPTER FIVE

WHY DID JESUS' MOM NEED TO BE A VIRGIN?

**Therefore the Lord himself will give you a sign.
Behold, the virgin shall conceive and bear a son,
and shall call his name Immanuel.**

ISAIAH 7:14

✝

Each Christmas the world celebrates the birth of Jesus to his young mother, Mary, and homes are adorned with nativity scenes. Nonetheless, the virgin birth of Jesus remains the second most controversial miracle in all of history, following the resurrection of Jesus from death. Some people do not believe in the virgin birth, some people do believe in the virgin birth, and still others believe in the scriptural virgin birth in addition to a host of myths, legends, fables, and folklore. Opinions about the virgin birth of Jesus include the following curious statements from the famous and infamous:

- Marilyn Manson: "I hate Christmas. I like to go around and replace Baby Jesus in the nativities with a boiled ham."
- Prince: "I don't understand what Christmas means. It seems to be a ridiculous convention that everyone assumes."
- Larry King, when asked if he could interview anyone from all of history, said, "Jesus Christ." "And what would you like to ask Him?" King

replied, "I would like to ask Him if He was indeed virgin-born. The answer to that question would define history for me."

⊚ Catholic Cardinal Robert Bellarmine at the trial of Galileo in 1615: "To assert that the earth revolves around the sun is as ridiculous as a claim that Jesus was not born of a virgin."

⊚ Harry Emerson Fosdick (influential pastor of Riverside Church in New York City): "I do not believe in the Virgin Birth and hope that none of you do."

⊚ Bishop Joseph Sprague of the United Methodist Church called the virgin birth a "myth."

⊚ Thomas Jefferson, in a letter to John Adams: "The day will come when the mystical generation of Jesus, by the Supreme Being as His father, in the womb of a virgin will be classed with the fable of the generation of Minerva in the brain of Jupiter."

⊚ Madonna wears a "Mary is my home girl" T-shirt.

⊚ Episcopalian bishop John Spong: "In time the virgin birth account will join Adam and Eve and the story of the cosmic ascension as clearly recognized mythical elements in our faith tradition whose purpose was not to describe a literal event."

⊚ Theologian Raymond Brown called it "folkloric."

⊚ Theologian Wolfhart Pannenberg called it an "aetiological legend."

⊚ Charles Haddon Spurgeon: "The greatest and most momentous fact which the history of the world records is the fact of his birth."

WHAT SCRIPTURE DOES TEACH ABOUT THE VIRGIN BIRTH OF JESUS

In light of the contradictory opinions, we will begin by examining what Scripture teaches about the virgin birth of Jesus. The genesis of the Bible's promise of the virgin birth is actually located in its opening pages. In Genesis 3:15, God tells the Serpent, "I will put enmity between you and the woman, and between your offspring and her offspring; he shall bruise your head, and you shall bruise his heel." God promises that Jesus would be born from a woman. This is unusual because the rest of Scripture speaks of children as being born from their father.[1] Here, however, no father is mentioned for Jesus, which implies that he would not have a biological earthly father. Paul speaks in the same manner, saying,

"But when the fullness of time had come, God sent forth his Son, born of a woman . . ."[2]

Some seven hundred years before the birth of Jesus, the prophet Isaiah further illuminated his virgin birth: "Therefore the Lord himself will give you a sign. Behold, the virgin shall conceive and bear a son, and shall call his name Immanuel."[3] This verse is the most hotly debated Old Testament verse regarding the virgin birth of Jesus on two fronts.

Some contend that the prophecy was not speaking of future events but rather the birth of the son of Ahaz. That is half true. An examination of the entire context reveals that the prophecy has a dual fulfillment; it speaks of the birth of a son to "Ahaz," as well as the birth of the Messiah to the "house of David."[4] Furthermore, by naming the son "Immanuel," God is promising more than just a male baby. Immanuel means "God is with us," which points to the son being God. In addition, a few pages later we read, "For to us a child is born, to us a son is given; and the government shall be upon his shoulder, and his name shall be called Wonderful Counselor, Mighty God, Everlasting Father, Prince of Peace. Of the increase of his government and of peace there will be no end, on the throne of David and over his kingdom, to establish it and to uphold it with justice and with righteousness from this time forth and forever more. The zeal of the LORD of hosts will do this."[5] This promise speaks to much more than just the birth of a male human baby.

Some also contend that the prophecy in Isaiah does not refer to a virgin. They argue that the Hebrew word *almah* (which is used in Isaiah 7:14) typically means "young woman," not "virgin," whereas the Hebrew word *bethulah* typically means "virgin." However, there are many reasons why the verse should be read as referring to a virgin. Even if the word does mean "young woman," that does not mean that she would not be a virgin. In that day, young women were virgins, making the terms synonymous for most young Hebrew women. Those unmarried women who were not virgins were subject to death under the Law. If there was any question about her virginity, a woman was subject to physical inspection, which we see in Deuteronomy 22:14–22.

Additionally, the word *almah* is used elsewhere in the Old Testament to refer specifically to a young virgin woman. One clear example is Rebekah, who is described as "very attractive in appearance, a maiden [*bethulah*] whom no man had known."[6] Further in the chapter we read that Rebekah was a "virgin [*almah*]."[7] While the two words are virtually synonymous, apparently *bethulah* required a bit more clarification that the woman was a virgin while *almah* did not. Furthermore, two centuries before Jesus was born, we find that the Jews understood exactly what *almah* means: the Septuagint, the Jewish 250 B.C. translation of the Hebrew Bible into Greek, translates *almah* as *parthenos*, which unambiguously means "virgin." Lastly, in the New Testament, Isaiah 7:14 is clearly interpreted to be a prophetic promise about the birth of Jesus to Mary, who was both a young woman and a virgin.

The fulfillment of the inference in Genesis and the promise from Isaiah are recorded in great historical detail in two of the four Gospels, namely Matthew 1:18–25 and Luke 1:26–38, which my children enjoy hearing Linus recite every year in the Charlie Brown Christmas cartoon special. Both sections of Scripture are listed below so you can read them for yourself. I have added emphasis to the repeated efforts the authors make to clearly identify that Jesus' mother, Mary, was a virgin who conceived by a miracle of God the Holy Spirit.

MaTTHeW 1:18–25

Now the birth of Jesus Christ took place in this way. When his mother Mary had been betrothed to Joseph, *before they came together she was found to be with child from the Holy Spirit.* And her husband Joseph, being a just man and unwilling to put her to shame, resolved to divorce her quietly. But as he considered these things, behold, an angel of the Lord appeared to him in a dream, saying, "Joseph, son of David, do not fear to take Mary as your wife, for *that which is conceived in her is from the Holy Spirit.* She will bear a son, and you shall call his name Jesus, for he will save his people from their sins." All this took place to fulfill what the Lord had spoken by the prophet: "Behold, the *virgin* shall conceive and bear a son, and they shall call his name Immanuel" (which means, God with us) [Isa. 7:14]. When Joseph woke from sleep, he did as the angel of the Lord commanded him: he took his wife, but *knew her not until she had given birth to a son.* And he called his name Jesus.

LuKe 1:26–38

In the sixth month the angel Gabriel was sent from God to a city of Galilee named Nazareth, to a *virgin* betrothed to a man whose name was Joseph, of the house of David. And the *virgin's* name was Mary. And he came to her and said, "Greetings, O favored one, the Lord is with you!" But she was greatly troubled at the saying, and tried to discern what sort of greeting this might be. And the angel said to her, "Do not be afraid, Mary, for you have found favor with God. And behold, you will conceive in your womb and bear a son, and you shall call his name Jesus. He will be great and will be called the Son of the Most High. And the Lord God will give to him the throne of his father David, and he will reign over the house of Jacob forever, and of his kingdom there will be no end." And Mary said to the angel, *"How will this be, since I am a virgin?"* And the angel answered her, *"The Holy Spirit will come upon you, and the power of the Most High will overshadow you*; therefore the child to be born will be called holy—the Son of God. And behold, your relative Elizabeth in her old age has also conceived a son, and this is the sixth month with her who was called barren. *For nothing will be impossible with God."* And Mary said, "Behold, I am the servant of the Lord; let it be to me according to your word." And the angel departed from her.

In summary, the Old Testament both quietly implies and loudly prophesies the virgin birth of Jesus. The writers of the New Testament go to painstaking detail to emphasize that in every way Jesus' mother, Mary, was a virgin woman who conceived Jesus solely through a miracle of God the Holy Spirit. Sadly, a number of doctrines without biblical justification have attached themselves to this glorious truth like barnacles. Therefore, we must also examine seven specific beliefs that Scripture does not teach about the virgin birth of Jesus but that many theologians do.

WHAT SCRIPTURE DOES NOT TEACH ABOUT THE VIRGIN BIRTH OF JESUS

1) SCRIPTURE DOES NOT TEACH THAT MARY DID NOT HAVE A NORMAL DELIVERY.

Some Catholic theologians have taught that Jesus was not born in the normal fashion through Mary's birth canal. Rather, they say he was born via something much like a miraculous C-section, as if Mary were some Messiah-in-the-box, and Joseph cranked her arm until the Messiah popped out of her gut. However, nothing in Scripture says this, but instead contradicts it: "But you, O Bethlehem Ephrathah, who are too little to be among the clans of Judah, from you shall come forth for me one who is to be ruler in Israel, whose coming forth is from of old, from ancient days. Therefore he shall give them up until the time when she who is in labor has given birth; then the rest of his brothers shall return to the people of Israel."[8]

Simply, the Scriptures give no indication that Mary's birth was in any way abnormal or miraculous. As a sinner, she experienced the same pain of childbirth felt by every daughter of Eve who has mothered a child, as was prophesied in Micah 5:3.

2) SCRIPTURE DOES NOT TEACH THAT MARY REMAINED A VIRGIN FOR THE REST OF HER LIFE.

Arguments for the perpetual virginity of Mary arose as early as the second century, became more popular in the fourth century, and culminated with the Second Council of Constantinople, which convened in 553 and declared Mary "ever virgin." Some early church fathers (e.g., Origen), some Catholic and Protestant theologians (such as Luther, Calvin, Zwingli, and Wesley), along with the Second Helvetic Confession and the Geneva Bible say that Mary was "ever virgin," or *semper virgo*. I am assuming that her husband, Joseph, was *semper bummo*, or "ever bummed."

The first time I learned of this doctrine was during one of my three years in Catholic grade school. I will never forget the day that one of the nuns told our entire fifth grade class that Mary was a virgin her entire life and that the girls should want to give their life to Jesus and be virgins forever. I was very disappointed to look around the room and see the girls nodding in agreement. It was at that moment that I decided that I needed to get back to the public school I had previously attended as quickly as possible so that I could one day find a wife who would have sex with me.

The implications of the perpetual virginity of Mary are important. Practically, this would mean that not only was Mary a virgin when she conceived Jesus, but that following his birth she never had intimate relations with her own husband, Joseph. This teaching is inaccurate for three reasons. First, God designed marriage to include physical union[9] and said that depriving marital intimacy is a sin.[10] Second, Matthew 1:25 says that they did have relations following Jesus' birth: "But [he] knew her not *until* she had given birth to a son.

And he called his name Jesus." The language here clearly implies that they did in fact have normal marital relations (as are celebrated in the Song of Soloman) after Jesus was born. Third, Scripture repeatedly states that Mary had other sons and daughters.[11] In no way are we ever led to believe that Mary produced a Suburban full of kids through a succession of virgin births. Jesus' conception was unique, whereas the conception of his siblings was via the ordinary way of a husband and wife listening to old Motown baby-making music and doing what married folks are supposed to do. Therefore, Scripture states that Mary was a virgin until the birth of Jesus, as was also taught by the church fathers Tertullian and Irenaeus. Much of the opposition to this simple and beautiful truth is based on the false assumption that loving, marital sexual intimacy is somehow unholy and therefore unfit for a woman like Mary.

3) SCRIPTURE DOES NOT TEACH THAT JESUS' VIRGIN BIRTH WAS A MYTH TAKEN FROM OTHER RELIGIONS.

In mythology there are stories such as Zeus begetting Hercules and Apollo begetting Ion and Pythagoras. As a result, some have speculated that Christians stole the virgin birth story from such myths. This speculation must be rejected on three grounds. First, some such myths came after the prophesy of Isaiah 7:14 and therefore could not have been the origination of the story. Second, the myths speak of gods having sex with women, which is not what the virgin birth account entails. Third, the myths do not involve actual human beings like Mary and Jesus, but rather fictional characters similar to our modern-day superheroes in the comics.

4) SCRIPTURE DOES NOT TEACH THAT BELIEF IN THE VIRGIN BIRTH PROVES THE DEITY OF JESUS.

Just because people believe in the virgin birth doesn't mean they believe in the deity of Christ. For example, Jehovah's Witnesses strongly affirm the virgin birth but also wrongly declare Jesus to be the incarnation of Michael, the archangel. In doing so, they follow the ancient heresy of the Arians. Even some Muslims believe in the virgin birth, but they certainly don't believe in the deity of our Lord.

5) SCRIPTURE DOES NOT TEACH THAT OUR SIN NATURE IS PASSED ONLY THROUGH THE MALE LINE.

Many Christian theologians, including Augustine, Ambrose, Aquinas, and Luther, believe the sin nature is imparted through the male line. If this is true, the reasoning goes, then Jesus had to be virgin born. An earthly father would have given him a sin nature and brought him under Adamic condemnation.

While Scripture clearly teaches that the sin of Adam brings death and condemnation to all humans,[12] it does not teach that our sin nature comes only from our dads. In fact, the Bible seems to connect sinfulness with the normal process of conception.[13] Furthermore, this line of teaching seems to assume that somehow women are not as depraved as men. Scripture flatly denies that. Both genders are equally sinful.[14]

Some have gone even further. To protect Jesus from any sort of sin, the Roman Catholic Church followed Augustine and said that Mary was not a sinner in her life. They say that she too was immaculately conceived, and therefore, she had no sin nature and was not a sinner. None of this is grounded in Scripture and flatly contradicts Mary's own words that she needed a savior.[15] If she had no sin of any kind, why would she have brought a sin offering to the temple?[16] Indeed, Jesus was without sin[17] and did not have a sin nature, not because Mary was without sin, but because he was protected by a miracle of the Holy Spirit in a way that was similar to the miracles of God, making Adam from dust and granting Sarah the ability to conceive Isaac. While this point may seem trivial, if science such as genetic engineering continues to advance, we may one day see people made without a father, and if so they should not be considered sinless like Jesus.

6) SCRIPTURE DOES NOT TEACH THAT MARY KNOCKED BOOTS WITH GOD.

The Mormons actually teach that God the Father had physical, flesh-and-bone sexual relations with Mary, thereby enabling her to conceive Jesus. If that were not weird enough, they also state that Mary remained a virgin because apparently if a woman knocks boots with a god it does not count, and she technically remains a virgin. Furthermore, I am surprised there is not an epidemic of boys changing their names to Zeus and then taking Mormon girls to prom.

7) SCRIPTURE DOES NOT TEACH THAT JESUS' VIRGIN BIRTH IS UNIMPORTANT.

In answer to the question, can a true Christian deny the virgin birth? Dr. Al Mohler has said: "The answer to that question must be a decisive No. . . . Christians must face the fact that a denial of the virgin birth is a denial of Jesus as the Christ. The Savior who died for our sins was none other than the baby who was conceived of the Holy Spirit, and born of a virgin. The virgin birth does not stand alone as a biblical doctrine[;] it is an irreducible part of the biblical revelation about the person and work of Jesus Christ. With it, the Gospel stands or falls."[18]

Ironically, however, perhaps the most curious doctrine to be undermined recently is the virgin birth, or more precisely the virgin conception, of Jesus Christ in the womb of his mother, Mary. One popular young pastor named Rob Bell speculates that if "Jesus had a real, earthly, biological father named Larry, and archaeologists find Larry's tomb and do DNA samples and prove beyond a shadow of a doubt that the virgin birth was really just a bit of mythologizing the Gospel writers threw in to appeal to the followers of the Mithra and Dionysian religious cults that were hugely popular at the time," we would essentially not lose any significant part of our faith because it is more about how we live.[19] To be fair, Bell does not deny the virgin conception of Jesus, but rather he does deny that it is of any notable theological importance. This, however, is a dangerous move for four reasons.

First, the only alternative to the virgin birth offered in Scripture is that Mary was a sexually sinful woman who conceived Jesus illegitimately, which was the accusation in Jesus' day.[20] In agreement with this line of reasoning, "theologian" and Jesus Seminar fellow Robert Funk has called Jesus a "bastard messiah."[21] Subsequently, since anyone with a devoutly Christian mother would not appreciate people calling her a slut, it seems reasonable to refrain from speculating about whether Jesus' mom was giving out freebies in the woods to some guy named Larry between her quiet times.

Second, if the virgin birth of Jesus is untrue, then the story of Jesus changes dramatically; we would have a sexually promiscuous young woman lying about God's miraculous hand in the birth of her son, raising that son to declare he is God, and then joining his religion.[22] If Mary is nothing more than a sinful con artist, then neither she nor her son Jesus should be trusted.

Third, Bell makes the assumption that DNA testing is somehow more trustworthy than the testimony of Scripture. In this, he is saying that there can and should be potential authorities above Scripture for our theological conclusions, which is a very dangerous move and a diminished view of the perfection, authority, and trustworthiness of Scripture. The Bible is emphatic that Jesus' mother, Mary, was a virgin who conceived by the Holy Spirit. If we deny the virgin birth, we are flatly and plainly stating that Scripture may contain mistakes, or even outright lies, used as marketing schemes to sell Christian faith to pagans. In his book *The Virgin Birth of Christ*, which is perhaps the greatest book ever written defending that fact, J. Gresham Machen said, "Everyone admits that the Bible represents Jesus as having been conceived by the Holy Ghost and born of the Virgin Mary. The only question is whether in making that representation the Bible is true or false."[23] Machen went on to argue that "if the Bible is regarded as being wrong in what it says about the birth of Christ, then obviously the authority of the Bible in any high sense, is gone."[24]

Fourth, in the early days of the Christian church, there was, in fact, a group who rejected the belief that Isaiah 7:14 spoke of a virgin and instead believed it referred only to a young woman. This heretical group was called the Ebionites. One scholar says, "Apart from the Ebionites … and a few Gnostic sects, no body of Christians in early times is known to have existed who did not accept as part of their faith the birth of Jesus from the Virgin Mary."[25] Another writes, "Everything that we know of the dogmatics of the early part of the second century agrees with the belief that at that period the virginity of Mary was a part of the formulated Christian belief."[26] Furthermore, the church father Ignatius, who was trained by the apostle John, testified to this fact, speaking of the "virginity of Mary."[27] Lastly, Machen summarizes the evidence for that fact saying, "There is good ground, we think, to hold that the reason why the Christian Church came to believe in the birth of Jesus without a human father was simply that He was a matter of fact so born."[28]

It is true that some doctrines are primary in that they are essential to Christian belief (e.g., Scripture, Trinity, Jesus' death and resurrection) and others are secondary in that people who love Jesus and believe

Scripture have differing opinions (e.g., details surrounding Jesus' second coming). However, if we lose the virgin birth, we do lose the very core of what it means to be Christian because we diminish the trustworthiness of Scripture, Jesus, and the witness of his own mother.

WHAT WE ARE TO MAKE OF MARY

Tragically, Mary has been either maligned or made over by seemingly everyone with a corrupt theological agenda. For example, in her book *The Illegitimacy of Jesus*, Jane Schaberg "accuses the church of inventing the doctrine of the virgin birth in order to subordinate women. As she summarizes: 'The charge of contemporary feminists, then, is not that the image of the Virgin Mary is unimportant or irrelevant, but that it contributes to and is integral to the oppression of women.'"[29] Schaberg goes on to declare that Jesus' conception was most likely the result of extramarital sex or rape.

The Mary of the Bible does not need to be maligned or made over. Scripture prophesied that Jesus would be Immanuel, God with us, born of the Virgin Mary. The birth of Jesus is unique, miraculous, and unprecedented in all of human history. Furthermore, it shows that God kindly works through us by his power and grace. It also shows that God honors motherhood and women of faith like Mary.

I too was guilty for many years of having a view of Mary that was not based on Scripture. Raised in a Catholic home, I prayed many prayers to Mary as a young boy like so many practitioners of the Catholic and Orthodox brands of Christian faith. Although many Catholics and Orthodox people are in fact Christians who love Jesus, I did not grow up as one of them but was merely a religious person who attended church infrequently and had no real devotion to the person of Jesus or appreciation for his work. Upon my conversion to both Jesus and Protestantism at the age of nineteen, something very sad happened in my heart for a few years. In essence, I despised Mary. Having prayed to her, I saw that I had elevated her to a status of veneration that caused her to be at least as important in my life as Jesus.

Over the years since, I have studied Scripture and prayed for God the Holy Spirit to give me a more biblical and correct view of Mary. I have come to believe that while Catholic and Orthodox Christians make too much of Mary, Protestants have been equally guilty of overreacting and making too little of Mary. This point was made evident to me when, after preaching a Christmas sermon from Luke's Gospel on Mary, a devout Protestant Christian brother essentially rebuked me for talking about Mary from the pulpit with anything more than a passing mention. He told me, "You should not preach about Mary because we are not Catholics so we don't need to hear all about her." Thankfully, God in his patient kindness has brought me to a new appreciation of Mary through my study of Scripture.

Mary is not to be our object of faith but rather our example of faith in Jesus. Imagine her emotions when she's told that she will be pregnant without being married in a society that shamed, humiliated, exiled, or even killed such women. Tradition says they would take her to the gate of the city, rip off her clothes, dress her in rags, tie her up, and bring all the women to see her and learn the lesson of shame through her suffering. Joining them as witnesses would have been the worst kind of vile men who simply enjoyed watching women getting stripped and beaten.

But Mary knew the promises of Isaiah. She lived by the power of God. So instead of saying, "Count me out. I just want a nice life," she immediately accepted God's very difficult call on her life, saying, "Behold, I am the servant of the Lord; let it be to me according to your word."[30] Hers is a faith for anyone to follow.

The first snapshot of the early church singles out Mary for mention as a woman of prayer. She is pointed out among the one hundred twenty people in the Upper Room worshiping Jesus as the only God before the Holy Spirit was poured out on the day of Pentecost.[31]

Mary is a wonderful example for all Christians, particularly women, and especially young women. She obviously loved God, and, while not sinless like her son, she did live in holiness as marked by her virginity until marriage. She is an inspiring example that our sexually promiscuous culture desperately needs to have modeled through women like her. We all need to follow her example of humble faith that fully trusted God's will for her life.

Martin Luther deftly commented that while the virgin conception was God's greatest miracle in Mary's life, the fact of her faith in God was perhaps her greatest miracle of all.[32] It is our prayer that you would, by God's grace, follow in the wonderful example of a remarkable teenage girl who was honored by God with the birth and raising of the Lord Jesus Christ, Immanuel, God with us, who came to save us sinners from our sins. Beautifully, our new birth through Jesus is patterned after the birth of Jesus in that both are miracles wrought entirely of God to be received in faith.

ANSWERS TO COMMON QUESTIONS ABOUT JESUS' VIRGIN BIRTH

WHAT DOES IT MEAN THAT JESUS IS CALLED GOD'S "ONLY BEGOTTEN SON"?

In the King James Version of the Bible, John 3:16 reads, "For God so loved the world, that he gave his only begotten Son, that whosoever believeth in him should not perish, but have everlasting life." The word "begotten" (*monogenes*) refers to a father producing a child. The idea of *mono* emphasizes the uniqueness of this child, as with Abraham and Isaac.[33]

There has been a raging controversy in the church about this term. Many see it as referencing the Trinitarian relation between the eternal Father and the eternal Son. The emphasis is that the Son is begotten, not made. When I beget a son, he is of the same essence as I am. But if I were to make a son, like a robot, he would be entirely different from me. But if the Son is really begotten, it certainly sounds like we are headed into a cultish, Mormon-like understanding of a God who fathers children. Worse yet, it would also mean that rather than being eternal, the Son had a beginning, which is a core tenet of the Jehovah's Witnesses cult.

Many contemporary scholars think the term *begotten* stresses the uniqueness of the child, and they drop the idea of fathering. So the ESV translates John 3:16 as "For God so loved the world, that he gave his only Son . . ." That translation avoids the problem of the Son's having a beginning, but it doesn't seem quite right to overlook the aspect of fathering.

Another possibility keeps the basic meaning of *monogenes* as "uniquely fathered," but focuses on what the Father did to conceive a son in the womb of Mary. Jesus is the only person in all of history to be fathered by the action of God. Adam and Eve were created by the Father. All other people were fathered by human fathers. This interpretation seems to fit every occurrence of the term in reference to Jesus.[34]

WHY DOES THE VIRGIN BIRTH APPEAR ONLY IN TWO GOSPELS?

The virgin birth is taught very clearly in Matthew and Luke. Critics have argued that if the other parts of the Bible are totally silent on it, perhaps they don't agree.

But look at the facts. It's alluded to in Genesis 3:15 and specifically prophesied in Isaiah 7:14. Matthew and Luke teach it with absolute clarity. John indicates it when he uses *monogenes*[35] and when he asserts the divine source of Jesus.[36] Paul alludes to it clearly in Galatians 4:4: "But when the fullness of time had come, God sent forth his Son, born of woman, born under the law . . ."

Lastly, every baptismal formula and creed in the early church includes the phrase "born of Mary the virgin." This truth was regularly repeated because it was believed as an essential truth of the Christian faith.

WASN'T A VIRGIN BIRTH A PRETTY COMMON IDEA IN THE ANCIENT WORLD?

Actually, no. While the ancients lived before the days of genetic engineering and DNA studies, they sure knew where babies came from.

Ancient religions often taught bizarre supernatural origins, but not virgin births. For example, the Greeks thought that Hercules came from the sexual union of the god Zeus and the woman Alcmene. But that is hardly a virgin birth.

Some sects of Hinduism believe Krishna is the virgin-born avatar or incarnation of Vishnu. But they also think Vishnu came as a fish, a turtle, a boar, a lion, and other bizarre things . . . just like Jesus?

Augustus Caesar also claimed a god impregnated his mother, Olympia, using a snake. . . . just like Jesus?

If you check the facts, it becomes obvious that the teaching of the virgin birth of Jesus is unique.

DOES GENESIS 3:15 REALLY SPEAK OF THE COMING OF THE MESSIAH?

This strange prediction of the "enmity" between the snake and the woman is understandable since most every woman hates snakes. But it is peculiar in that it says that a snake will also hate a woman, and women do not generally have snakes inform them of their hatred. But Genesis

3:15 says a lot more. There is also enmity between the "offspring" (_zera_) of the snake and the "offspring" of the woman. But then it changes: the offspring of the woman will crush not the head of the snake's offspring, but the head of the snake itself.

Who is the snake that the offspring will crush? Later Bible writers reveal that Satan is the one behind the cursed snake.[37]

More significantly, we immediately wonder who this offspring of Eve is.

The Septuagint has a very normal translation of _zera_ into _sperma_, a neuter noun. But then there's a big surprise. Though you would expect the next phrase to be "it [neuter] will crush your head," the ancient translators actually use "he," the masculine noun. They expected a male head-bruiser.

Some of the equally ancient Jewish Targums (Aramaic paraphrases of the Hebrew Bible) take the serpent as symbolic of Satan and look for a victory over him in the days of King Messiah.[38] Similar interpretations show up in other Jewish writings, such as _Jubilees_ 16:17–18 (about 125 B.C.) and _Pseudo-Philo_ 8:3 (about the time of Jesus).[39] It's very significant that these are pre-Christian writings because they prove that this idea of the Messiah is not a Christian invention.

The early Christian commentators, beginning with Justin (about A.D. 160) and Irenaeus (about A.D. 180), usually interpret this passage as the _protoevangelium_, or the first gospel and the foundational messianic prophecy.

Unfortunately, some church fathers and the Vulgate (the old Latin translation of the Bible), greatly confused the issue. Instead of using "he," as the Septuagint did, or "it," as grammar would lead, they translated the phrase "she shall bruise your head," suggesting it is Mary who is Eve's offspring. Even _The Da Vinci Code_'s Dan Brown, who makes a legion of errors about Jesus, does not make this mistake.

It seems wisest to agree with many commentators that the question asked throughout the whole of the Old Testament is "where is he whose coming is foretold?" Furthermore, offspring (_zera_) is a critical term throughout the Pentateuch. For example, it is used to reveal that the appointed offspring would come from Seth who replaced Abel (who was murdered by his older brother, Cain, the first son of Adam and Eve),[40] Noah's offspring,[41] and the continually repeated promise that the Messiah would come from the family line of Abraham.[42]

When the New Testament authors allude to Genesis 3:15, they understand it in a broadly messianic sense.[43] One example plainly clarifies that the promised offspring is Jesus Christ alone: "Now the promises were made to Abraham and to his offspring. It does not say, 'And to offsprings,' referring to many, but referring to one, 'And to your offspring,' who is Christ."[44]

CHAPTER SIX

WHAT DID JESUS ACCOMPLISH ON THE CROSS?

**He himself bore our sins in his body on the tree,
that we might die to sin and live to righteousness.
By his wounds you have been healed.**

1 PETER 2:24

✝

Jesus the God-man taught the foolish, fed the hungry, healed the sick, encouraged the brokenhearted, counseled the wayward, and loved the sinner. Yet, Jesus was emphatic that the primary purpose of his coming to earth was to suffer and die. In John 12:27–28, which chronicles the week leading up to Jesus' death, he says, "Now is my soul troubled. And what shall I say? 'Father, save me from this hour'? But for this purpose I have come to this hour. Father, glorify your name." In that moment, Jesus was setting his gaze on the cross.

Crucifixion was invented by the Persians around 500 B.C., perfected by the Romans in the days of Jesus, and not outlawed until the time of Emperor Constantine, who ruled Rome in the fourth century A.D. In the days of Jesus, crucifixion was reserved for the most horrendous criminals. Even the worst Romans were beheaded rather than crucified. The Jews also considered crucifixion the most horrific mode of death, as Deuteronomy 21:22–23 says: "And if a man has committed a crime punishable by death and he is put to death, and you hang him on a tree, his body shall not remain all night on the tree, but you shall bury him the same day, for a hanged man is cursed by God."

The ancient Jewish historian Josephus called crucifixion "the most wretched of deaths."[1] The ancient Roman philosopher Cicero asked that decent Roman citizens not even speak of the cross because it was too disgraceful a subject for the ears of decent people.[2]

Under the leadership of Adolf Hitler, German soldiers crucified Jews at Dachau by running bayonets and knives through their legs, shoulders, throats, and testicles. Under the leadership of Pol Pot, the Khmer Rouge performed crucifixions in Cambodia. Today, crucifixion continues in Sudan and online with the multiplayer video game *Roma Victor*.

On television, the hit show *CSI: Crime Scene Investigation* had an episode called "Double-Cross." In that episode, the star of the show, Gil Grissom, investigated the death of a woman who had died by crucifixion on a cross in a Catholic church. Curiously, Grissom said, "Jesus died for our sins," before seeking to uncover why the woman died. The episode had some very accurate medical discussions about the nature of death by crucifixion. The characters correctly concluded that Jesus died on the cross from asphyxiation.

The pain of crucifixion is so horrendous that a word was invented to explain it: *excruciating* literally means "from the cross." A crucified person could hang on the cross for days, passing in and out of consciousness as their lungs struggled to breathe while laboring under the weight of their body. It was not uncommon for those being crucified to slump on the cross in an effort to empty their lungs of air and thereby hasten their death.

To ensure maximum suffering, scourging preceded crucifixion. Scourging itself was such a painful event that many people died from it without even making it to their cross. Jesus' hands would have been chained above his head to expose his back and legs to an executioner's whip called a cat-o'-nine tails. The whip was a series of long leather straps. At the end of some of the straps were heavy balls of metal intended to tenderize the body of a victim, like a chef tenderizes a steak by beating it. Some of the straps had hooks made of either metal or bone that would have sunk deeply into the shoulders, back, buttocks, and legs of the victim. Once the hooks had sunk deeply into the tenderized flesh, the executioner would rip the skin, muscle, tendons, and even bones off the victim as he shouted in agony, shook violently, and bled heavily. Hundreds of years prior, the prophet Isaiah predicted the results of Jesus' scourging: "many were astonished at you—his appearance was so marred, beyond human semblance, and his form beyond that of the children of mankind."[3]

Jesus then had a crown of lengthy thorns pressed into his head as onlookers mocked him as the "King of the Jews."[4] With that, blood began to flow down Jesus' face, causing his hair and beard to be a bloodied and matted mess, and his eyes to burn as he strained to see through his own sweat and blood. Jesus' robe was then used as the pot in a gambling dice game.

Jesus was then forced to carry his roughly hewn wooden crossbar of perhaps one hundred pounds on his bare, traumatized, bloodied back and shoulders to the place of his own crucifixion. The cross was likely already covered with the blood of other men. Timber was so expensive the crosses were recycled, so Jesus' blood mixed with the layers of blood from countless other men who had walked that same path before him.

Despite his young age and good health, Jesus was so physically devastated from his sleepless night, miles of walking, severe beating, and scourging that he collapsed under the weight of the cross, unable to carry it alone. A man named Simon of Cyrene was appointed to carry Jesus' cross. Upon arriving at his place of crucifixion, they pulled Jesus' beard out—an act of ultimate disrespect in ancient cultures—spat on him, and mocked him in front of his family and friends.

Jesus the carpenter, who had driven many nails into wood with his own hands, then had five-to-seven-inch, rough, metal spikes driven into the most sensitive nerve centers on the human body in his hands and feet. Jesus was nailed to his wooden cross. At this point Jesus was in unbearable agony. Nonetheless, Hindus are prone to deny that Jesus suffered at all.

Jesus was then lifted up, and his cross dropped into a prepared hole, causing his body to shake violently on the spikes. In further mockery, a sign was posted above Jesus that said, "Jesus of Nazareth, the King of the Jews."[5] A painting later discovered from a second-century Roman graffito further shows the disrespect of Jesus at his crucifixion. The painting depicts the head of a jackass being crucified, with a man standing alongside of it with his arms raised. The caption reads, "Alexamenos worships his god."

At this point during a crucifixion, the victims labored to breathe as their body went into shock. Naked and embarrassed, the victims would often use their remaining strength to seek revenge on the crowd of mockers who had gathered to jeer at them. They would curse at their tormentors while urinating on them and spitting on them. Some victims would become so overwhelmed with pain that they would become incontinent and a pool of sweat, blood, urine, and feces would gather at the base of their cross.

Jesus' crucifixion must have been a grotesque scene. Hundreds of years in advance, the prophet Isaiah saw it this way: "He was despised and rejected by men; a man of sorrows, and acquainted with grief; and as one from whom men hide their faces he was despised, and we esteemed him not. Surely he has borne our griefs and carried our sorrows; yet we esteemed him stricken, smitten by God, and afflicted."[6]

None of this was done in dignified privacy, but rather in open public places. It would be like nailing a bloodied, naked man above the front entrance to a grocery store. Not only was crucifixion excruciatingly painful and publicly shameful, it was also commonly practiced. Tens of thousands of people were crucified in the ancient world. For example, when Spartacus died in battle, six thousand of his followers were crucified in one day. They were lined up along a road that stretched for one hundred and twenty miles, not unlike the shoulder of a modern freeway.

As a general rule, it was men who were crucified. Occasionally a man was crucified at eye level so that bored high school kids could look him directly in the eye and cuss him out, spit on him, and make fun of him for crying and messing his pants. In the rare event of a woman's crucifixion, she was made to face the cross. Not even such a barbarous culture was willing to watch the face of a woman in such excruciating agony.

On the day Jesus was crucified, two men were hung with him, one on each side. Some years later, when the leader of Jesus' disciples, Peter, was to be crucified, he reportedly did not consider himself worthy of dying like Jesus and therefore requested that he be hung upside down. His request was granted, and he hung upside down until he closed his eyes in death and opened them to gaze upon his scarred Savior and heard, "Well done, good and faithful servant."

Among the scandals of the cross is the fact that Christians have called it their *gospel*, or good news. Indeed, there are many additional opinions regarding Jesus' death by crucifixion:

- Jean-Jacques Rousseau: "If Socrates lived and died like a philosopher, Jesus lived and died like a god."
- Gandhi: "His death on the cross was a great example to the world, but that there was anything like a mysterious or miraculous virtue in it, my heart could not accept."
- Mark Twain: "Jesus died to save men—a small thing for an immortal to do—and didn't save many, anyway. But if he had been damned for the race, that would have been [an] act of a size proper to a god, and would have saved the whole race."
- John Knox: "To remember Jesus is to remember first of all his Cross."
- Friedrich Nietzsche: "Jesus died too soon. If he had lived to my age he would have repudiated his doctrine."
- An 1892 United States Supreme Court decision declared "[Jesus] the redeemer of mankind."
- Puritan John Owen: "There is no death of sin without the death of Christ."
- The medieval motto of the Carthusian Order was "the world is my crucifix."
- Martin Luther King Jr.: "In that dramatic scene on Calvary's hill three men were crucified. We must never forget that all three were crucified for the same crime—the crime of extremism. Two were extremists for immorality, and thus fell below their environment. The other, Jesus Christ, was an extremist for love, truth and goodness."

Perhaps most peculiar is the fact that the cross, which represents Jesus' torturous death, has become the most famous and popular symbol in all of history. Beginning with the church father Tertullian, early Christians would make the sign of the cross over their bodies with their hand. They would also adorn their necks and homes with crosses to celebrate the brutal death of Jesus. In our day, this would be akin to an AIDS-infected drug needle or used condom becoming the world's most beloved symbol and adorning homes, churches, and bodies. American satirist Lenny Bruce once quipped, "If Jesus had been killed twenty years ago, Catholic school children would be wearing little electric chairs around their necks instead of crosses."

Today, the symbol of the cross remains a powerfully controversial religious image. For example, the Mujahideen Shura Council, led by Iraq's branch of Al-Qaeda, recently threatened the "worshipers of the cross" saying, "We shall break the cross . . . [and] slit their throats."[7]

The cross was at the center of controversy about perhaps the most hotly debated piece of "art" ever produced. In 1989, Andres Serrano ignited a cultural war when he used tax dollars provided by the National Endowment for the Arts to create the "Piss Christ." The work was a photograph of a crucifix supporting the body of Jesus submerged in what was apparently the artist's own urine. The disrespect of the symbol of Jesus' death caused a national uproar rarely seen in the world of art, which spilled over to the floor of the United States Senate, where Senators Al D'Amato and Jesse Helms nearly blew a gasket airing their displeasure with the piece.

In the world of pop culture, the cross has ironically become a trendy fashion statement. Both old-school rocker Axl Rose of Guns N' Roses and rapper 50 Cent wore crosses at the 2006 MTV Video Music Awards. In 2006, Madonna concluded each concert during her $193 million-grossing *Confessions* tour by being laid upon a disco cross. She defended it by saying, "I believe in my heart that if Jesus were alive today he would be doing the same thing."[8]

The question begs to be answered: how can Christians celebrate the crucifixion of Jesus as good news, the best news they have ever heard? To answer this question we must move from the historical fact of Jesus' death to the theological meaning of that fact.

To understand the doctrine of Jesus' death on the cross, also known as the atonement, we must connect it to the doctrines of God's character, God's creation, human sin, and the responses of God to sin and sinners. To do this we will briefly examine seven truths that are absolutely essential to rightly understanding the significance of Jesus' cross.

1) GOD IS HOLY AND WITHOUT ANY SIN.

When we survey the death, evil, and injustice that plague our world and then hear that it was made by God, we could rush to conclude that the world reflects the evil nature of God. However, the Bible tells us exactly the opposite, namely that God is holy, without any sin, and only altogether good. In fact, the holiness of God is his most frequently mentioned attribute in Scripture.[9]

2) GOD MADE US HOLY AND WITHOUT ANY SIN.

Not only is God good, but everything God made was originally good, including human beings, who were made in his image and likeness.[10]

3) SIN RESULTS IN DEATH.

Sin is us separating ourselves from God. Because God is the living God and the source of life, sin results in death. This is similar to a piece of technology being unplugged from its power source; it continues to exist but is functionally dead. In the same way, the Bible says that because of sin we are physically alive but spiritually dead. Furthermore, we will all die physically, just as God promised our first parents in the garden.[11]

4) JESUS IS SINLESS.

One of the things that makes Jesus distinct from and morally superior to everyone who has or will ever live is that he alone is without sin. He said this about himself, and it is confirmed in additional Scriptures.[12]

5) WE ARE SINFUL.

Despite the fact that God made us sinless, everyone but Jesus is a sinner both by nature and by choice. Anyone who says he is not a sinner is in fact proud; and according to the church father Augustine, pride (also known as self-esteem) is the worst of sins and was the cause of Satan's fall from heaven. Our sin includes our words, deeds, thoughts, and motives. Our sin also includes omission (not doing what God commands) and commission (doing what God forbids). Even non-Christians tend to agree that everyone is sinful and declare so with the oft-repeated statement, "nobody is perfect," which agrees with Scripture.[13]

6) Jesus Became Our Sin.

This point is perhaps the most controversial and debated in this entire chapter because it is so shocking. On the cross as our substitute, Jesus was made to be the worst of what we are. This does not mean that Jesus ever sinned. Rather, it means that he was made sin. As a result, in that moment when Jesus cried out that he had been forsaken by God the Father, Jesus became the most ugly, wicked, defiled, evil, corrupt, rebellious, and hideous thing in all creation. In that moment, Jesus became a homosexual, alcoholic, thief, glutton, addict, pervert, adulterer, coveter, idol worshiper, whore, pedophile, self-righteous religious prig—and whatever else we are. Martin Luther is one of the few theologians who does not lessen the blow of this truth and calls it the "great exchange." As shocking as this fact is, Scripture declares that on the cross Jesus exchanged his perfection for our imperfection, his obedience for our disobedience, his intimacy with God the Father for our distance from God the Father, his blessing for our cursing, and his life for our death. As Isaiah 53:6 says, "All we like sheep have gone astray; we have turned—every one—to his own way; and the Lord has laid on him the iniquity of us all." Furthermore, "For our sake he made him to be sin who knew no sin, so that in him we might become the righteousness of God."[14]

7) Jesus Died For Us.

The fact that Christians celebrate the murder of Jesus as "good news" is disgusting unless we understand the reason why Jesus died. The Bible teaches that in perfect justice, because Jesus was made to be our sin, he died for us. The little word *for* has big implications. In theological terms, it means that Jesus' death was substitutionary (or, as some used to call it, vicarious). His death was in our place solely for our benefit and without benefit for himself. Just to be perfectly clear, this means that Jesus took the penalty for our sins in our place so we do not have to suffer the just penalty ourselves. The wrath of God that should have fallen on us and the death that our sins merit fell on Jesus. This wasn't something forced on him. Rather, he took it willingly.[15] Scripture repeatedly stresses this point, which theologians call *penal substitutionary atonement*:

- "But he was wounded *for* our transgressions; he was crushed *for* our iniquities; upon him was the chastisement that brought us peace, and with his stripes we are healed" (Isa. 53:5).

- "He poured out his soul to death and was numbered with the transgressors; yet he bore the sin of many, and makes intercession *for* the transgressors" (Isa. 53:12).
- "[He] was delivered up *for* our trespasses" (Rom. 4:25).
- "But God shows his love for us in that while we were still sinners, Christ died *for* us" (Rom. 5:8).
- "Christ died *for* our sins" (1 Cor. 15:3).
- "For Christ also suffered once *for* sins, the righteous *for* the unrighteous, that he might bring us to God" (1 Pet. 3:18).
- "He is the propitiation *for* our sins, and not *for* ours only but also *for* the sins of the whole world" (1 John 2:2).
- "Christ redeemed us from the curse of the law by becoming a curse *for* us" (Gal. 3:13).

Because death is the penalty for sinners, the only way that the death of the sinless Jesus can be understood is in terms of substitution. The sinless Jesus literally stood in our place to suffer and die for us. In doing so, Jesus is our savior who alone can take away the curse we deserve because of our sin. Conversely, Unitarian Universalists wrongly believe that "No savior can carry away the sin and punishment. No savior can bear the penalty in our place."[16] But the Scriptures are emphatic and clear that Jesus is our savior who did die in our place, bearing our punishment and taking away our sin.

Some will protest that a loving God could not possibly pour out his wrath on Jesus. Yet this is precisely what Scripture says: "Yet it was the will of the LORD to crush him; he has put him to grief."[17] Others will protest that a loving God would never sanction the bloody, unjust murder of Jesus. Scripture plainly states, however, that it is at the cross of Jesus that the love of God for us is most clearly seen. Jesus himself said precisely this: "This is my commandment, that you love one another as I have loved you. Greater love has no one than this, that someone lay down his life for his friends."[18] Other Scriptures echo the words of Jesus—his death on the cross is the place where love is most clearly seen in all creation. John 3:16 says, "For God so loved the world, that he gave his only Son, that whoever believes in him should not perish but have eternal life." Romans 5:8 says, "but God shows his love for us in that while we were still sinners, Christ died for us." Finally, 1 John 4:9–10 says, "In this the love of God was made manifest among us, that God sent his only Son into the world, so that we might live through him. In this is love, not that we have loved God but that he loved us and sent his Son to be the propitiation for our sins." Clearly, Jesus' bloody death on the cross is about love.

One of the things that confused me the most when I first began reading the Bible in college was all the mention of blood. Furthermore, when I went to church I heard Christians singing about blood with smiles on their faces, which frankly weirded me out. But as I have studied over the years, I have learned two things about why the Bible speaks so much about blood. One, God connects sin and blood to show that sin results in death. Two, God is sickened by sin like we are sickened by blood; he connects the two so we know how he feels. When I preached the sermon on which this chapter is based, I actually had someone pass out and another person puke, just because I was talking in some detail about blood. Their strong aversion to blood is akin to God's strong reaction to sin, which explains in part why God continually connects sin and blood throughout Scripture.

The Old Testament often used the theme of blood to prepare people for the coming of Jesus to die for our sins. Among the central events in the Old Testament is the act of atonement, including the annual celebration of the Day of Atonement (Yom Kippur), according to the regulations of the book of Leviticus.

The Day of Atonement was the most important day of the year. It was intended to deal with the sin problem between humanity and God. Of the many prophetic elements on this special day, one stands out. On that day, two healthy goats without defect were chosen; they were therefore fit to represent sinless perfection. The high priest would slaughter one goat, which acted as a substitute for the sinners who rightly deserved a violently bloody death for their many sins. The high priest treated the first goat as a sin offering. He slaughtered the innocent goat and sprinkled some of its blood on the mercy seat on top of the ark of the covenant inside the Most Holy Place. But the goat is no longer innocent when it takes the guilt of our sin because it is a sin offering for the people.[19] Subsequently, its blood represents life given as payment for sin. The result is that the dwelling place of God is cleansed of the defilement that resulted from all of the transgressions and sins of the people of Israel and God's wrath is satisfied.

The bloody slaughter of the goat on the Day of Atonement represents *propitiation*. Propitiation means that God's wrath, which is mentioned more than six hundred times in Scripture, was turned away, or propitiated, from sinners and diverted to Jesus Christ. This was made possible because Jesus substituted himself in our place as both our high priest and the lamb of God to pay the penalty for our sins.[20] Many Scriptures speak of Jesus' assuming God's wrath and thereby propitiating it from sinners. The English Standard Version of the Bible actually maintains the word "propitiation," unlike some other translations.[21]

The high priest, acting as the representative and mediator between the sinful people and their holy God, would take the second goat and lay his hands on the animal while confessing the sins of the people. This goat, called the scapegoat, would then be sent away to run free into the wilderness away from the sinners, symbolically taking their sins with it. Theologically, we call this the doctrine of *expiation*, whereby our sin is expiated, or taken away so that we are made clean.

Throughout the Bible, some dozen words are frequently used to speak of sin in terms of staining our soul, defiling us, and causing us to be filthy or unclean.[22] The effect of sin, particularly sins committed against us, is that we feel dirty. I had one rape victim explain to me, for example, that after being raped she took a shower because she just felt dirty. What she was referring to was much deeper than just her body; somehow her soul had also been stained by the sin committed against her. The scapegoat illustrates for us how Jesus takes away our sin so that we can become new people who live new lives. Scripture uses a variety of verbs, such as "cleanse"[23] and "purify"[24] to explain this aspect of Jesus' work on the cross. The Bible also frequently mentions God's people wearing white as a symbol that they have been cleansed from sin by Jesus.[25]

Subsequently, only by rightly understanding that the entirety of Yom Kippur is fulfilled in Jesus do we appreciate Jesus as our high priest who mediates between us and God the Father, our substitute who died for our sins, and our scapegoat who takes away our sin so that we can live new lives of freedom and joy.

In considering the crucifixion of Jesus, it is also tempting to have pity on Jesus as a weak victim. But, not only was Jesus fully man, he also went to the cross and took his beating like a man. With the cross impending, Jesus said, "For this reason the Father loves me, because I lay down my life that I may take it up again. No one takes it from me, but I lay it down of my own accord. I have authority to lay it down, and I have authority to take it up again."[26] Therefore, Jesus is not to be pitied like a loser, but rather honored as a hero. He is like the bravest soldier in a platoon who courageously throws himself on a grenade to save others and bleeds out on the battlefield with his dignity intact.

Curiously, some people in the more left-leaning side of our dysfunctional Christian family are backing away from the doctrine of penal substitutionary atonement. Those in the more established liberal churches, along with their emergent offspring, are routinely decrying the concept that Jesus paid the penalty (death) for our sin in our place on the cross. They say it is too gory, too scary, too bloody, too masculine, and too violent. Furthermore, they say that in our tender little world of kindness, such teachings won't help further the kingdom of meek and mild Jesus.

Meanwhile, non-Christians in the culture seem to have an insatiable appetite for the doctrine. The storyline of masculine sacrifice of one's life to save others in love remains one of the most powerfully moving themes in pop culture. It was amazing, for example, to sit in a theater watching *The Chronicles of Narnia* and observe the reaction of a largely non-Christian audience to Aslan. If you remember, Aslan is the Christ figure in the story, or the lion that represents Jesus as "the Lion of the tribe of Judah."[27] In the story, Aslan willingly and nobly lays down his life as a substitute for those he loves to save them from the rule of evil. The theater became quiet and still at the sacrifice of Aslan—even non-Christians were moved to deep sorrow and tears. Later in the story, when Aslan returns back to life as a victorious king, a heartfelt joy returned to the crowd, and some people even broke out in applause and cheers.

Why? Because deep down, even though we are sinners, we remain God's image bearers. Like Solomon said, God has set eternity in our hearts and we cannot shake our yearning to be delivered from evil and death by a conquering hero who loves us enough to give us new life through his death.[28]

Likewise, the sixth season of the hit television show 24 was preceded by online trailers showing the main character, Jack Bauer, "sacrificing" himself by laying down his life as a substitute to defeat evil and save the lives of a multitude. Without being blasphemous and saying anything that makes Jack into Jesus, it is curious to note the parallels that the show makes between the two. Both are healthy, young men who work in construction, tell the truth, accomplish their mission, oppose evil, are betrayed by a close friend who dies as a result of sin, are saviors who lay down their life to save people they love, and both resurrect from death (Jack having been essentially brought back from death in one season in an effort to escape capture).

The first episode of season six opened with Jack, imprisoned by the Chinese, with long hair and a scruffy beard that made him look a lot like the images of Jesus in pop culture. Taking off his shirt, Jack revealed that his entire back was scarred like Jesus' from brutal flogging. Returning to the United States, Jack was asked to "sacrifice" himself by dying at the hands of terrorists in exchange for their promise not to unleash a nuclear attack on civilian targets. In so many ways, 24, like many other popular cultural stories, echoes the true story of Jesus the hero substituting himself to be our savior by suffering in our place.

Today, the message of the cross is seen as foolish and offensive (as Paul himself predicted it would be).[29] Tragically, some who profess to be Christians see the cross not as an efficacious loving atonement for sin; rather, they see it as little more than a sentimental symbol for the battle against the oppression of marginalized peoples, such as homosexuals and feminists.

Sadly, some Christians and some Christian leaders, while not denying the cross, prefer to keep it out of plain view because they wrongly believe that nice, decent people hate to have their sensibilities offended by such violence and gore. Consequently, the word has gotten out that being a Christian is about avoiding the suffering, pain, and horrors of this life by living in a safe, zip-locked Christian plastic bag filled with diversionary worship songs to prom-date Jesus so we don't have to pick up any cross or shed any tears.

Such Christianity rings hollow for those who have suffered and know the horrors of our sinful world. I have witnessed firsthand a growing appetite for a rigorous theology of the cross. While preaching a series on the cross in Seattle, which is among the least churched cities in America with more dogs than evangelicals, I saw our attendance grow by as many as eight hundred mainly young, single, college-educated twenty-something hipsters in a single week. I yelled for well over an hour in each of our Sunday church services about the depth of sin, wrath of God, and propitiation of Jesus.

At the foot of Jesus' cross, we learn that ours is a faith not of victorious life, but rather victorious life only through excruciating pain and death. Subsequently, Jesus welcomes us to pick up our cross and die. In our age of religious gimmicks and tricks that promise a victorious life without pain and death, the invitation to die won't help sell a lot of copies of this book, but it will help ensure that you continue to walk with Jesus, who said, "If anyone would come after me, let him deny himself and take up his cross and follow me. For whoever would save his life will lose it, but whoever loses his life for my sake and the gospel's will save it."[30]

To be a Christian is to be a "little Christ." In fact, the name *Christian* was originally a term of mockery given to us by our enemies. But Jesus said that to be a Christian is to pick up our cross and die. Die to sin, die to pride, die to comfort, die to anything and everything that fails to glorify God alone as the object of our affection and the source of our joy. With great insight, Walter Wink has said that killing Jesus was like trying to destroy a dandelion seed-head by blowing on it.[31] At the cross, what was intended as eradication was used by God for multiplication, and we pray that you would always be loyal to Jesus, our hero, and his revolution.

ANSWERS TO COMMON QUESTIONS ABOUT JESUS' CRUCIFIXION

WHAT ELSE DID JESUS ACCOMPLISH ON THE CROSS?

Throughout church history, much ink has been spilled as various theologians and Christian traditions debated the effects of Jesus' death. One theologian has called the cross the great jewel of the Christian faith, and like every great jewel it has many precious facets that are each worthy of examination for their brilliance and beauty. Therefore, you will be well served to see each side of this jewel working together for the glory of God in complimentary, not contradictory, fashion. Most false teaching surrounding the cross results from someone's denying one of these facets, ignoring one of these facets, or overemphasizing one of these facets at the expense of the others, often due to an overreaction to someone else's overreaction.

Furthermore, the cross is not a pagan jewel. Tragically, some have argued that the crucifixion of Jesus is little more than the makeover of ancient pagan concepts borrowed from other religions. It is then argued that since the Bible itself adapts pagan thinking, we should do the same and reinterpret the work of Jesus on the cross through modern-day paganism such as goddess worship, atheistic therapy, secular feminism, and Marxism. This leads to a wholesale departure from any understanding of the cross that has previously been accepted as faithfully Christian. Both the Old and New Testaments clearly declare that our understanding of the cross is the result of God's revelation to us and not human speculation borrowed from pagan culture.[32]

Some of the glorious sides of this jewel (in addition to the sides previously examined in this chapter) include the following:

- Jesus died to reveal God's justice,[33] glory,[34] and pleasure,[35] along with his wisdom and power.[36]
- Jesus died as our new covenant sacrifice.[37]

- Jesus died for our justification.[38]
- Jesus died as our redemption.[39] This redemption includes redemption from sin,[40] condemnation,[41] the curse of the law,[42] Mosaic code,[43] and Satan and demons.[44]
- Jesus died to remove sin that separates people from God and each other so that there can be reconciliation.[45]
- Jesus died to crush Satan, demons, sin, and the world as our *Christus Victor* who achieved cosmic triumph.[46]
- Jesus died to ransom sinners by paying their debt.[47]
- Jesus died to exchange our sin for his righteousness and give us imputed righteousness.[48]
- Jesus died as an example of how we should live our lives as *Christus Exemplar*.[49]

At the cross, God satisfies himself through substitution and propitiation, inspires us through Christ's example and revelation, redeems us from entrapment in sin, and triumphs over evil of all kinds. It begins with objective or satisfactory themes, proceeds to subjective or regenerative themes, and finishes with classic or triumphant themes. An adequate biblical understanding of atonement requires all of these facets for the true brilliance of the great jewel of our faith to shine out.

In the cross we see God's self-giving love, goodness, mercy, justice, and holiness. It demonstrates his justice in judging sin and his mercy in justifying the sinner. The cross is the purest act of love ever committed in this world. It alone shows true wisdom and redemptive power. John Calvin put it this way: "For in the cross of Christ, as in a splendid theater, the incomparable goodness of God is set before the whole world. The glory of God shines, indeed in all creatures on high and below, but never more brightly than in the cross. . . . If it be objected that nothing could be less glorious than Christ's death, I reply that in the death we see a boundless glory which is concealed from the ungodly."[50]

DID JESUS GO TO HELL AFTER HE DIED ON THE CROSS?

It has been wrongly taught by some that following his death on the cross, Jesus went to hell for three days. Building on this error, some have even said that Jesus was tormented by Satan in hell in the time between his crucifixion and resurrection. Much of this is a misunderstanding of the Apostles' Creed. It is easily cleared up by a faithful reading of Scripture. First, Jesus paid the penalty for our sins on the cross and said his work was "finished."[51] Therefore, there was nothing else to be done for us, such as going to hell to suffer for our sins yet again.[52]

Second, Jesus told us from the cross where he was going ("today you will be with me in Paradise"[53]), which was not hell. Third, in Luke 16:19–31, Jesus explains that before his death there were two places (divided by a great chasm) where people would go when they died. These were holding places until heaven and hell were opened for eternal occupancy. One was a place of joy for believers called "Abraham's side,"[54] also called "paradise" by Jesus on the cross. The other holding place was hades or the place of torment for unbelievers. Ephesians 4:8–10 says that after his death, Jesus went into that place of holding for believers called paradise for three days and then upon his ascension into heaven he took the Christians with him. Today, paradise is in heaven and when we die we go to heaven, for as Paul says, "to be absent from the body is to be present with the Lord."

Fourth, Revelation 20:11–15 explains that at the end of time, hades (the holding place for unbelievers) will be opened up and unbelievers will be judged before they are sent into the lake of fire, which is hell and the second death. Until that time, which we are still awaiting, no one, including Jesus, is in hell. Fifth, at no time does Satan ever rule over Jesus, even in hell. We see in Revelation 14:10 that Jesus Christ the Lamb rules over hell, and in Revelation 20:10 that Jesus rules over the punishment of Satan and demons in hell.

Furthermore, the earliest version of the Apostles' Creed (roughly A.D. 140) did not have the phrase "He descended into Hell" and neither did the Nicene Creed (roughly A.D. 325). Most scholars believe that the phrase was a later addition, perhaps around A.D. 390.

WHAT IS THE RELATIONSHIP BETWEEN THE CROSS AND THE RESURRECTION OF CHRIST?

Jesus' death on the cross paid the penalty for our sin. The result is forgiveness, justification, imputation of righteousness, and our acceptance as children into God's family with Jesus as our Lord and brother.

Jesus' resurrection from death brings formerly dead people to life. The result is life, regeneration, and a new heart imparted to us by the power of the Holy Spirit. If the cross were the only work, then we'd be forgiven corpses. But through the resurrection, the very life of God has broken into this world to give us life that is new in character and eternal in duration.

Perhaps the most illustrative act that pictures the death and resurrection of Jesus is Christian baptism. In going under the water, the Christian is identified with the death and burial of Jesus for their sin. In being brought up out of the water, the Christian is identified with the resurrection of Jesus in triumph over sin and death.

The death, burial, and resurrection of Jesus are in many regards different aspects of the total work of Jesus that includes both forgiveness and new life. This explains why all of the gospel stories include both Jesus' death and resurrection.[55]

Sadly, there are those who err in emphasizing either the crucifixion or the resurrection of Jesus at the expense of the other. Some preach only the cross and its result of forgiveness of sin and justification. Without preaching the resurrection of Jesus as well, Christians are prone to overlook the mission of Jesus and the new life he has for them on the earth. They tend to see Christian life as little more than going to church to soak in teaching until they get to heaven. This is the perennial error of Christian fundamentalism.

Conversely, there are others who preach only the new kingdom life that Jesus offers through his resurrection. These Christians excel at helping the poor and handing out hugs and muffins, but fail at repenting of personal sin and calling others to repent of personal sin so that they might be forgiven and reconciled to God through Jesus. This is the perennial error of Christian liberalism.

HOW CAN I WORSHIP AN UNLOVING, CRUEL, PRIMITIVE, AND BLOODTHIRSTY GOD?

If this picture were true, then everyone would rightly have great difficulty in loving the God of the Bible. He would be like the gods of the world, who hurt you unless you give them things to make them happy. I (Gerry) am writing this portion of the book while teaching in Manila. While here we went by a funeral tent set up at a squatter village. They had bright lights on to scare away the spirits that would cause disease or death if they could. We heard that the workers constructing a new building at Faith Academy sacrificed a rooster and poured its blood around the excavation so the gods living there would not be mad at the construction workers for disturbing them. Later this week, I also will be in Taiwan. There they do things like burn ghost money so the gods can buy nice things. Otherwise, it is believed the gods will become angry and create a great deal of trouble. These capricious, mean gods who need to be kept happy are tragically typical of the gods all over the world.

Conversely, the God of the Bible reveals himself in Exodus 34:6 as "a God merciful and gracious, slow to anger." God himself says that his typical state is compassionate and gracious. People have to work really hard at doing evil to make him angry because he is slow to anger. Unfortunately, we do exactly that with our sin. Just for a moment, think of the times when your anger has been aroused for righteous reasons. The time when a child you love was molested, a woman you know was raped, a politician you voted for was embroiled in scandal, a church you supported was proven to have crooked leaders, or a person you had given your heart to slept with someone else. Alongside of that, put the more common sins of idolatry, lying, gossip, stealing, fornication, adultery, and the like. Now, imagine that you are God and not only altogether holy but also all-knowing and constantly aware of all the sin and evil of the entire world. The fact that we who are sinners become rightly angry at a few snapshots of sin is by virtue of the fact that we are God's image bearers with a conscience that cannot accept evil.

How then can we not love God for his anger rather than in spite of it? How could we possibly worship a God who looks at rapists, pedophiles, murderers, slave traders, thieves, and the like and simply smiles with pointless nicety because none of it bothers him? That kind of god, and not the God who becomes angry, is an ugly accomplice to injustice that no one with even a barely functioning conscience could or should worship.

Our ultimate problem is that we are alienated from the Lord because of our own sin. It is not God who turned his back on us and severed our loving relationship. It is we who sinned and gave God the finger. As a result, while God remains fully loving, his anger has been rightly aroused along with his just wrath.

If we are honest, this makes complete sense, because if anyone treated us the way we have treated God, we would be angry as well and would want justice.

What doesn't make sense is that the Lord decided to take the penalty of sin on himself. He decided to die so we wouldn't have to.[56] His death enables our reconciliation. How and why would he do that? If he were just paying some huge monetary debt, it would be an incomprehensible act of love. But he went much further and took a moral debt to himself. This mind-blowing act of love is the most unprecedented and unimaginable act of both justice and love ever. No one is as glorious as the God of the Bible and therefore worthy of our worship.

CHAPTER SEVEN

DID JESUS RISE FROM DEATH?

"I am the resurrection and the life. Whoever believes in me, though he die, yet shall he live."

JESUS (JOHN 11:25)

✝

Dustin was a tall young man topped by a head of thick, curly, brown hair. He devoted himself to Jesus a few years ago and zealously began pursuing a relationship with Jesus. His mother said that he changed quickly for the good while keeping his loving disposition and screwball sense of humor.

He met the girl of his dreams—a cute, shy jazz singer named Rachel. He adored this young woman and began pursuing her with honor and kindness by respecting her and her family and friends. They all quickly grew to love him and thanked God for bringing him into Rachel's life.

The first time I met them, the sun was shining and they were holding hands and giggling as they ran into the church for a premarital Bible study. As their wedding day approached, Dustin broke out with a rash on his hand. Not thinking much of it, he went to the doctor, who gave him a salve and expected it to go away. When it did not, he was sent to a specialist; he was told the shocking news that, although he was a rugged and healthy young man in his early twenties, he had leukemia.

Subsequently, the couple had to postpone their wedding day while Dustin was undergoing treatment. Dustin's condition worsened and they had to cancel their wedding again because of his deteriorating health and treatment.

Dustin, and those who loved him, prayed fervently in faith that God would heal him. Dustin continued to fight valiantly but was losing the battle of his life. He and Rachel finally decided not to wait any longer and to get married while he was hospitalized; they desperately wanted to spend however many days God would give them together as husband and wife. They were married at the hospital by one of our pastors, James, thanks to the kind nurses who organized their simple ceremony.

Each night, family and friends along with pastors and members of our church joined Rachel around Dustin's bed, praying for a miraculous healing. Many months into his battle, however, Dustin's body essentially lost the ability to fight anymore, and it seemed that his death was imminent. One of our pastors, who had spent a considerable amount of time at the hospital, including staying the night on some occasions, sent me a heartbreaking e-mail detailing Dustin's decline.

Upon entering his hospital room, my heart broke to see his lovely wife, Rachel, staring at him with the face of an angel while family and friends crowded around his dying body. I was hoping to remain strong for the family, but when I saw Dustin I could not hold back my tears. He was virtually unrecognizable; his locks of long, curly hair were gone and all that remained was his bald head. His body was bloated, and his eyes were swollen shut. He could not speak because a breathing tube was down his throat, but I do believe he could hear me, so I spoke to him as best I could through my weeping. As I opened my mouth, Jesus said, "Tell Dustin I have been where he is and I have been where he is going." So, not wanting to discourage his family with the certainty of his death, I held Dustin's head close and whispered in his ear what Jesus told me to tell him while I cried and kissed his head.

I then turned to his loving mother, who was visibly shaken, and asked her if there was anything I could do to serve her. "Preach his funeral," she asked, to which I agreed.

Dustin died.

His funeral opened with Rachel singing a song in tribute to the husband with whom she never had the opportunity to consummate her marriage. I preached from John 11 about how Jesus went to the funeral of his friend Lazarus and how Jesus himself later died, which means that he alone can help both those who die and those who are left behind.

What I found most striking about Dustin's funeral was that there were actually few tears shed considering the circumstances surrounding his death and the large size of the crowd. Even Rachel smiled as she spoke and sang about Dustin, remembering how well he loved her in the few days he had with her as her husband.

Following the funeral, the reason behind the scarcity of tears became apparent as I spoke to those who knew Dustin best. Amazingly, nearly every person I met had either been brought to Jesus, brought back to Jesus, or brought closer to Jesus through their friendship with Dustin, including his little sister who seemed perhaps to love him most affectionately. He obviously had the spiritual gift of evangelism and had used his few days far more effectively for spreading the good news of Jesus than many people who live to a ripe old age. Person after person said that even though they missed Dustin, they knew that Jesus had died a brutal death as a young man like Dustin, and that Dustin was with Jesus because Jesus had risen from death to give eternal life to Dustin. Dustin was so certain of the resurrection of Jesus that he persuaded those he loved to place their faith in that fact, which gave them comfort in his death.

Sadly, not everyone has faith in the fact of Jesus' resurrection like Dustin did. For example, serving in stark contrast to Dustin is Hugh Hefner. In *Playboy* magazine, which he founded and publishes, Hefner was asked what happens to people at the moment of their death:

PLAYBOY: What do you believe happens after death?

HEFNER: I haven't a clue. I'm always struck by the people who think they do have a clue. It's perfectly clear to me that religion is a myth. It's something we have invented to explain the inexplicable. My religion and the spiritual side of my life come from a sense of connection to the [sic] humankind and nature on this planet and in the universe. I am in overwhelming awe of it all: It is so fantastic, so complex, so beyond comprehension. What does it all mean—if it has any meaning at all? But how can it all exist if it doesn't have some kind of meaning? I think anyone who suggests that they have the answer is motivated by the need to invent answers, because we have no such answers.[1]

Hefner's answer is both common and tragic. Our culture wrongly bifurcates fact and faith. Subsequently, many people think that facts are only to be found in arenas such as science and banking. Meanwhile, faith is relegated to the worlds of spirituality and religion. Practically, this means that we can only have certainty about truth in the world of fact and are left with little more than hunches and hopes in the world of faith. Furthermore, if we allow the resurrection of Jesus Christ to be relegated to the marginalized world of faith, then it is assumed that we cannot know whether Jesus actually did rise, or as Hefner said, "we have no such answers."

Conversely, Scripture is clear that the resurrection of Jesus is both a matter of fact and faith. The historical fact is that Jesus Christ alone has risen from death. For that fact to be of any benefit to us, though, we must receive it by personal faith in the person of Jesus and fact of his resurrection. Rather than saying, "I haven't a clue" about what happens after death, through the fact of Jesus' resurrection we have the answer about what awaits us on the other side of the grave. We can live with assurance in our own eternal life and resurrection like Dustin did.

The resurrection of Jesus is the most known and celebrated miracle in the history of the world. There has always been consensus that it is in many ways the core issue of our Christian faith:

- Thomas Arnold (professor of modern history at Oxford): "No one fact in the history of mankind . . . is proved by better and fuller evidence of every sort" than the fact that "Christ died and rose from the dead."
- Bishop B. F. Westcott: "Indeed, taking all the evidences together . . . it is not too much to say that there is no historic incident better or more variously supported than the resurrection of Christ."
- John Locke: "Our Savior's resurrection . . . is truly of great importance in Christianity; so great that His being or not being the Messiah stands or falls with it."
- Billy Graham: "The entire plan for the future has its key in the resurrection."
- Martin Luther: "Our Lord has written the promise of the resurrection not in words alone, but in every leaf in springtime."
- John R. Stott: "Christianity is in its very essence a resurrection reli-

gion. The concept of resurrection lies at its heart. If you remove it, Christianity is destroyed."

- ⊚ William Lyon Phelps (Yale professor): "In the whole story of Jesus Christ, the most important event is the resurrection."
- ⊚ Benjamin Warfield (Princeton professor): "The resurrection of Christ is a fact."

Perhaps the lengthiest biblical account of the implications of Jesus' resurrection is found in 1 Corinthians 15. There we are told that if Jesus did not bodily rise in victory over death, then Christianity is nothing more than a cruel hoax dreamt up by liars to give false hope to gullible fools. Consequently, in this chapter we will answer the question, did Jesus rise from death? We will examine the biblical evidence, circumstantial evidence, and the non-Christian historical evidence. It is my objective to establish the resurrection as a historical fact. Once we have established the fact of Jesus' resurrection, it is our prayer that your personal faith will be in him and in the fact that he is alive today.

BIBLICAL EVIDENCE FOR JESUS' RESURRECTION

1) JESUS' RESURRECTION WAS PROPHESIED IN ADVANCE.

Roughly seven hundred years before the birth of Jesus, the prophet Isaiah promised that Jesus would be born into humble circumstances to live a simple life, die a brutal death, and then rise to take away our sin.[2]

2) JESUS PREDICTED HIS RESURRECTION.

On numerous occasions Jesus plainly promised that he would die and rise three days later.[3]

3) JESUS DIED ON THE CROSS.

Mary Baker Eddy, founder of Christian Science (which has no Christians or science and reminds me of Grape-Nuts, which has no grapes or nuts), said that Jesus did not die but only went through "what seemed to be death."[4]

However, the biblical record is emphatic that Jesus died. First, he underwent a sleepless night of trials and beatings that left him exhausted. Second, he was scourged—a punishment so horrendous that many men died from it before even making it to their crucifixion. Third, Jesus was crucified, and a professional executioner declared him dead. Fourth, to ensure Jesus was dead, a spear was thrust through his side and a mixture of blood and water poured out of his side because the spear burst his heart sac.[5] Fifth, he was wrapped in roughly one hundred pounds of linens and spices, which, if he was able to somehow survive beatings, floggings, crucifixion, and a speared heart, would have killed him by asphyxiation. Sixth, even if through all of this Jesus somehow survived (which would in itself be a miracle), he could not have endured three days without food, water, or medical attention in a cold tomb carved out of rock. In short, Jesus died.

4) Jesus was buried in a tomb that was easy to find.

Some seven hundred years before Jesus was even born, God promised through Isaiah that Jesus would be assigned a grave "with a rich man in his death."[6] This was incredibly unlikely because Jesus was a very poor man who could not have afforded an expensive burial plot. Following Jesus' death, though, a wealthy and well-known man named Joseph of Arimathea gifted his expensive tomb for the burial of Jesus.[7] As a result, the place of Jesus' burial was easy to confirm. For example, Joseph who owned the tomb, governmental leaders and their soldiers who were assigned to guard the tomb, and the disciples and women who visited the tomb and found it empty all knew exactly where Jesus' dead body was laid to rest. Had Jesus truly not risen from death, it would have been very easy to prove it by opening the tomb and presenting Jesus' dead body as evidence.

5) Jesus appeared physically alive three days after his death.

The Jehovah's Witnesses religion began in 1872 in Pittsburgh with a number of doctrines that have been widely considered heretical throughout the history of the Christian church. One of their beliefs includes rejecting the physical resurrection of Jesus while maintaining that he rose spiritually. This alternative explanation for Jesus' resurrection, however, simply does not agree with the historical facts.

Following Jesus' resurrection, many people touched his physical body: his disciples clung to his feet,[8] Mary clung to him,[9] and Thomas the doubter put his hand into the open spear hole in Jesus' side.[10] Jesus also appeared to his disciples after his resurrection, yet they were uncertain if he had truly physically risen from death. But Jesus was emphatic about his bodily resurrection and went out of his way to prove it:

> As they were talking about these things, Jesus himself stood among them, and said to them, "Peace to you!" But they were startled and frightened and thought they saw a spirit. And he said to them, "Why are you troubled, and why do doubts arise in your hearts? See my hands and my feet, that it is I myself. Touch me, and see. For a spirit does not have flesh and bones as you see that I have." And when he had said this, he showed them his hands and his feet. And while they still disbelieved for joy and were marveling, he said to them, "Have you anything here to eat?" They gave him a piece of broiled fish, and he took it and ate before them.[11]

It is also significant to note that no credible historical evidence from that period exists to validate any alternative explanation for Jesus' resurrection other than his literal bodily resurrection.[12]

6) JESUS' RESURRECTION WAS RECORDED AS SCRIPTURE SHORTLY AFTER IT OCCURRED.

Mark's Gospel account of the days leading up to Jesus' crucifixion mentions the "high priest" without naming him.[13] It can logically be inferred that Mark did not mention the high priest by name because he expected his readers to know of whom he was speaking. Since Caiaphas was high priest from A.D. 18–37, the latest possible date for the tradition is A.D. 37.[14] This date is so close to the death of Jesus that there would have not been sufficient time for a "legend" of his resurrection to have developed. This proves that the biblical record of Jesus' resurrection was penned while the eyewitnesses were still alive to verify the facts. His resurrection is not a mythical legend that developed long after the time of Jesus. In fact, John Rodgers, former dean of Trinity Episcopal School for Ministry, says, "This is the sort of data that historians of antiquity drool over."[15]

7) JESUS' RESURRECTION WAS CELEBRATED IN THE EARLIEST CHURCH CREEDS.

In 1 Corinthians 15:3–4, Paul says, "Christ died for our sins in accordance with the Scriptures, that he was buried, that he was raised on the third day in accordance with the Scriptures." This statement is widely accepted as the earliest church creed, which began circulating as early as A.D. 30–36, shortly after Jesus' resurrection. Considering the early age of this creed, there was not sufficient time between the crucifixion and the creed for any legend about Jesus' resurrection to accrue. In addition, the witnesses mentioned were still alive and available to be questioned about the facts surrounding the resurrection. The early date of this creed also proves that the church did not corrupt the truth about Jesus with fables and folklore like the resurrection. Rather, the early church simply clung to the plain and incontrovertible facts of Jesus' death, burial, and resurrection.

8) JESUS' RESURRECTION CONVINCED HIS FAMILY TO WORSHIP HIM AS GOD.

James, Jesus' half-brother, was originally opposed to the claims of his brother.[16] A transformation occurred in James, though, after he saw his brother resurrected from death.[17] James went on to pastor the church in Jerusalem and authored the New Testament epistle bearing his name.[18] He was also actively involved in shaping the early church, which suffered and died to proclaim to everyone that Jesus is the one true God.[19] Also, Jesus' mother, Mary, was part of the early church that prayed to and worshiped her son as God,[20] as was Jesus' other brother, Jude, who wrote a book of the New Testament bearing his name.[21] While it is not impossible to imagine Jesus convincing some people that he is God if he were not, it is impossible to conceive of Jesus convincing his own mother and brothers to suffer persecution in this life and risk the torments of hell in eternal life for worshiping him as the one true God unless he truly is.

9) JESUS' RESURRECTION WAS CONFIRMED BY HIS MOST BITTER ENEMIES, SUCH AS PAUL.

Paul was a devout Jewish Pharisee who routinely persecuted and killed Christians.[22] After an encounter with the risen Christ, Paul was converted and became the most dynamic defender and expander of the church.[23] Had Jesus not truly risen from death, it is absurd to assume that Paul would have ever worshiped him as God, particularly when Paul rightly believed that worshiping a false God would send one into the eternal flames of hell. Simply, Paul hated Jesus and would never have changed his religious practice unless Jesus had risen from death to prove him wrong. Furthermore, Paul insisted that Jesus had risen in almost all of his letters that are saved for us in the New Testament.

CIRCUMSTANTIAL EVIDENCE FOR JESUS' RESURRECTION

In addition to the clear teachings of the Bible that Jesus did resurrect from death, changes occurred after Jesus' resurrection that could not have taken place unless he had truly risen. Conversely, to deny his resurrection also raises the burden of explaining how these things could have occurred without his truly rising to life.

1) THE TRANSFORMATION OF THE DISCIPLES

Prior to the resurrection, his disciples were timid and fearful, even hiding when Jesus appeared to them.[24] Following the resurrection, however, they were all transformed into bold witnesses to what they had seen and heard, even to the point of dying for their convictions. Had they not truly witnessed the risen Jesus, they undoubtedly would have recanted of their teachings and opted for a simpler life, free of suffering. They certainly would have told the truth rather than dying for a lie. Is it really plausible to assert that a group of scattered liars would remain loyal to one another and die for their lie in poverty and disgrace when riches and power could be obtained by their recanting? Apart from the resurrection, is there any way to account for the transformation of Peter—a coward who denied even knowing Jesus before his crucifixion and resurrection, but afterwards became the fearless leader of the early church and was himself crucified upside down?

Regarding the apostles' eyewitness testimony to Jesus' resurrection, Simon Greenleaf, professor of law at Harvard University and a world-renowned scholar on the rules of legal evidence, said that it was "impossible that they could have persisted in affirming the truths they have narrated, had not Jesus actually risen from the dead, and had they not known this fact as certainly as they knew any other fact."[25]

2) THE DISCIPLES' LOYALTY TO THEIR MESSIAH

Our culture is filled with various people who are proclaimed to be, in varying degrees, messiahs. These messiahs include, for example, politicians who propose to save and deliver us from a terrible fate such as terrorism, poverty, or unreasonable taxation. Such messiahs are surrounded by passionate followers who make sacrifices to support their messiah. However, once their messiah fails to get elected, their support base dwindles and people either give up hope or go searching for another messiah to trust in.

Curiously, the disciples of Jesus did neither. They did not give up hope that there was truly a real Messiah. Nor did they walk away from their commitment to Jesus in search of another messiah following his death. Instead, they claimed that he rose from death and remained loyal to him even though most of them suffered horrendously painful deaths marked by torture inflicted to coerce them into recanting of their belief in the resurrection of Jesus.

3) THE CHARACTER OF THE DISCIPLES

To claim that the disciples preached obvious lies and deluded people into dying for the world's greatest farce, one would first have to find credible evidence to challenge the character of the disciples. These men were devout Jews who knew that if they worshiped a false god and encouraged others to do the same, they would be sentenced by God to the fires of eternal hell for violating the first two commandments. Furthermore, does not such egregious lying conflict with the character of men and women who gave their lives to feeding the poor, caring for widows and orphans, and helping the hurting and needy?

4) THE DAY OF WORSHIP

The early church stopped worshiping on Saturday, as Jews had worshiped for thousands of years, and suddenly began worshiping on Sunday in memory of Jesus' Sunday resurrection.[26] The Sabbath was so sacred to the Jews that they would not have ceased to obey one of the Ten Commandments unless Jesus had resurrected in fulfillment of their Old Testament Scriptures.

5) THE OBJECT OF WORSHIP

Not only was the day of worship changed after the resurrection of Jesus, but so was the object of worship. Considering that one of the Ten Commandments also forbids the worship of false gods, it is impossible to conceive of devout Jews simply worshiping Jesus as the one true God without the proof of Jesus' resurrection.

According to even non-Christian historians, multitudes began worshiping Jesus as the one true God after his resurrection. Pliny the Younger (A.D. 61 or 62–113) was the nephew of the encyclopedist Pliny the Elder. Pliny the Younger became governor of Bithynia (northwestern Turkey) in the early second century. In a letter written around 111 to the emperor Trajan, he reports on early Christian worship meetings, saying: "They were in the habit of meeting on a certain fixed day before it was light, when they sang in alternate verses a hymn to Christ, as to a god . . ."[27]

Lucian of Samosata was a non-Christian Assyrian-Roman satirist who, around A.D. 170, wrote:

> The Christians, you know, worship a man to this day—the distinguished personage who introduced their novel rites, and was crucified on that account. . . . You see, these misguided creatures start with the general conviction that they are immortal for all time, which explains their contempt of death and voluntary self-devotion which are so common among them; and then it was impressed on them by their original lawgiver that they are all brothers, from the moment that they are converted, and deny the gods of Greece, and worship the crucified sage, and live after his laws.[28]

The question persists, if Jesus simply died in shame on a cross like tens of thousands of other men in his day and had not risen from death, why would people shortly thereafter begin worshiping him as God?

6) THEOLOGICAL CHANGES IN THE CHURCH

The resurrection of Jesus was accompanied with numerous theological changes among the worshipers of the God of the Old Testament. They include everything from the sacraments to the view of the purpose of the Old Testament laws.

Baptism shows that Christians will be buried and raised, cleansed from sin by Jesus. Communion remembers the body of Jesus that died on the cross for our sins and rose from the grave for our salvation. Both baptism and communion are related to the resurrection and would have been meaningless apart from it. They would not have become so endearing to early Christians without the resurrection.

Additionally, the early church rejected the observances of the law because they saw it as having been fulfilled in Jesus and no longer binding upon them in the same way as it previously had been for over a thousand years. This was a cataclysmic shift in belief that was only considered possible because a new epoch had begun following the resurrection of Jesus.

7) WOMEN DISCOVERING THE EMPTY TOMB

The women who discovered the tomb were mentioned by name, well known in the early church, and could have easily been questioned to confirm their findings if they were untrue.[29] Moreover, since the testimony of women was not respected in that culture, it would have been more likely for men to report discovering the empty tomb if the account was fictitious and an attempt were being made to concoct a credible lie about Jesus' resurrection. Therefore, the fact that women are said to have been the first to arrive at Jesus' empty tomb is confirmation that the account of Scripture is factual and not contrived.

8) EARLY CHURCH PREACHING

Undoubtedly, if the empty tomb had not been a widely accepted fact, the disciples would have reasoned with the skeptics of their day to defend the central issue of their faith. Instead, we see the debate occurring not about whether the tomb was empty, but why it was empty.[30] Also, nowhere in the preaching of the early church was the empty tomb explicitly defended for the simple reason that it was widely known as an agreed-upon fact. Furthermore, a reading of the book of Acts shows that on virtually every occasion that preaching and teaching occurred, the resurrection of Jesus from death was the central truth being communicated because it had changed human history and could not be ignored. Jesus' resurrection appears in twelve of the twenty-eight chapters in Acts, which records the history of the early church.

9) THE TOMB NOT ENSHRINED

In the days following the death of Nirvana lead singer Kurt Cobain, our local television news was filled with scenes of fans gathering to honor him at a memorial that was erected outside of the home in which he died. Fans left numerous cards, poems, letters, flowers, and various gifts.

In the same way, it was common in Jesus' day for the tombs of holy men to be enshrined. In Palestine at that time, the tombs of at least fifty prophets or other religious figures were enshrined as places of worship and veneration.[31] Yet, according to James D. G. Dunn, there is "absolutely no trace" of any veneration at Jesus' tomb.[32] The obvious reason for this lack of veneration is that Jesus was not buried but instead resurrected.

10) GROWTH OF THE CHURCH

There must be an explanation for the rapid growth and extraordinary level of commitment of the early church. Every effect has a cause, and such a world-changing effect would have necessitated a phenomenal cause. What else could have caused the commitment, perseverance, and rapid expansion of the early church other than Jesus' resurrection from death? On the same day, in the same place, and in the same way, two other men died, one on Jesus' left and one on his right. Despite the similarities, we do not know the names of these men, and billions of people do not worship them as God. Why? Because they remained dead and Jesus alone rose from death and ascended into heaven, leaving the Christian church in his wake.

We will now examine the non-Christian historical evidence for the resurrection of Jesus. In doing so, we are confirming that even those without a proclivity toward Christianity confirm the account of Christian Scripture.

NON-CHRISTIAN HISTORICAL EVIDENCE FOR JESUS' RESURRECTION

Despite their many differences, one thing that the ancient Romans, Greeks, and Jews all agreed upon was that they opposed Jesus and wanted him dead.[33] Because of this, Jesus' death was widely known and reported among these cultural groups of people. So, to help confirm the historical fact that Jesus rose from death, we will examine some of the more celebrated ancient historical accounts of Jesus' death and resurrection, taken from people who were simply telling the news of the day though they themselves were not Christians. The testimony of these Romans, Greeks, and Jews is helpful because it confirms the truthfulness of the biblical accounts of Jesus.

1) JOSEPHUS (A.D. 37–100)

Josephus was a Jewish historian born just a few years after Jesus died. His most celebrated passage, called the "Testimonium Flavianum," says:

> Now there was about this time Jesus, a wise man, if it be lawful to call him a man; for he was a doer of wonderful works, a teacher of such men as receive the truth with pleasure. He drew over to him both many of the Jews and many of the Gentiles. He was [the] Christ. And when Pilate, at the suggestion of the principal men among us, had condemned him to the cross, those that loved him at the first did not forsake him; for *he appeared to them alive again the third day*, as the divine prophets had foretold these and ten thousand other wonderful things concerning him. And the tribe of Christians, so named from him, are not extinct at this day.[34]

2) SUETONIUS (A.D. 70–160)

Suetonius was a Roman historian and annalist of the Imperial House. In his biography of Nero (Nero ruled A.D. 54–68), Suetonius mentions the persecution of Christians by indirectly referring to the resurrection: "Punishment was inflicted on the Christians, a class of men given to *a new and mischievous superstition* [the resurrection]."[35]

3) PLINY THE YOUNGER (A.D. 61 OR 62-113)

Pliny the Younger wrote a letter to the emperor Trajan around 111 describing early Christian worship gatherings that met early on Sunday mornings.in memory of Jesus' resurrection day:

> I have never been present at an examination of Christians. Consequently, I do not know the nature of the extent of the punishments usually meted out to them, nor the grounds for starting an investigation and how far it should be pressed. . . . They also declared that the sum total of their guilt or error amounted to no more than this: they had met regularly *before dawn on a fixed day* [Sunday in remembrance of Jesus' resurrection] to chant verses alternately amongst themselves in honor of Christ as if to a god . . . [36]

4) THE JEWISH EXPLANATION

The earliest attempt to provide an alternative explanation for the resurrection of Jesus did not deny that the tomb was empty.[37] Instead, Jewish opponents claimed that the body had been stolen, thus admitting the fact of the empty tomb. But this explanation is untenable for the following reasons. One, the tomb was closed with an enormous rock and sealed by the government, and there is no explanation for how the rock was moved while being guarded by armed Roman soldiers. Two, if the body had been stolen, a large ransom could have been offered to the thieves and they could have been coerced to produce the body. Or, if it had been taken by the disciples, then the torture and death they suffered should have been sufficient to return the body. Three, even if the body was stolen, how are we to account for the fact that Jesus appeared to multiple crowds of people, proving that he was alive? In conclusion, the theft of the body is unlikely and still fails to account for it returning back to life.

Summarily, the historical testimony of those who were not Christians stands in agreement with Scripture that Jesus died and rose because those are the simple and incontrovertible facts. Having examined the biblical, circumstantial, and historical evidence for Jesus' resurrection, it is apparent that the resurrection of Jesus is a historical fact. We will now consider the practical implications of Jesus' resurrection, and why it is imperative that our personal faith be in Jesus and his resurrection.

PRACTICAL IMPLICATIONS OF JESUS' RESURRECTION

There have been many disagreements among Christians on secondary matters of their faith through the history of the church. But on the primary issues related to Jesus, such as his bodily resurrection from death, there has always been consistent agreement.

The resurrection of Jesus is more than just another amazing historical fact. It has unprecedented practical implications for our life in this world and beyond our grave.

Sadly, there is apparently a great deal of confusion on this matter. Every year people celebrate the resurrection of Jesus at Easter. Nonetheless, many people believe in the historical fact of Jesus' resurrection but have not become Christians by placing their personal faith in him. Even some who claim to be Christians oddly deny the historical fact of Jesus' resurrection. For example, a poll conducted by *Newsweek* magazine asked the question, "Do you believe that Jesus Christ rose from the dead after dying on the cross?"[38] Of those who answered, only 88 percent of people who claimed to be Christians answered yes. But, fully 32 percent of people who claimed to be non-Christians answered yes.

Jesus promised that he would not only rise from death to prove beyond any doubt he is God, but also that he would judge everyone who has ever lived and determine their fate.[39] His first promise came true when he rose from death, and his second promise will come true upon either our death or his return. This makes the opportunity he grants us in this life to repent and turn from sin and judgment to him all the more urgent. Plainly stated in loving concern, if someone has not come to know and love the living Jesus who has conquered both sin and death for us, they are sadly destined to die and spend eternity in the torments of hell. Forgiveness and eternal life are made possible only through Jesus' own death and resurrection for us.

ANSWERS TO COMMON QUESTIONS ABOUT THE RESURRECTION OF JESUS CHRIST

IS IT POSSIBLE THAT JESUS MERELY SWOONED ON THE CROSS AND DID NOT DIE?

Some have argued that Jesus did not in fact die on the cross, but rather swooned or basically passed out and therefore appeared dead. This is also what the Muslim Koran teaches as fact. Regarding this claim, theologian John Stott has asked if we are to believe

> that after the rigours and pains of trial, mockery, flogging and crucifixion he could survive thirty-six hours in a stone sepulchre with neither warmth nor food nor medical care? That he could then rally sufficiently to perform the superhuman feat of shifting the boulder which secured the mouth of the tomb, and this without disturbing the Roman guard? That then, weak and sickly and hungry, he could appear to the disciples in such a way as to give them the impression that he had vanquished death? That he could go on to claim that he had died and risen, could send them into all the world and promise to be with them unto the end of time? That he could live somewhere in hiding for forty days, making occasional surprise appearances, and then finally disappear without explanations? Such credulity is more incredible than Thomas' unbelief.[40]

Also, crucifixion is essentially death by asphyxiation, because the prisoner grows too tired to lift himself up and fill his lungs with air. This explains why the Romans would often break a prisoner's legs, thus preventing him from continuing to fill his lungs with air. Since the professional executioners did not break Jesus' legs, these professional executioners must have been convinced of his death. The only way Jesus could have deceived the executioners would have been to stop breathing, which in itself would have killed him.

Lastly, John 19:34–35 tells us that the Roman soldier thrust a spear into Jesus' side to confirm his death. The water that poured out was probably from the sac surrounding his heart, and the blood most likely came from the right side of his heart. Even if he had been alive, this would have killed him.[41]

IS IT POSSIBLE THAT JESUS DID NOT RISE BUT THAT HIS BODY WAS STOLEN?

The original explanation given for the empty tomb by those Jews who did not choose to worship Jesus as God was that the tomb was indeed empty but not because of a resurrection; rather, it was empty because of a theft of Jesus' dead body.[42] For this to be true, a number of impossibilities would have had to occur. First, despite the fact that it would have cost them their lives, all of the guards positioned at the tomb would have had to fall asleep at the same time. Second, each of the guards would not only have had to fall asleep but also remain asleep and not be awakened by the breaking of the Roman seal on the tomb, the rolling away of the enormous stone which blocked the entrance, or the carrying off of the dead body. Third, even if Jesus' body was stolen, there is no way to account for its returning to vibrant and triumphant life.

The issue of motive is also a key factor in refuting this hypothesis. What benefit would there be for the disciples to risk their lives to steal a corpse and die for a lie as a result? What motive would there be for the Jews, the Romans, or anyone else to steal the body? And, if the body had been truly stolen, could not a bounty have been offered and someone enticed to provide the body in exchange for a handsome cash reward? Lastly, even if the dead body had been stolen, how does that explain the fact that Jesus reappeared alive, walking around, talking to people, and eating meals for forty days until he returned to heaven?

IS IT POSSIBLE THAT A TWIN BROTHER, OR A LOOK-ALIKE, DIED IN JESUS' PLACE?

It has been suggested by some Muslim scholars along with various other people that Jesus was not the one crucified, but rather a brother or other man who looked like him. However, there is not a shred of evidence to prove that someone who looked like Jesus existed at that time. Additionally, Jesus' mother was present at his crucifixion, and the likelihood of fooling his mother is minimal. Also, the physical wounds he suffered during the crucifixion were visible on Jesus' resurrection body and carefully inspected by the disciple Thomas, who was very doubtful that Jesus had risen until he touched scars from the crucifixion evident on Jesus' body.[43] In addition, the tomb was empty and the burial cloths were left behind. So, even if it was not Jesus who resurrected from death, someone else who simply looked like him did rise, and we should worship him as God instead.

IS THE IDEA OF JESUS' RESURRECTION A MYTH BORROWED FROM OTHER RELIGIONS?

Those wanting to determine the truth on this point should simply check out the facts for themselves and demand the evidence. Rather than believing us or any other expert, you can simply go to the web and look at the "resurrection" stories of the other religions.

You will find the story of a corn-god who died. Priests performed a funeral for the god and buried an image of it made of dirt and corn so that it would come to life again with the new crops.

You will also find the Osiris story. Osiris upset Seth who murdered him and threw his body into the Nile. Isis and her sisters magically located Osiris's body, which further upset Seth. So he tore the body into fourteen pieces and scattered them throughout Egypt. According to the story, Isis once again found every part of his body, save his phallus, which the fish had eaten. She magically reassembled Osiris and resurrected him long enough to be impregnated by him so that she could give birth to the new king Horus.

Ask yourself, is the story of Jesus' resurrection truly stolen from these myths as evidenced by their numerous parallels?

According to noted historian Edwin Yamauchi, there is no possibility that the idea of a resurrection was borrowed because there is no definitive evidence for the teaching of a deity resurrection in any of the religions prior to the second century.[44] In fact, it seems they stole the idea from Christians! Lastly, this theory completely ignores the historical facts of the empty tomb and post-resurrection appearances of Jesus that need an explanation if they are not to be believed.

COULD THE DISCIPLES HAVE MISSED JESUS SO MUCH THAT THEY HALLUCINATED HIS RESURRECTION?

Some people have suggested that the disciples did not actually see Jesus risen from death but rather they hallucinated, or projected their desires for his resurrection into a hallucination that it had occurred. One example is John Dominic Crossan, cochairman of the Jesus Seminar. He told *Time* magazine that after the crucifixion, Jesus' corpse was probably laid in a shallow grave, barely covered with dirt, and eaten by wild dogs. The subsequent story of Jesus' resurrection, he says, was merely the result of "wishful thinking."[45]

This thesis is unbelievable for five reasons.

First, a hallucination is a private, not public, experience. Yet Paul clearly states that Jesus appeared to more than five hundred people at one time.[46] Second, Jesus appeared at various times in a variety of locations, whereas hallucinations are generally restricted to individual times and places. Third, certain types of people tend to be more prone to hallucination than others. Yet Jesus appeared to a great variety of personalities, including his brothers and mother. Fourth, after forty days, Jesus' appearances suddenly stopped for everyone simultaneously. Hallucinations tend to continue over longer periods of time and do not stop abruptly. Fifth, a hallucination is a projection of a thought that preexists in the mind. However, the Jews had a conception of resurrection that applied to the raising of all people at the end of history,[47] not the raising of any particular individual in the middle of history.[48] Therefore, it is inconceivable that the witnesses to the resurrection could have hallucinated Jesus' resurrection.

CHAPTER EIGHT

WHERE IS JESUS TODAY?

"I came from the Father and have come into the world, and now I am leaving the world and going to the Father."

JESUS (JOHN 16:28)

✝

Jesus' image is practically everywhere today—television, movies, T-shirts, magazines, web sites, blogs, books, artwork, and tattoos. But where is Jesus today?

Christian author Philip Yancey wisely said, "By ascending, Jesus took the risk of being forgotten."[1] His words seem tragically accurate. For the first nineteen years of my life until I became a Christian, I don't remember ever really thinking about whether Jesus was alive today, and if so, where.

In preparation for this book, I decided to simply interview people on the street to get their opinions about Jesus. I wanted to see if they had forgotten him now that he is no longer visibly here on the earth with us. My favorite interviews were at the legendary Seattle Hempfest, where some quarter-million people gather together under the banner of getting higher than Sputnik. I took a film crew to the event to interview people about Jesus, while wearing my very favorite T-shirt, which has a picture of Jesus and says, "Jesus is watching you smoke that weed!"

I was humored to discover that almost everyone I spoke with knew at least two Scriptures—the one from Genesis where every seed-bearing plant is good, and the one from the Gospels about not judging anyone. People gave me some interesting answers when I asked them where they thought Jesus is today. One guy, who had been smoking forever and ever like the biblical *gehenna*, swore that he had seen Jesus at the Hempfest, and as I looked around, it did seem like nearly every other guy did look a little bit like the stereotypical, long-haired hippie Jesus. The most common answer I received was that Jesus did not rise from death and is little more than legendary mulch in a hole somewhere.

Likewise, in Jesus' day, some Jews believed that Jesus never did rise and that his body was stolen, which would mean that he is still very much dead today. Later pseudo-Christians who denied the possibility of miracles generally agreed. For example, president Thomas Jefferson sat down in the White House with a razor in one hand and the Bible in the other. He cut out those parts of Scripture that he decided were untrue. The result was *The Philosophy of Jesus of Nazareth*, or *The Life and Morals of Jesus of Nazareth*. Only one in ten verses survived, zero miracles were considered factual, and the resurrection of Jesus was systematically cut from the pages of Scripture. Jesus was left as a mere Zen-like, humanist, sage philosopher. Similarly, Thomas Paine said he went "through the Bible as a man would go through a wood with an axe on his shoulders and fell trees."[2]

Following in Jefferson's and Paine's fatal footsteps, in 1985 the two hundred fellows (a.k.a. kindling) of the Jesus Seminar gathered to vote on the probability of the truthfulness of the words and deeds of Jesus as recorded in Scripture. By the time they were finished, they surmised that only 18 percent of what is recorded as Jesus' words in the Gospels were actually said by Jesus. Only one statement from the Gospel of Mark got voted in. Even the most critical of scholars think that the trustworthiness of Scripture is a lot better than this. These guys were obviously educated beyond their intelligence.[3]

Bahá'ís believe that Jesus was a great man but not God and think his spirit rose from death but not his body. Likewise, the Jehovah's Witnesses also believe that Jesus did not rise physically but did rise spiritually and returned to the earth in 1914 and now rules the world from the Watchtower headquarters in Pittsburgh (which may explain why the Steelers won the 2006 Super Bowl, thanks in part to the horrendous officiating). Some Muslims believe Jesus did not die and though he was not God was simply taken up to heaven like Enoch and Elijah.

Mormons believe Jesus is hanging out in heaven with his wives like some rapper with a bootylicious entourage. According to assorted *Da Vinci Code* conspiracy nuts, Jesus ran off to France, got married, filled up an entire minivan with kidlets, and later died and remains to this day metaphysically challenged.

The Bible has much to say about where Jesus is today and what he is doing. As the second member of the Trinity, Jesus Christ ruled from eternity past as God exalted in glory. He then humbly entered into history as a man to identify with us. Throughout his life on the earth, Jesus repeatedly said that following his death, burial, and resurrection, he would ascend back into heaven where he had come from.[4] As the counterpart to the humble incarnation of Jesus, this is the glorious exaltation of Jesus.

Sadly, when many people think of Jesus they only understand his past humble incarnation and neglect his current glorious exaltation. The tragic result is that for many, Jesus is little more than a "[hippie] in a world of Augustan yuppies" as John Crossan has said.[5]

Indeed, if we were to see Jesus today, we would not see a homeless and humble, marginalized Galilean peasant on earth. Instead, we would see Jesus in his glorious exaltation in heaven. Hundreds of years before Jesus' humble incarnation, Isaiah was given an opportunity to see the Lord Jesus in his state of glorious exaltation:

> I saw the Lord sitting upon a throne, high and lifted up; and the train of his robe filled the temple. Above him stood the seraphim. Each had six wings: with two he covered his face, and with two he covered his feet, and with two he flew. And one called to another and said: "Holy, holy, holy is the LORD of hosts; the whole earth is full of his glory!" And the foundations of the thresholds shook at the voice of him who called, and the house was filled with smoke. And I said: "Woe is me! For I am lost; for I am a man of unclean lips, and I dwell in the midst of a people of unclean lips; for my eyes have seen the King, the Lord of hosts!"[6]

Jesus' disciple John later revealed that Isaiah saw none other than Jesus Christ.[7]

John was not only present as an eyewitness to the life of Jesus during his humble incarnation but was also given an opportunity much like Isaiah to see Jesus following his ascension back into heavenly glory. His report of Ultimate Fighter Jesus in glorious exaltation is recorded in Revelation 19:11–16. There, Jesus is not revealed as a glass-jawed hippie wearing a dress. Rather, he is an Ultimate Fighter warrior king with a tattoo down his leg who rides into battle against Satan, sin, and death on a trusty horse, just like every decent Western from Pecos Bill to the Rifleman, the Cisco Kid, the Lone Ranger, Buffalo Bill, and Wild Bill Hickok. If we were to see Jesus today, we would see him in glory, not in humility. We would see a Jesus who will never take a beating again, but is coming again to open a can on the unrepentant until their blood flows upon the earth like grapes crushed in the violence of a winepress. Echoing John's vision, one Christian author has perceptively compared the ascension of Jesus to the journey home of a valiantly triumphant soldier after a great victory in war.[8] That Soldier is also coming back again.

Too often Christology (doctrines about the person and work of Jesus) is derived almost exclusively from the four Gospels. While they do faithfully record the earthly life of Jesus, the pictures that emerge of Jesus from such a Christology are incomplete because they only see him in humble incarnation and do not see him in glorious exaltation. The book of Revelation is therefore an incredibly important book because it is a book about Jesus, no less than the four Gospels, and the primary book that reveals to us the picture of Jesus in heaven today as opposed to on the earth yesterday. Sadly, the book of Revelation has become the fishing pond for Christian wingnuts with an affinity for goofy charts to string together endless debates about what the mark of the beast is, who the antichrist is, and whether or not locusts are really code word for Blackhawk helicopters. Such people need both new hobbies and the right meds. Revelation is a book about Jesus and emphatically declares that in the opening line of the book, which describes the entire book as "the revelation of Jesus Christ."[9]

To arrive at a proper picture of what Jesus appears like today requires that we journey with him from his life, death, burial, and resurrection to his ascension back onto his throne in Revelation. Curiously, there are relatively few books written on the ascension of Jesus and his present exaltation, which may contribute to the weak opinions of Jesus.

To help clarify where Jesus is today we will trace the biblical account beginning with his final moments on the earth.

JESUS PHYSICALLY ASCENDED INTO HEAVEN

Following his bodily resurrection from death, Jesus spent forty days living his life in open, public visibility to assure people that he had in fact conquered sin and death.[10] He then said his final words to his followers and "when he had said these things, as they were looking on, he was lifted up, and a cloud took him out of their sight. And while they were gazing into heaven as he went, behold, two men stood by them in white robes, and said, 'Men of Galilee, why do you stand looking into heaven? This Jesus, who was taken up from you into heaven, will come in the same way as you saw him go into heaven.'"[11]

Having completed his mission on the earth, Jesus punched his round-trip ticket and returned to heaven where he had come from. This is precisely what Jesus had said would happen: "I came from the Father and have come into the world, and now I am leaving the world and going to the Father."[12]

Not only did Jesus enter into human history in a physical body for his incarnation, but he also died, rose, and ascended back into heaven in a physical body. Furthermore, Acts 1:11 says that Jesus will return one day in the same way that he left. This means that today Jesus continues to have a resurrected and glorified body that is the pattern for ours. When Jesus returns he will come in his glorified human body.

This point is important because so much false Greek thinking has bled into some Christian concepts of heaven. One of the essential flaws of Greek philosophy was that it divided creation into the material and immaterial and considered the immaterial or spiritual world to be good and the material world to be essentially bad. The logical outgrowth of this lens is that heaven is the place where we shed our physical bodies to live forever in our immaterial spirit. However, the view of heaven in the Bible is essentially a redeemed creation, free of sin, death, and the curse, where we live together with Jesus in our physical bodies in God's physical creation. Therefore, it is important for us to see that Jesus ascended into heaven and that his ascension was physical because he is the pattern for our future resurrection, which is further explained in 1 Corinthians 15.

JESUS IS IN HEAVEN WITH DEPARTED CHRISTIANS

Not only did Jesus Christ ascend into heaven, but he also took his Old Testament people with him, according to what many Christians believe. Luke 16:19–31 seems to indicate that before Jesus died for our sins, God's people were held in a temporary holding place. They were waiting for Jesus to come and take them to heaven upon his ascension. In some ways this was like the waiting area at the airport—your flight is already booked and you've made it past security, but you have to hang out for a long time until you can board your flight and embark on your journey to your final destination.

Upon his ascension into heaven following his resurrection, Jesus took with him those who had previously died with faith in him. This is because heaven was essentially closed until Jesus opened it with his return in victory over sin. On this matter, Ephesians 4:8 says, "When he ascended on high he led a host of captives." As a result, today there is no holding place, including purgatory, other than heaven for God's people to reside in following their death. There remains, however, a place of holding for those who die apart from faith in Jesus. That place, called hades, is a place of justice and torment. It will ultimately be thrown into the hellish lake of fire once the final judgment of non-Christians is completed by Jesus.[13]

JESUS SITS AT THE RIGHT HAND OF GOD THE FATHER

Throughout Scripture the right hand is denoted as special. It is used for taking oaths[14] and giving blessing.[15] God's right hand is the place of righteousness[16] and might.[17] To be at the right side is to be in a place of honor.[18] Therefore, it is not surprising to hear that following his ascension, Jesus was seated at the right hand of God the Father.[19]

Two Scriptures are particularly pertinent on this point. Psalm 110:1 says, "The LORD [God the Father] says to my Lord [God the Son]: 'Sit at my right hand, until I make your enemies your footstool.'" Picking up on the theme of Psalm 110:1, Jesus said, "I tell you, from now on you will see the Son of Man seated at the right hand of Power and coming on the clouds of heaven."[20]

Today, Jesus is seated at the right hand of God the Father. As such, he will never again be subject to the disrespect that he humbly endured during his earthly life.

JESUS SITS ON A THRONE

The imagery of a throne is used roughly 196 times in Scripture, with 135 occurrences in the Old Testament and sixty-one occurrences in the New Testament. Of the New Testament occurrences, forty-five of the sixty-one are in the book of Revelation. The imagery of the throne appears in seventeen of its twenty-two chapters, most frequently in Revelation 4. The person sitting on the throne in heaven throughout Revelation is the ascended Jesus Christ.

In a day when most people sat on the floor, squatted, or reclined, thrones were reserved for kings, priests, and warriors. Throughout Revelation, Jesus is portrayed in each of these roles. As king, Jesus rules over all creation from his throne. As priest, Jesus mediates between us and God the Father. As warrior, Jesus sits in triumph over Satan, sin, and death.

JESUS RULES AND REIGNS AS SOVEREIGN, KING, AND LORD

From his throne in heaven at the right hand of God the Father, Jesus Christ is presently ruling and reigning as Sovereign, King, and Lord. Consequently, everything and everyone is under the rule of the exalted Jesus Christ. Simply, nothing is beyond the rule and authority of Jesus Christ. The Bible says this repeatedly and emphatically by explaining Jesus' sovereign rule over "all things."[21]

In the early days following the ascension of Jesus, it was the exclusive claim of Jesus' unparalleled supremacy as the only king and only God who alone ruled over all other kings and their kingdoms, gods, and religions that made Christians incredibly controversial and hated. Much like the past days of the Old Testament and present days of postmodern pluralism, there was great pressure on the followers of Jesus to reduce his rule solely to their hearts, their family, and their church. But the Scriptures clearly, repeatedly, and unashamedly declare that Jesus rules over all peoples, times, places, cultures, things, and perspectives as the preeminent Lord of all.

JESUS INTERCEDES AS OUR LIVING
GOD-MAN MEDIATOR

Not only is Jesus alive, he also continues to minister for us in his glorified, resurrected body. In John 14:6 Jesus said, "I am the way, and the truth, and the life. No one comes to the Father except through me." Likewise, in 1 Timothy 2:5, Paul says, "For there is one God, and there is one mediator between God and men, the man Christ Jesus." And Hebrews 7:25 says, "[Jesus] always lives to make intercession."

As our living exalted Lord of all, Jesus is the only one who can mediate between people and God because he alone is both God and man, having humbly become a human being in his incarnation. Subsequently, it is only through Jesus that we have a relationship of forgiven sin and new eternal life with God the Father.

The mediation of Jesus alone between us and God the Father is repugnant to some because it seems both discriminatory and exclusive. It is seen as discriminatory against all other religions and beliefs that have mediators in addition to or instead of Jesus. Examples include beliefs that the church, morality, karma, good works, sincere intent, or religious devotion are sufficient to close the distance between us and God the Father without the help of a mediator to settle the conflict caused by our sin. Furthermore, many people today are looking for spirit guides, or guardians, who will do the mediation between themselves and the spirit world. The guardians can read our "akashic record" or our "Book of Life." They can remind us of our past lives or protect us if or when we leave our bodies for astral travel. Most importantly, they promise to be there to help us get to the spirit dimension when we die.

There is much to be said as to why discrimination is not, in and of itself, necessarily a bad thing, though it can and has been sinfully applied. For example, we regularly discriminate in our homes by choosing who can and cannot enter, as well as what is and what is not acceptable conduct. Therefore, if strangers should knock on our door and demand that we allow them to move in with us, eat our food, make a mess, ignore our house rules, and do what they tell us, we would discriminate and decline their demands. In doing so, we are being exclusive. We do not want everyone in our home acting as they please because it is our home, and we have the subsequent right to decide who is permitted to enter and how they are expected to conduct themselves.

Curiously, those who protest the mediation of Jesus alone as discriminatory and exclusive are hypocritically denying God the same freedoms they enjoy. Because heaven is God's home, he too has the right to discriminately choose who he allows in, and he has the exclusive right to declare how they are to behave once accepted. Rather than being unhappy with an exclusive and discriminating God, we should be thankful that God allows any of us into his home. We should also celebrate that his invitation goes out in a very inclusive way to everyone on the earth, welcoming them to turn to Jesus for salvation. In this way, God is far more inclusive than any of us, as he has welcomed all people to his eternal home through Jesus Christ, the mediator he has made available to us.

In a conversation I once had with a non-Christian friend, it became apparent to me that by not taking everyone to heaven, God is actually being very gracious. My friend said that God should take everyone to heaven. I then asked him if he wanted to spend eternity under God's rule worshiping Jesus with other Christians. He replied, "That sounds like my hell and I would be furious if God stuck me in a place like that forever."

JESUS GRANTS HIS SPIRITUAL AUTHORITY TO CHRISTIANS

One of the most stunning truths of Scripture is not only that Jesus is seated at the right hand of God the Father exalted in glory, but that we who are by grace in Christ are also seated with him positionally. Ephesians 2:6 says that God has "seated us with him in the heavenly places in Christ Jesus." From this position, Paul says to Christians, "Do you not know that we are to judge angels?"[22] Amazingly, today Christians possess the delegated spiritual authority of the exalted Jesus Christ. Furthermore, one day we will join Jesus in the judgment of angels and demons.

Practically, this means that even though we remain physically upon the earth, we are positionally seated with Jesus in heaven. Subsequently, we are granted use of Jesus' spiritual authority over Satan and demons. As a result, we need not succumb to Satan's temptations, believe Satan's lies, or receive Satan's accusations and condemnations. Because Jesus has ascended and rules over all, and because his unparalleled authority has been delegated to us, we who are his people can walk in his spiritual power and victory. Consequently, any Christian has the authority to resist a demon, commanding it to get away in Jesus' name.[23]

JESUS IS PREPARING A ROOM FOR US IN HIS FATHER'S HOUSE

Jesus' ascension into heaven is also the pattern for our own future if we belong to him. Consequently, for those who die today with faith in Jesus, their spirit immediately goes to be with the Lord in heaven.[24] One day their spirit will reenter their body when they rise from death to live forever in God's kingdom in a glorified, resurrected body like Jesus.[25] Jesus himself described heaven as a glorious home owned by God the Father that includes a well-prepared room for each of us to live in forever as part of God's family the church.[26]

JESUS IS ENJOYING AN URBAN PARADISE

When our first parents sinned, creation was also implicated in the curse. As a result, though it is glorious and does reveal something of the glory of God,[27] creation is nonetheless cursed and subject to futility.[28] However, in addition to lifting the curse, upon his return Jesus will unveil a new creation that will include a new earth free of any effects of sin.[29]

Jesus' redemption of the earth generally in addition to his redemption of me personally is interesting in light of the worldview of many people who are committed to environmental activism and a green lifestyle. The result can often be an intense self-righteousness enabled by a gospel that proclaims justification by recycling and promotes worship of the Trinitarian god of biking to work, eating organic food, and naturopathy. While each of these efforts is good, they are not sufficient to lift the curse, erase the effects of sin in the world, and restore earth to the Edenic paradise that is deeply lodged in the memory of God's image bearers who do not believe the true creation story of Scripture. Therefore, the environmentalist dream of a perfect and perfectly stewarded creation will only be fulfilled with the return of Jesus.

As an aside, it is important to note that the new creation will not be the idyllic rural lifestyle that has dominated so much American vision of faithful Christianity. Rather, at the center of the new creation will be a grand metropolis from which Jesus will rule over the earth.[30] The entire storyline of the Bible is not from garden to garden, but rather from garden to city.[31] The Bible opens in its first few pages with a beautiful garden paradise. But the Bible closes in its final few pages with the vision of heaven as a dense city filled with people—the ultimate goal of creation is an urban paradise.

Practically speaking, a city is marked by both greater density and diversity than suburban or rural areas. For the first time in the world's history, roughly half of the world's population is urban. That number is expected to swell to 60 percent by the year 2030.

Sadly, most Christians associate the city with vice, not virtue. In truth, cities have long been seen as a haven for violent crime, sexual sin, and drug abuse. But sin is often most clearly seen in the city because it is more concentrated in the city than in suburban and rural areas. As a result, the related need for God is most clearly seen in the city. The rawness of the city makes it exactly the kind of place that God would use to convince people of their need for him. Furthermore, by revealing the unveiling of a city upon his return, Jesus intends for Christians to love cities in the meantime.

Unlike today where Christians have largely fled the cities in favor of homeschooling about the rapture amidst large stacks of canned goods readied for a hunkering down at the unleashing of Armageddon, Christianity has historically been an urban religion. A reading of the history book of early Christianity, Acts, reveals that Christianity began as an urban movement led by Paul, whose itinerant church planting ministry was almost exclusively urban as he moved from city to city and bypassed the rural areas.

Historians like Rodney Stark[32] and Wayne Meeks[33] say that by A.D. 300, upwards of half of the people living in major Roman cities were Christian, while more than 90 percent of those living in the countryside were still pagan. Curiously, our word *pagan* likely came from the Greek word *paganus*, which meant "someone who lives on the farm." Most of the Christians lived in cities and most pagans lived on farms.

Indeed, God's people should bring the gospel to any place where there are people, because God loves all people. But since there are more people in the city, it also makes sense that bringing the gospel to cities would be a priority.

One of the reasons Christians in our day are to love the city as they await the unveiling of Jesus' city is that the city is the most strategic place for Christians and the gospel. If culture is like a river, then cities are upstream, creating culture that then flows downstream to the masses. Because government, law, education, healthcare, information, media, arts, sports, entertainment, trade, travel, population, and industry are concentrated most in a city, cities are the fountains from which culture flows. Therefore, for Christians to flee from cities then to only complain about the kind of culture that is flowing into the culture from the cities is both foolish and hypocritical. The answer is for Christians to love the city, move to the city, pray for the city, and serve the city until Jesus returns with his city from which all culture will emanate throughout the new earth.

JESUS IS WITH US AS WE BRING THE GOSPEL TO THE WORLD

Shortly before his ascension into heaven, Jesus gave some final orders for his people to follow: "All authority in heaven and on earth has been given to me. Go therefore and make disciples of all nations, baptizing them in the name of the Father and of the Son and of the Holy Spirit, teaching them to observe all that I have commanded you. And behold, I am with you always, to the end of the age."[34] Jesus' declaration that he alone possesses all authority both in heaven and on earth is an unparalleled claim that is devastating to our current postmodern mood. Rather than seeing the world as a muddied mess of equally valid and authoritative perspectives, cultures, opinions, spiritualities, philosophies, genders, generations, races, and the like, Jesus boldly revealed that he alone rules over all with all authority and without any exception.

Subsequently, today Jesus Christ is alive and well, seated on a throne at the right hand of God the Father being worshiped as God by angels and departed saints. Today Jesus alone rules and reigns in exalted glory as Lord over man and beast, male and female, gays and straights, young and old, rich and poor, black and white, simple and wise, powerful and powerless, Republicans and Democrats, married and single, chaste and unchaste, modern and postmodern, Christians and non-Christians, angels and demons, the living and the dead, every religion, every spirituality, every philosophy, every thought, every word, every deed, every dollar, and every inch of creation, which he claims as his possession under his throne that is over all. Practically, this means that Jesus has authority over the sex we have, money we spend, food we eat, web sites we browse, words we speak, places we journey, attitudes we project, ideas we entertain, friends we embrace, shows we watch, drinks we consume, hobbies we enjoy, and work we do, because Jesus has all authority over all people and all things without any exception.

By grace we love and are loved by this glorious and exalted Jesus whom we worship unceasingly, serve unwaveringly, and proclaim unashamedly until our face is at his feet. We will explore that theme more fully in the next chapter.

ANSWERS TO COMMON QUESTIONS ABOUT JESUS' ASCENSION

IS JESUS REIGNING AS KING TODAY?

Jesus is anointed king today but is not yet reigning as king. He won't be until he comes in glory to set up his millennial kingdom. The situation is a little like David in the Old Testament. Samuel anointed him king in 1 Samuel 16. Rather than ruling as king, though, David spent some years running for his life, surrounded by a posse of malcontent dudes. Despite the fact that Saul was the guy on the throne in Jerusalem, they had eyes of faith to realize that David was the rightful king. They were loyal to him and did their work in his authority until the day he entered Jerusalem to take the throne.

Likewise, God the Father has anointed Jesus as King.[35] As Christians, our citizenship is in heaven.[36] Today, we live here on earth with the blessings of his heavenly authority. We can proclaim forgiveness of sins, command demons away from us, and experience the kingdom power of the Holy Spirit at work in us.

As we live for the anointed king in this world where evil still dominates, we will face persecution. As Jesus said, "I have said these things to you, that in me you may have peace. In the world you will have tribulation. But take heart; I have overcome the world."[37]

So we live in hope for the day when Jesus will come to reign personally here on the earth over a kingdom where justice will roll down like waters and righteousness like an ever-flowing stream.[38] In the meantime, we say no to ungodliness in all its forms and live self-controlled and godly lives while we wait for the blessed hope—the glorious appearance of our great God and Savior, Jesus Christ, who gave himself for us to redeem us from all wickedness and to purify for himself a people that are his very own, eager to do what is good.[39]

ARE WE UNDER THE POWER OF CURSES?

Actually, we are not. The Father rescued us from the dominion of darkness where the curses have their dark power and transferred us to the kingdom of his beloved Son, the kingdom of light.[40] Because we are in the authority realm of the Son and not in darkness, curses have no authority over us. However, if we believe the curses have power, then they will. It's a little like parents believing that they have to obey their young child. It isn't true, but watching parents today shows us the power of such a false belief.

To be freed from the curses, we only need to stand on our rightful authority as Christian believers. Jesus is far above all rule and authority and power and dominion, and above every name that is named, not only in this age but also in the one to come. The Father put all things under Jesus' feet and gave him as head over all things to the church.[41] Therefore, the cross, resurrection, and ascension of Jesus is the greatest triumph in the history of the human race that liberates us from the power of curses.

CAN PEOPLE WHO ARE WITH JESUS SEE US?

Many appeal to the "great cloud of witnesses" in Hebrews 12:1 to argue that people are sitting in the heavenly stands, watching us and cheering us on like spectators in a cosmic sports stadium. The question is whether they are witnesses to the faith in their day on earth or spectators witnessing us today from heaven. The normal use of the word "witness" meant Jesus' followers telling the glory of God and bearing witness to God's faithfulness and the power of the faith.[42] They were certainly not passive spectators. As F. F. Bruce notes, "It is not so much they who look at us as we who look to them—for encouragement."[43] Whether or not God's faithful servants who have gone before us can see us run the race of our life, the important thing is that we run well because the proverbial baton of the gospel has been handed to us.

CHAPTER NINE

WHY SHOULD WE WORSHIP JESUS?

"Worthy is the Lamb who was slain, to receive power and wealth and wisdom and might and honor and glory and blessing!"

REVELATION 5:12

✝

A downside to being a pastor is that you never get to attend pro football games on Sundays. While I thank God for TiVo, I do long to attend the occasional game to join other lazy people in complaining about the performance of highly trained athletes.

God answered my prayers when our hometown Seahawks were playing a Monday-night game, and someone in the church had an extra ticket, which made me as happy as a redneck getting a ticket to a motorcycles-on-ice show. As a hometown homey I was thrilled because our team won. As a Christian I found it to be an intriguing example of worship.

As I sat among nearly seventy thousand fans, I wondered what the impression of Old Testament Hebrew worshipers would be if they could have been teleported to the game. My guess is that they would have assumed they were at the worship service of an enormous cult.

While zoning laws in our city essentially forbid us from building a large church, the football stadium was built at a cost of 450 million dollars (with roughly 300 million dollars of that money coming from public monies such as taxes). Every ticket for the entire season is expensive yet sold out. Our seats at the game I attended were in what Paul calls the "third heaven" and cost about forty dollars each. In addition, parking, a hot dog, and a beer cost about the same as a year's tuition at a state college. The help of a Sherpa was required to haul it all to the high altitude where the seats were.

People walked many blocks in a driving rain that was so Old Testament that parts of the city were flooded, rivers had spilled over their banks, and mudslides were leading the nightly newscasts. Nonetheless, seemingly every seat in the stadium was filled, and fans stood in the rain for the entire game—not even using the seat they paid for—wearing the team colors and screaming, while music blared through the sound system and half-naked young women provided the eye candy.

In short, I was at a worship service with a congregation that was larger, more devoted, more generous, and more vocal than any church in America.

As I enjoyed the game I was reminded of words spoken to me some years before. A dear friend of mine is a pastor who also runs an orphanage and a Bible college in India. He converted to Christianity after being raised a Hindu. We have spent a considerable amount of time together over the years in both the United States and India.

When I was in India, the false worship that permeated the culture was disturbingly obvious to me. As I walked through the villages I continually came upon small shrines alongside the road dedicated to various local gods. Inside the small huts were food gifts along with blood from various animal sacrifices. As we drove near the beach I also saw large crowds of Hindus with their faces painted, undergoing ceremonial washings in the sea, seeking to appease their angry gods. There were ongoing feasts and festivals throughout the villages that included loud music and cheering, along with excessive alcohol and food consumption. It seemed that people spent much of their time and money in worship to idols and demons, which was heartbreaking.

Some days later I was teaching church-planting pastors from the local villages who were an incredible encouragement. In a private discussion with one pastor's wife, I asked her if she had ever been to the United States. She replied that she had been once but had been deeply troubled by all of the idolatrous worship she witnessed in the United

States. At first, I was stunned that she would accuse my culture of being idolatrous, but as I sat at the Monday-night football game, it became apparent to me that sometimes we see only the errors of worship in someone else's culture while neglecting to be as objective in our own culture. I too was surrounded by people no less religiously zealous who had painted their faces to gather together and cheer on their gods who happened to play quarterback, tailback, and such, while wearing replica jerseys in tribute and giving one another high-fives in celebration whenever one of their gods made a great play.

Therefore, the subject of worship is one that needs examination in light of the person and work of Jesus. We will begin by defining some key concepts to ensure that there is understanding on this very important matter.

WHAT WORSHIP IS NOT

We will define what worship is but must first define what worship is not. This is because there is a tendency among some Christians to define worship too narrowly and thereby overlook the fullness of what worship is according to Scripture.

First, worship is not something done solely by Christians or "spiritual" people. Rather, because everyone was made to worship God, everyone is in fact a worshiper whether or not he or she has any religious or spiritual devotion.

Second, worship is not merely a style of music. There have been so-called worship wars among various Christians in recent years, although the body count between those preferring hymns and those preferring prom songs to Jesus is rather low. Those wars are essentially battles over styles of music played in church for the purpose of corporate singing. Sadly, such conflicts can reduce the concept of worship to little more than a style of music or preferred kinds of instrumental accompaniment. When the Bible speaks of worship, it does include God's people gathering to sing praises to God,[1] but worship is also something much bigger than simply singing or musical tastes.

Third, worship is not something that is connected to a time and place. In John 4 there is a discussion between Jesus and a woman who is uncertain of where and when worship is to occur. Jesus responds to her by stating that worship is an ongoing, unbroken life of communion with God empowered by the Holy Spirit and informed by the truth. Therefore, while worship does happen in specific places at specific times, such as Sunday morning services at a church building, worship is not limited to any time or any place. Rather, worship is to exist as a ceaseless lifestyle of God's people in every time and every place. Furthermore, by using words such as "Holy Land," Christians can give the false impression that one part of the earth is somehow more sacred and appropriate for worship than others. Jesus' own words deny that.

Fourth, worship is not something that starts and stops. Church worship services may start and stop but the worshipful life of a Christian is to continue unceasingly. A. W. Tozer once said, "If you will not worship God seven days a week, you do not worship Him one day a week."[2]

WHAT WORSHIP IS

Worship is living our life individually and corporately as continuous living sacrifices to the glory of a person or thing. This connection between glory and worship is clear in verses such as Romans 11:36–12:1, which says, "To him be *glory* forever. Amen. I appeal to you therefore, brothers, by the mercies of God, to present your bodies as a living sacrifice, holy and acceptable to God, which is your spiritual *worship*." In this packed section of Scripture, Paul connects a number of vital truths regarding worship. First, we hold a person or thing in a place of glory. Second, we then worship that person or thing. Third, our worship of that person or thing we hold in glory is done by means of making sacrifices.

Glory means weightiness, importance, preeminence, priority, or that which is our greatest treasure, deepest longing, and fountain of hope. Functionally, what we hold in the place of glory is in effect our real god. People can and do hold various people and things in a position of glory and then worship them by making sacrifices. Because we have limited resources (time, energy, money), we must allocate those things to what we consider most important or glorious to us and in so doing make sacrifices for our functional god. Whatever we hold in the position of highest glory is by definition our god(s). Practically, worship is making sacrifices for what we are living to glorify.

Also, the biblical word for worship is sometimes translated "sacrifice." This insight is helpful because what we make the greatest sacrifices for reveals what we truly live to glorify and worship. For example, if we eat and drink in excess, we are worshiping our stomach and sacrificing our health. If we sacrifice relationships with God and people for a hobby (e.g., sport, music, craft), then we are worshiping that hobby. If we are giving our bodies to sexual sin, we are worshiping sex and/or another person whose glory is our highest aim, sacrificing holiness and intimacy with God in the process. In short, we give our time, energy, body, money, focus, devotion, and passion to that which we glorify most, and we make sacrifices to worship that person or thing. Because we were made for the express purpose of worshiping God, everyone is a worshiper. The only difference is who or what we worship.

For example, I am writing this chapter the day after the PlayStation 3 video game console went on sale. Despite the fact that it cost five hundred dollars and an additional sixty dollars per game, people slept outside of stores waiting for the doors to open so that they could purchase one and spend their ensuing days and nights calling in sick to work while giving themselves in worship to a video game. One of the most legendary episodes of the adult cartoon *South Park* was based on this very same subject. The boys who star in the show became so addicted to the game World of Warcraft that it consumed their entire life, taking both their sleep and health in hilarious scenes that would have been even funnier if they were not true of so many people.

EXAMPLES OF FALSE WORSHIP

According to the first two commandments, there is only one God, and that God alone is to be worshiped.[3] Martin Luther said that we break the rest of the commandments only *after* we have broken the first two. What he means is that if the One True God is my only God, and I worship only that God, then I will not end up committing idolatry by worshiping my job (and not taking a Sabbath), worshiping my anger (and becoming violent), worshiping sex (and committing adultery), worshiping things (and stealing them), or worshiping success (and coveting what other people have).

The opposite of worship is idolatry, or the worshiping of something or someone other than the One True God of the Bible alone. On this point, Christian philosopher Peter Kreeft has said, "The alternative to theism is not atheism but idolatry."[4] This theme of worship versus idolatry is in some ways the theme of the entire Old Testament.

In addition, Paul articulates the pattern of false worship as failing to glorify God, which leads to an overinflated and arrogant view of self that ends in worshiping created things rather than the Creator God alone:

> For although they knew God, they did not honor him as God or give thanks to him, but they became futile in their thinking, and their foolish hearts were darkened. Claiming to be wise, they became fools, and exchanged the glory of the immortal God for images resembling mortal man and birds and animals and creeping things. Therefore God gave them up in the lusts of their hearts to impurity, to the dishonoring of their bodies among themselves, because they exchanged the truth about God for a lie and worshiped and served the creature rather than the Creator, who is blessed forever! Amen.[5]

At the root of all sin is the confusion, or inversion, of creator and creation. The worship of created things can be either the worship of things God has made, such as the environment or the human body, or the worship of things we have made, such as the television (which usually sits in the middle of the living room with all of the seats facing it so that hours can be paid in homage to the glowing deity that demands sacrifices not unlike the little shrines present in Buddhist and Hindu homes that are eerily familiar minus the remote control). The result of this error is that a good thing becomes inordinately elevated to a god thing and therefore a bad thing. Often times the god we worship is simply the one we see in the mirror every morning as we brush our teeth.

To help us uncover our possible idols, the following questions are helpful:

- Who or what do I make sacrifices for?
- Who or what is most important to me?
- If I could have any thing or experience I wanted, what would that be?
- Who or what makes me the most happy?
- What is the one person or thing I could not live without?
- What do I spend my money on?
- Who or what do I devote my spare time to?

The human heart is an idol factory for everything from political causes to hobbies, recreation, sports, and crafts. As a result, some men worship old cars and houses and spend all of their time and money to renovate them while neglecting time with God and the people he has called them to love, such as their wife and children. Some women worship their beauty and spend so much of their time, energy, and money on their looks that they are prone to neglect God and others such as their husband, children, and friends. Others are prone to worship their favorite band and even spend hours every day online gathering the latest news, downloading the latest songs, tuning in to the latest interviews, buying the latest merchandise, and even traveling around the country and world to catch the latest concert.

In my own city of Seattle, I have seen two very popular and peculiar idols that are worshiped by seemingly everyone. The first is the e-mail- and text message-enabled cell phone. At a recent dinner with my family at a restaurant, it was troubling to see that nearly every family seated around us was not engaged in conversation, but the father was either talking on the phone or busy returning e-mail. That piece of technology ruled over him like a god stealing time from his family and demanding to be answered and served at any time.

Additionally, many people in our city worship created things like their pet. In fact, there are more dogs than either Christians or children in our city. People spend huge sums of money for organic doggy food, drop their dogs at doggy daycares when they go to work, and even meet with doggy therapists who seek to help depressed doggies get out of their funk. Such people even follow their doggies around picking up their poop in little bags and then carry it with them, not unlike a slave following around a poorly mannered god. The latest insanity includes a forthcoming bill that would allow people to bring their doggies into restaurants to eat with them because they actually believe that the dog is basically human and akin to a spouse or child. While I love doggies, I cannot fathom worshiping something that licks its own private parts.

None of these examples, however, can compete with our cultural worship of good old-fashioned naked crazy-making. In Paul's day, he accused some people of worshiping their stomachs as their god, and in our day it appears that our god has simply moved a short distance south. Americans spend more money each year on pornography than country music, rock music, jazz music, classical music, Broadway plays, and ballet combined.[6] Additionally, some researchers have even said that we spend more money on pornography than we do on professional baseball, basketball, and football combined.[7] Clearly, perversion is officially America's favorite pastime and a ten-billion-dollar business.

The annual rentals and sales of adult videos and DVDs now top four billion dollars annually.[8] Fully eleven thousand porno movies are made every year, twenty times the number of mainstream movies made by Hollywood![9] The porn industry now claims over 30 percent of all video rentals on the east and west coasts.[10] Nationally, there are now over 2,400 strip clubs. Some of those clubs generate as much as eight million dollars a year in revenues and employ as many as two hundred dancers.[11]

On the Internet, the top word searched for is "sex," with "porn," "nude," "Playboy," and "erotic stories" also in the top twenty.[12] Furthermore, 70 percent of porn traffic occurs between 9 a.m. and 5 p.m. while people are sitting at work unable to focus on their job because the god of Eros continually beckons.[13] The top research priority in the porn business is getting good quality porn to a cell phone or mobile device so that everyone can feed any twisted desire anytime and anywhere.[14]

The National Council on Sexual Addiction Compulsivity estimated that 6 to 8 percent of Americans are sex addicts, which is 16 to 21.5 million people. Their numbers include young people.[15] Sixty-one percent of all high school seniors have had sexual intercourse, about half are currently sexually active, and 21 percent have had four or more partners.[16] Adolescents have the highest sexually transmitted disease (STD) rates. Approximately one out of four sexually active adolescents becomes infected with an STD each year, for a total of three million cases.[17] People under the age of twenty-five account for two-thirds of all STDs in the United States.[18]

By their graduation date, students will have watched fifteen thousand hours of television, compared to only twelve thousand hours in the classroom.[19] While watching, they will see fourteen thousand sexual references every year, with only 165 of those occasions encouraging birth control, self-control, abstinence, or mentioning anything about the risk of pregnancy or STDs.[20]

Undeniably, people are worshipers and will worship someone or something. Thankfully, Jesus came to enable us to worship God through him.

WORSHIPING THROUGH JESUS

Though we bought the Serpent's lie that we can be our own god and live for our own glory,[21] we remain worshipers. However, as Martin Luther said, we are now bent in toward ourselves, worshiping ourselves and incapable of breaking the horrendously depressing loop of Me-ism. But because Jesus lived the perfectly sinless life of unceasing worship that fully glorified God the Father, his life, death, and resurrection alone can reconcile us to God. Therefore, only through Jesus can we be made worshipers instead of idolaters and glorify God. In short, Jesus saves us from the worship of self to the worship of God.

The Bible speaks of this wondrous work of Jesus in the worshipful term "glory." Speaking of this transformation, Hebrews 2:10 says, "For it was fitting that he, for whom and by whom all things exist, in bringing many sons to glory, should make the founder of their salvation perfect through suffering." Romans 6:4 teaches that our worship includes a new life lived to the glory of God the Father patterned after the life of Jesus: "We were buried therefore with him by baptism into death, in order that, just as Christ was raised from the dead by the glory of the Father, we too might walk in newness of life."

WORSHIPING LIKE JESUS

Not only do we worship through Jesus, we must also worship like Jesus. Jesus is the person who has worshiped God the Father with the most glory of anyone who has ever lived. Jesus is the perfect worshiper. Jesus lived in glory before time began as the second member of the Trinity. Jesus spoke about his glorious worship, saying, "And now, Father, glorify me in your own presence with the glory that I had with you before the world existed. . . . Father, I desire that they also, whom you have given me, may be with me where I am, to see my glory that you have given me because you loved me before the foundation of the world."[22]

The Trinity is our perfect model for worship because each member honors and glorifies the other ceaselessly and perfectly. That Trinitarian God made us male and female in his image, which means in part that we were made for unceasing communion with him in a life of continual worship to his glory. Our unceasing worship has been broken by sin, which has separated us from God. As a result, Jesus entered into human history to take away our sin and reconnect us to God as we were created to be.

Jesus lived a life of perfect glory to his Father, and thus we can look at everything in his life—from the ordinary to the extraordinary—as born out of a life of ceaseless worship that glorified God the Father. Jesus' life destroys any notion that worship is a sacred thing we do at a special time or special place. Cutting our grass and cleaning our dishes are as sacred and God-glorifying as raising our hands in church. Jesus himself modeled this. He spent roughly 90 percent of his earthly life doing chores as a boy and working a carpentry job as a man. All of life is to be lived as ceaseless worship: "So, whether you eat or drink, or whatever you do, do all to the glory of God."[23]

WORSHIPING JESUS

Mormons do not pray to or worship Jesus, according to Bruce McConkie, one of the Twelve Apostles of the LDS Church.[24] Mormons are reverentially grateful to Jesus, but worship in the true sense is reserved only for the Father.

Conversely, according to Scripture, not only should we worship like Jesus and worship through Jesus, we should also worship Jesus. This is because Jesus is both the glory of God and the God of glory. As John 1:14 says, "And the Word became flesh and dwelt among us, and we have seen his glory, glory as of the only Son from the Father, full of grace and truth."

To fully understand the importance of worshiping Jesus, we must begin by examining the Old Testament to see how Jesus was worshiped in heaven before his entrance into human history as a man. We see that angels worshiped Jesus as the only God. Hundreds of years before the birth of Jesus, Isaiah gives us one of the most glorious snapshots of heaven in all of Scripture:

> I saw the Lord sitting upon a throne, high and lifted up; and the train
> of his robe filled the temple. Above him stood the seraphim. Each had
> six wings: with two he covered his face, and with two he covered his

feet, and with two he flew. And one called to another and said: "Holy, holy, holy is the LORD of hosts; the whole earth is full of his glory!"[25]

John later clarifies that whom Isaiah saw worshiped in glory was none other than Jesus: "Isaiah said these things because he saw his glory and spoke of [Jesus]."[26] Jesus was indeed worshiped in heavenly glory before his humble incarnation. Echoing Isaiah's grand vision, Queen Victoria, the longest reigning British monarch (from 1837 to 1901), said, "I wish [Jesus] would come in my lifetime so that I could take my crown and lay it at his feet."

In addition to being worshiped in heaven before his entrance into human history, Jesus was also worshiped as the only God by many people during his life on the earth. Worshipers of Jesus include the magi,[27] the blind man,[28] the previously demonized man,[29] Thomas the doubter,[30] his best friend John,[31] all of the disciples,[32] a group of women,[33] the mother of James and John,[34] angels,[35] entire churches,[36] his own mother[37] and brothers,[38] little children,[39] and even his former enemies such as Paul.[40] Jesus repeatedly accepted the worship of people throughout the course of his life without rebuking them for being wrong or correcting them.

Today, Jesus is worshiped both on the earth and in heaven. An unprecedented few billion people, fully one-third of everyone alive on the earth today, worship Jesus as God.[41] The heavenly scenes of Revelation unveil for us the ongoing worship of Jesus Christ as he is seated on his throne in glory. This theme of the worship of Jesus culminates and builds throughout the book in magnificent fashion.

In Revelation 4:10–11, we see the Lord God Almighty himself being worshiped by the twenty-four elders as their Creator God. As spiritual leaders, they set the example for all of God's people, falling down before the throne, laying their crowns before him, and saying, "Worthy are you, our Lord and God, to receive glory and honor and power, for you created all things, and by your will they existed and were created."

It is striking that in Revelation 5, the attention turns to the one at the right hand of the Father's throne—Jesus. Rather than quieting down, the worship rings even louder. Jesus is as fully worthy of worship as the Father. In Revelation 5:11–13, a seemingly endless choir of angels join the human elders in the worship of Jesus. Together they worship

Jesus for being not only creator, but also redeemer, singing, "Worthy is the Lamb who was slain, to receive power and wealth and wisdom and might and honor and glory and blessing!" Joining both humans and angels in the worship of Jesus are also every bird of the air, beast of the field, and fish of the sea, like some unprecedented episode of *The Lion King*, all singing in unison, "To him who sits on the throne and to the Lamb be blessing and honor and glory and might forever and ever!"

In Revelation 7:11–12, the worship of Jesus expands. Every angel joins in his praise as they all encircle the throne upon which he sits in glory. John reports that "they fell on their faces before the throne and worshiped God, saying, 'Amen! Blessing and glory and wisdom and thanksgiving and honor and power and might be to our God forever and ever! Amen.'"

In Revelation 15:2–4, those who had been martyred for their devotion to Jesus arrive at the throne and are handed instruments by God himself to play in the band that leads all creation in the worship of Jesus. That worship team leads the unprecedented heavenly chorus in singing, "Great and amazing are your deeds, O Lord God the Almighty! Just and true are your ways, O King of the nations! Who will not fear, O Lord, and glorify your name? For you alone are holy. All nations will come and worship you, for your righteous acts have been revealed."

The worship continues to increase in volume until in Revelation 19:1 we hear "what seemed to be the loud voice of a great multitude in heaven, crying out, 'Hallelujah! Salvation and glory and power belong to our God.'"

In one of the closing scenes of the Bible and human history, we read of nothing less than the unveiling of the glory of Jesus Christ over all creation as the source of our light and object of our love. Peering into heaven, John reports, "And I saw no temple in the city, for its temple is the Lord God the Almighty and the Lamb. And the city has no need of sun or moon to shine on it, for the glory of God gives it light, and its lamp is the Lamb."[42]

In conclusion, the reason that many people are prone to hold someone or something in glory above Jesus is that they believe the lie that God's glory and our joy are in conflict, so that if we live for God's glory it comes at the cost of our joy. Thus, people who want to live for the "pursuit of happiness" are prone to glorify and worship what they wrongly believe will give them joy. But tragically the result is misery. Because we were made to worship Jesus Christ the God of glory, it is only in being worshipers of Jesus that we can find joy. This glorious truth means that in worshiping Jesus, God is glorified and we are satisfied. The result, as Luther said, is that if we do not break the first two commandments (which lovingly instruct us that there is only one God and we should worship only that God), we are satisfied to the degree that we do not need to break the other commandments chasing our joy in stuff, sex, or self-esteem.

Sadly, as a pastor of thousands of young single women, I have seen one particular tragic example many times. It occurs when a young woman holds in glory either the fantasy of a relationship or a young man who is not godly and not fit for a Christian relationship. Believing that if she just had a boyfriend or the affection of a particular boy she would be happy, the young woman begins to worship a boy instead of Jesus by making sacrifices for the young man. Subsequently, she gives the boy her time, energy, heart, mind, money, and even her body as acts of worship to her functional god, the young man. She does so believing the lie that his touch, his time, his approval, his affection, and the like will satisfy her longings and make her happy. But over time the young woman begins to realize that she is unhappy because her god is not sufficient for her joy. Her god is not good or holy and even cheats on her, demeans her, neglects her, abuses her, gives her a venereal disease, has no intention of ever marrying her, or gets her pregnant with no intention of making a family with her.

Too many young men arrange their life around video games, sports, the latest sex experience, or just hanging out. They take women as instruments of their pleasure and discard them when it's not fun anymore. Jobs, when they have one, are just to provide dollars for another buzz of excitement. They seek better living through chemistry. Their false trinity of Frank and Beans is a demanding god, taking everything in exchange for a few thrills. But soon the thrill isn't what it used to be. The lie that the ultimate thrill is just ahead begins to pale. At this point, many young men realize that they are miserable and dissatisfied because their god is a robber, not a giver like Jesus. But apart from Jesus, the addictions defy change; despite the misery, credit card debt soars and friends disappear. To cope, many listen to music that makes them either violently angry or suicidally depressed as their sin marches them to death.

I have spoken to numerous young people for whom these stories are biography. The only hope for them and every other sinner prone to break the first two commandments is to believe the truth that only when God is glorified will we be truly satisfied. Through the worship of Jesus Christ alone there is joy, freedom, holiness, and life. Only by worshiping God our Creator are we free to enjoy creation by rightly eating, drinking, sleeping, playing, working, laughing, loving, weeping, marrying, parenting, living, and dying to the glory of God. I am a Christian because I want to be happy and, after trying lesser things, I am convinced that my desires are from God and can find their satisfaction in him alone.

ANSWERS TO COMMON QUESTIONS ABOUT WORSHIPING JESUS

WHY DO WE WORSHIP DIFFERENTLY FROM THE PEOPLE IN THE OLD TESTAMENT?

The Old Testament regulations regarding worship were very attentive to the outward forms of worship and the inward heart of the worshiper. In the New Testament, the outward forms of worship are virtually deleted while the concern for the inward heart of the worshiper is kept intact. This is because all of the outward Old Testament forms of worship were fulfilled in Jesus, just as he promised they would be.[43]

Therefore, because we have Jesus, we do not need a tabernacle,[44] a temple,[45] a priest,[46] or a lamb to sacrifice,[47] because Jesus is each of those things. All we need in order to worship God is a relationship with Jesus.

WHY ARE CHURCH WORSHIP SERVICES BORING AND NOT LIKE REVELATION?

In Revelation we see such things as singing, musical instrumentation, brilliant lighting, and visual imagery incorporated in the worship of Jesus. Elsewhere in Scripture, we also see that the worship of God includes God's people bowing and kneeling,[48] clapping and shouting,[49] and raising their hands.[50] In comparison, many churches today seem committed to being as boring as possible. Others seem just as committed to doing the latest cool thing and make one wonder who they are actually worshiping.

Nonetheless, in being reconciled to Jesus we are also reconciled to his people and made part of the church. So God expects every Christian to find a congregation of people who are devoted to real Jesus-directed worship and join them. While the style of architecture and music may be important, what is most important is that you connect with both Jesus and his people. But remember, worship is about Jesus, not about us.

IS SINGING ALL THERE IS TO WORSHIP?

Not at all. Joining with God's people to proclaim the wonder of Jesus is important. But probably the most sincere worship is how we live our life after we disperse from the church building.

Romans 12:1 makes this point. Paul tells us to use our bodies to do *latreia*, worship or service. The word can mean doing religious rituals, but it is also doing acts in the world that make God's character concretely visible. The word is used to refer to a monetary gift that was collected for the Jerusalem Christians when famine hit, and also for Epaphroditus's delivery of the gift for Paul from the Philippians. So when you serve people out of compassion or grace or love or kindness or justice, you are doing worship. You are glorifying God, making God's glory, his character, visible.

In Isaiah 1, the Lord got angry at Judah. They were going to church, singing songs, spreading their hands in prayer, even giving tithes. But the Lord wouldn't receive their adoration. The rest of their life wasn't glorifying to him. They needed to do whole life worship and not just a few hours one day a week. So God commanded them to remove the evil of their deeds from before his eyes, cease to do evil, learn to do good, seek justice, correct oppression, bring justice to the fatherless, and plead the widow's cause as acts of true worship.[51] God is right—serving people in the name of Jesus and in the character of Jesus is the most satisfying form of worship ever.

WHY DOES GOD NEED ALL THAT PRAISE? IS HE THE ULTIMATE NARCISSIST? OR DOES HE JUST HAVE A WEAK EGO THAT NEEDS PROPPING UP?

Worship isn't about meeting God's needs. He was doing just fine without us. In fact, I think there's a lot of truth in this bumper sticker: "Please save me from my worshipers. —God."

Worship is first of all about direction for our lives. Worshiping God means honoring or valuing him above everything else. So someone who worships Jesus will refuse to give honor to anything that dishonors Jesus. They will not do things that don't promote his character and honor.

Worship is also about devotion or relationship. From the beginning, God made us like himself.[52] He made us for relationship with each other and with him. When we build the relationship between God and ourselves, then we are doing worshipful things.

Because we were made for worship, God allows us to worship him both for his glory and our good. Through the worship of God we are liberated to live freely and joyfully without worshiping people and things that would make us miserable.

WHY DOES GOD JEALOUSLY REQUIRE THAT WE WORSHIP ONLY HIM?

Cornelius Plantinga has a great illustration of why God says, "You shall have no other gods before me. . . . You shall not bow down to them or serve them, for I the LORD your God am a jealous God."[53] God is like a home in a tough neighborhood. The loving parents in the home tell their kids to honor them only, in a sense to worship them alone. Therefore they also tell the kids to finish their homework and to do their chores. There are others in the neighborhood who would never make their children finish their homework and do their chores. Instead, they would allow or even encourage their children to sin and spend their time drinking, doing drugs, having sex, and making trouble.

The reason godly parents ask for exclusive obedience and worship is not that they have insatiable egos that need constant stroking, but that they are the only ones who really love the kids, who want to give good things to them for the kids' deepest pleasure. Likewise, God is a jealous Father who wants only the best for us, his children, and his jealousy is nothing but his love seeking our good.

CHAPTER TEN

WHAT MAKES JESUS SUPERIOR TO OTHER SAVIORS?

"For unto you is born this day in the city of David a Savior, who is Christ the Lord."

LUKE 2:11

✝

A savior is someone or something that delivers us from a terrible plight. In ancient Greek culture, philosophers like Epicurus, gods like Zeus, and rulers like Ptolemy were heralded as saviors. Likewise, in ancient Roman culture, the emperors from Nero's family line were also considered saviors.

In current pop culture, the concept of a savior remains a popular theme. There are movies called *Saved!* (a comedy), *Sweet Savior* (a horror film), and *Savior* (a drama).

In music, "savior" is a song title for works by Bob Dylan, Lisa Marie Presley, 30 Seconds to Mars, Billy Bob Thornton, and the Red Hot Chili Peppers. There's also a Christian rock opera group called Saviour Machine and a brutal death metal band called Severed Savior. Additionally, "Save Me" is a song title by artists such as Dave Matthews, Queen, Fleetwood Mac, American Hi-Fi, Aretha Franklin, k. d. lang, and Kelly Osbourne.

The Killers have a song called "When You Were Young," in which they sing about a young girl "waiting on some beautiful boy to save you from your old ways, you play forgiveness, watch him now, here he comes," but the problem is "he doesn't look a thing like Jesus."

The band My Chemical Romance had a hit song titled "Welcome to the Black Parade." The lyrics say, "When I was a young boy, my father took me into the city, to see a marching band, he said, 'Son, when you grow up, will you be the saviour of the broken, the beaten and the damned?' He said, 'Will you defeat them, your demons, and all the non-believers, the plans that they have made?'"

In the world of comics, *Saviour* was published by Trident Comics. The software world includes RD1 BIOS Savior Software to save your hard drive. On television, *Law and Order* had an episode called "Savior." There are role-playing games called Savior Knight, Vampire Savior, and Dark Savior, and there is a "cloak of the savior" in World of Warcraft. In the world of fashion, Savior jeans are made for women in sizes 14–30, to save them from not looking good in casual attire.

In the world of sports, it seems that every seven-foot center is heralded as the savior of his basketball team, along with every pitcher who can throw in the mid-90s, and every quarterback who can move his team down the field and put points on the board. Various news stories have declared Howard Stern as the savior of satellite radio and Kanye West as the savior of the music biz.

In every election it seems that candidates are presented as nothing short of saviors. Joining them are CEOs of companies who are hired as nothing less than saviors who will snatch a company and its investors from a fiery hell of decreased profits. Additionally, it seems like every pharmaceutical commercial on television touts yet another pill as some sort of savior to make life in a cursed world sheer bliss.

The human desire for a divine human savior is seemingly insatiable. This explains why we invent comic book heroes who are in many ways both human and divine, and we deify our heroes like Martin Luther King Jr. and John F. Kennedy, who were both well-known philanderers, not sinless like Jesus. This desire for human saviors also explains why little boys always want to be saviors when they grow up so they dress up like firemen, soldiers, police officers, Batman, Spiderman, Superman, or Wolverine.

As we grow older we are even prone to label the next life stage as a functional savior. Whether it is getting your driver's license, graduating from high school, obtaining your college degree, moving out of your parents' home, getting married, having children, buying a home, or one day retiring to eat nothing but Viagra and do nothing but golf, there is a perennially popular myth that in time a savior is coming and life will get better if we just hang in there.

Many religions also have their own concepts of a savior. In Buddhism you save yourself by ceasing all desire. In Confucianism you save yourself through education, self-reflection, self-cultivation, and living a moral life. In Hinduism you save yourself by detaching yourself from the separated ego and making an effort to live in unity with the divine. In Islam you save yourself by living a life of good deeds. In Orthodox Judaism you save yourself through repentance, prayer, and working hard to obey the Law. In New Ageism you save yourself by gaining a new perspective, through which you see how you are connected to all things as a divine oneness. In Taoism you save yourself by aligning yourself with the Tao to have peace and harmony in and around you. What nearly all religions and spiritualities hold in common is the theme that if there is a savior, it is the people saving themselves.

If you are a Scientologist, apparently Tom Cruise is your savior. The head of Scientology, David Miscavige, was the best man at Tom's wedding to Katie Holmes. Miscavige said that he "believes that in [the] future, Cruise will be worshiped like Jesus for his work to raise awareness of the religion."[1]

In contrast to all of the other saviors, Christianity repeatedly speaks of a savior in very distinct ways. We will build a case that Jesus alone is our savior, and there are many things that he saves us from. It must be stressed that we need a savior, that there is a savior, but that that savior is not us; it is God alone. Therefore, the innate human desire for a savior is a good thing, but it can only be satisfied in the person and work of Jesus alone.

GOD ALONE IS OUR SAVIOR

The concept of God alone being our savior and therefore the only source of our hope is a common theme throughout the Old Testament, especially in the books of Psalms and Isaiah. For example, Isaiah 43:11 says, "I, I am the LORD, and besides me there is no savior." Isaiah 45:21

says, "There is no other god besides me, a righteous God and a Savior; there is none besides me." And Isaiah 62:11 says, "Behold, the LORD has proclaimed to the end of the earth: Say to the daughter of Zion, 'Behold, your salvation comes; behold, his reward is with him, and his recompense before him.'" In summary, God himself says that there is no savior apart from him, no savior like him, and that he alone is the savior for all the nations of the earth. Furthermore, our Savior God was promised to come into human history to gift salvation to us. From the days of Isaiah forward, God's people were then awaiting the coming of that savior, Jesus Christ.

JESUS IS OUR SAVIOR GOD

The word *savior* appears twenty-four times in the New Testament, with eight occurrences referring to God in general and sixteen referring to Jesus in particular. One example is Titus 2:13, which speaks of "our great God and Savior Jesus Christ."

In addition to the word *savior*, related words such as *save* and *salvation* also appear frequently throughout the New Testament. They too point to Jesus as our God and Savior. Those instances include the declaration by an angel that Jesus would be born to "save his people from their sins."[2] In this instance, God himself announces the coming of Jesus through an angel as the fulfillment of the promises given through Isaiah hundreds of years prior. Furthermore, it was commanded by God that the boy born to the Virgin Mary be named "Jesus," which means God saves his people from their sins.

At the birth of Jesus, an angel also declared that "a Savior" had been born.[3] Upon seeing the newborn Jesus, the godly old man Simeon, who had been longing for the coming of the Savior, held the baby Jesus in his arms and said, "My eyes have seen your salvation."[4] Therefore, God promised in the Old Testament that Jesus was coming as our savior, announced his imminent arrival through the womb of Mary, and then declared his arrival at the birth of Jesus.

JESUS SAVES MANY PEOPLE

Not only is Jesus our Savior, but he is also a global savior who is sufficient for the salvation of peoples from every age, nation, race, culture, tribe, and tongue. This is significant because many religions have a false concept of a savior who is only concerned with their people group and essentially disinterested or even opposed to peoples from other races, nations, and cultures. In this way, while in one sense Christianity is exclusive in that it recognizes only one savior, it is also very inclusive in that Jesus is the savior who invites all peoples to be saved by him.

Scripture speaks of Jesus as the savior of the Jews.[5] Jesus came into history as a Jew, lived his life as a Jew, and was seen by many Jews as the fulfillment of the Old Testament promises about the coming of a savior. As a result, much of the early church was comprised of Jews.

Jesus is also the savior of the church.[6] This means that while there are expressions of the global church in various local churches, denominations, and networks, Jesus is in fact the savior of all Christians who would come to him in repentant faith. He is the savior of the church and all of its expressions throughout various periods of history and cultures of the earth.

Jesus is the savior of the world.[7] Perhaps the song sung in worship to Jesus in Revelation 5:9 paints this picture of Jesus as the global, multicultural savior most beautifully: "By your blood you ransomed people for God from every tribe and language and people and nation." Simply, Jesus is in fact the glorious savior of all races, all genders, all intellects, and all incomes.

Jesus is the savior of the lost.[8] Because we have sinned, we have essentially run away from God our Father and are subsequently like foolish children who are utterly incapable of finding our way home. But Jesus in his great mercy has come to earth to find us and save us from the devastation that lies before us because of sin. In this way, Jesus is utterly unlike the view of a savior offered by religion. Religion says that we have gotten ourselves lost and we need to follow the path laid out for us by religion and rediscover our way home. Unlike religion, Jesus knows that we are hopelessly lost, and without his coming to seek us and save us, we are forever doomed.

Lastly, Jesus is the savior of sinners like us. The man who perhaps most clearly understood this was Paul, who had gone from a murderer of Christians to a Christian pastor. If ever there was a man who was unfit for God to save, it was Paul. But by saving Paul, Jesus demonstrated what a glorious savior he is. Paul wrote, "The saying is trustworthy and deserving of full acceptance, that Christ Jesus came into the world to save sinners, of whom I am the foremost. But I received mercy for this reason, that in me, as the foremost, Jesus Christ might display his perfect patience as an example to those who were to believe in him for eternal life. To the King of ages, immortal, invisible, the only God, be honor and glory forever and ever. Amen."[9]

One of the wonderful encouragements of Jesus' being our savior is that God can and will save even the most guilty of wretched sinners who turn to Jesus in repentant faith. I have personally seen rapists, pedophiles, wife beaters, adulterers, strippers, thieves, and cult leaders saved by Jesus. No one and nothing is beyond his saving hand. They serve as illustrations of Paul's great truth that "everyone who calls on the name of the Lord will be saved."[10]

Without Jesus' salvation by grace alone, all we are left with is the pathetic false god of religion that only loves the good guys and not the bad guys, offering no hope for sinners. The hard truth is that we are all sinners. As a result, we cannot save ourselves but need our sinless Savior to do our saving.

Sadly, not everyone recognizes the saving work of Jesus. For example, Satanist Anton LaVey said, "Christ has failed in all his engagements as both savior and deity."[11] Simply, Jesus is not a failed savior, but a failure to turn to Jesus results in not being saved from the many things that he alone saves us from.

JESUS SAVES PEOPLE FROM MANY THINGS

While there is only one savior, he saves us from many things. For the sake of brevity we will mention only four.

Jesus saves us from sin.[12] Because of Jesus' death for sin, we can be saved from sin to live in victory over sin. Practically, this means that rather than accepting or managing our sin, we can be so saved from our sin that we can actually put sin to death and live new lives with Jesus. Sadly, our day is filled with a host of excuses for sin—everything from our addictions to our unpleasant disposition is the result of our personality type, ethnic heritage, and genetic predisposition. A sort of fatalism is predominant, whereby we cannot be saved from our sins because we are locked into an unchanging life pattern that rules over us instead of God. Or, we do get saved from one sin only to then be enslaved to another. For example, we might stop smoking only to start eating too much, which leads to depression and then drinking too much; in turn, we work hard to get our life back under control only to become wrongly proud of our holiness, whereas pride/self-esteem is the root that nourishes the fruit of all sin.

Jesus saves us from death.[13] Because death is the penalty and consequence of sin, Jesus' death was, as the Puritan John Owen said, "the death of death." When Jesus died in our place, he saved us from death. By trusting in Jesus, we are granted eternal life at the end of this life. Our greatest enemy, death, no longer rules over God's children because Jesus has saved them from death.

Jesus saves us from Satan.[14] Because of our sin, we are captive to Satan. Much of Satan's captivity is done through general spirituality. Spirituality can in fact be synonymous with demonism because to be spiritual is simply to be spiritually connected. However, that spiritual connection is often solely with Satan and demons and not God and angels. Knowing that he would not be widely loved if clearly seen, Satan has, in the words of the Bible, taken upon himself disguises and schemes. He pretends to be good and trustworthy to gullible people who find spirituality, not salvation, to be sufficient. But Jesus' authority has been delegated to his people so that they can live in victory over Satan and demons.

Jesus saves us from God's wrath and hell.[15] To be a Christian is to be a guilty person saved from God's holy and just wrath.[16] God's wrath, expressed by some twenty various words, appears more than six hundred times in the Old Testament alone. God's wrath is also repeatedly mentioned throughout the New Testament.[17] God's wrath is ultimately poured out on the unrepentant in hell. The crucifixion of Jesus was a precursor of the eternity awaiting the unrepentant and a compelling reason for us to turn to Jesus so that we might be saved from the penalty for our sin. There is no reason that anyone should evade the deserved wrath of God. While some people struggle with the idea of a loving God sending people to hell, what I truly struggle with is how a holy God could allow anyone into heaven. Through the work of Jesus our savior who endured the wrath of God in our place for our sins after living the life we should have lived, we can and will be saved.

JESUS IS OUR ONLY SAVIOR

In our day of tolerance and diversity, it is perhaps most controversial to state that Jesus is the only savior, which makes him distinct from and superior to any other proposed savior. For example, the Buddha taught that there are eighty-four thousand paths to enlightenment, which makes as much sense as saying eighty-four thousand different roads going in different directions all lead to the same destination. Nonetheless, the opinion that Jesus is only one among many saviors and not the only Savior is a very popular spiritual concept:

- John Lennon: "I believe that what Jesus and Mohammad and Buddha and all the rest said was right. It's just that the translations have gone wrong."
- Homer Simpson: "I'm gonna die! Jesus, Allah, Buddha—I love you all!"
- Mahatma Gandhi: "All paths leading to God are equally good."
- Oprah Winfrey: "One of the biggest mistakes humans make is to believe there is only one way. Actually, there are many diverse paths leading to what you call God."
- Stephen Colbert: "And though I am a committed Christian, I believe everyone has the right to their own religion—be you Hindu, Jewish, or Muslim, I believe there are infinite paths to accepting Jesus Christ as your personal savior."

Are we to believe that the atheist road (which says there is no God), the agnostic road (which is unsure if there is a God), and the Hindu road (which says there are millions of gods) all lead to the same place? Are we to believe that the road that says there is no life after death, the road that says you reincarnate, and the road that says you stand before Jesus for judgment and sentencing to eternal heaven or hell all lead to the same place? Are we truly to believe that the road that says we save ourselves leads to the same place as the road that says only Jesus can save us?

The exclusivity, superiority, and singularity of Jesus are precisely the teaching of Scripture. This anchoring truth, that Jesus is our only savior, is in many ways responsible for much of the opposition and persecution that Christians from the early church to the present have encountered. This point was a heralding cry of the early church. For example, Peter, filled and led by God the Holy Spirit, proclaimed with all certainty, "There is salvation in no one else, for there is no other name under heaven given among men by which we must be saved."[18] Indeed, when we are speaking of salvation we must speak only of Jesus, always of Jesus, and assuredly of Jesus.

In this cry, the early Christians and every faithful Christian since are simply echoing the very words of Jesus himself, who said that he was the only savior and suffered death for not recanting that truth. For example, Jesus said, "Enter by the narrow gate. For the gate is wide and the way is easy that leads to destruction, and those who enter by it are many. For the gate is narrow and the way is hard that leads to life, and those who find it are few."[19] When Jesus was asked, "Lord, will those who are saved be few?" he responded, "Strive to enter through the narrow door."[20] In saying that being saved is akin to walking on a narrow path or entering through a narrow door, Jesus was declaring that he was not merely a way to salvation, but rather the only way to salvation. All other paths, doors, and functional saviors lead only to destruction. Jesus was emphatically clear on being the only savior: "I am the way, and the truth, and the life. No one comes to the Father except through me."[21]

Simply, people are by nature going to hell. But Jesus came as our savior to save us. We are to respond to him by worshiping him. As a result, he will save us from hell and deliver us to heaven.

Curiously, marketing and advertising take these very same themes from the Christian gospel and use them to pitch people, products, and experiences as functional saviors to be worshiped. Among the best places to witness the popularity of false saviors is at the magazine rack of your local grocery store. Practically speaking, the cover of each magazine is a snapshot of what a group of people considers to be their heaven. The rest of the magazine is filled with similar snapshots of what a perceived heaven is like, along with snapshots of what a perceived hell is like. Functional saviors are then presented for our worship; they will deliver us from our hell and grant us a new life in our self-defined heaven.

Because this point is important and easily misunderstood, I will give a few examples from various magazines. The breadth of maga-zine categories is by itself an interesting revelation of how various people apparently view heaven. There are magazines for art, business, cars, children, cigars, cooking, crafts, entertainment, fashion, fitness, gardening, health, hobbies, home décor, investing, men, motorcycles, nature, news, pets, photography, politics, religion, science, sex, sports, teens, travel, vacations, wine, and women, to name a few.

The examples are legion, but a few will suffice. We will start with women's magazines. *Teen* magazine is targeted to junior high–aged girls. In flipping through a recent issue, it seems that for young women, hell is a place where your face has zits, your closet has outdated clothes, and your life has no boyfriend. The heavenly life of a cute young guy who is your committed boyfriend can only be had by worshiping various functional saviors. Those saviors include shaving your legs, getting a cute haircut, maintaining that cut with the right product, using the right medications to have flawless skin, wearing the latest fashionable clothes and shoes, applying the right makeup in just the right way, and watching what you eat so that you can be skinny enough to attract the most heavenly boy.

Glamour magazine is targeted for the mothers of junior high–aged girls. Its pages seem to define hell in terms of facial wrinkles, unseemly body hair that makes a woman appear to have Don King in a head lock, cold sores, a few extra pounds, and unwieldy frizzy hair on top of her chubby, wrinkled, fuzzy, open-sored, flatulent body. Conversely, heaven is apparently having sex by the third date, finding just the right perfume, having perfectly white teeth, perky breasts, impeccable nails, frequent orgasms, and the occasional bisexual fling just for fun. The journey from heaven to hell requires obtaining various functional saviors, such as birth control pills, sex toys, hair care products, fashionable clothes, makeup to cover wrinkles, the right lotion for your skin type, year-round Brazilian waxes, jeans that hug your curves, the right diet to ensure your curves are not too curvy, and a list of the right questions to ask a guy on the first date.

Redbook magazine is targeted for the mothers of the mothers of the junior high girls. Its portrait of hell includes grey hair, bad breath, sweating, cat odor around the house, infrequent sex, being a single mother, getting fat, having scaly dry skin, and not being able to sleep at night because you are a wreck. Conversely, heaven is looking younger than you are, living in a home you own with a glorious kitchen that is outfitted with the right appliances, being able to make simple and nutritious family dinners, and having frequent orgasms possibly even while cooking said dinner. The saviors scattered throughout the pages of the magazine include age-defying makeup, bras that have some kind of pulley system that as far as I can tell can not only pull a woman's breasts up to her neck but also pull her vehicle out of a ditch if needed, a new car, Tidy Cats, a child, a great daycare for that child, Weight Watchers, sleeping pills, and a husband who likes to snuggle and listen attentively while somehow remaining heterosexual.

For those with a mild case of obsessive-compulsive disorder, *Simply Perfect Storage* magazine serves as a heavenly savior from your home of clutter hell. In it, the gospel of shelves, drawers, baskets, canisters, and label makers is preached because Home Depot loves you and has a wonderful plan for your neatnik life.

For men, there are a lot of magazines, and most of them have a lot more pictures than words, and most of those pictures include at least one woman who is nearly naked and barely old enough to vote, although she probably could not read the ballot anyways. *Stuff* magazine is filled with saviors such as hot chicks, good razors, motorcycles, sneakers, sexual positions, alcohol, cool haircuts, a fit body, a nice truck, indestructible condoms, porn, fast cars, tobacco, fishing gear, and more hot chicks (but not a word about marriage or children or doing anything for anyone but yourself). Likewise, *FHM* magazine, which I think stands for Fool-Hearted Machismo, is more of the same with the addition of golf, video games, car stereos, home media systems, boxing, wrestling, hockey, threesomes with two hot chicks, baseball caps, but yet again not one word about such things as reading a book or feeding the homeless.

In the geek bible, *Wired* magazine, there is a very different heaven from the one advertised in many men's magazines. This heaven is specially designed for guys who tuck their shirts in and do their own tech support. The *Wired* heaven is access to the latest information and innovation. Subsequently, the geek saviors include the most cutting-edge wireless mobile device in your hand, iPod in your pocket, GPS device in your car, entertainment system in your home, video game console in your entertainment system, laptop in your cubicle, and flat screen television in your bedroom, all ensuring that you are continually plugged in to the heavenly world of information and entertainment with the technology functioning in a mediatorial capacity not unlike Jesus.

Any number of magazines and advertised products could be

explored, but they all reveal that the question is not whether we will run to a functional savior. Rather, the question is whether the savior we are trusting in can actually save us. While a diet may help us lose weight, a spouse may cure our loneliness, and a child may give us joy and improve our quality of life, they work best as gifts from God to be enjoyed and not as functional savior-gods. David Powlison has formulated some questions[22] to help us uncover our functional saviors, and the following questions are based on them:

- What am I most afraid of?
- What do I long for most passionately?
- Where do I run for comfort?
- What do I complain about most?
- What angers me most?
- What makes me happiest?
- How do I explain myself to other people?
- What has caused me to be angry with God?
- What do I brag about?
- What do I want to have more than anything else?
- Who do I sacrifice the most for in my life?
- If I could change one thing in my life what would that be?
- Whose approval am I seeking?
- What do I want to control/master?
- What comfort do I treasure the most?

In speaking of a savior, we must also speak of the urgent need for our rescue. If our home were on fire, we would urgently call out for a firefighter to save us. If our body were failing, we would urgently call out for a doctor to save us. If our home were broken into, we would call out to a police officer to save us. If we were drowning, we would cry out to a lifeguard to save us. Tragically, the sense of urgency that we rightly have in our physical life is lacking in our spiritual life, where the consequences are even direr. For this reason, if you are reading this and are not a Christian, we must in loving concern ask, who and what are you trusting to save you? Can they truly save you?

For those who are Christians, it is important that we acknowledge that Jesus has also saved us from ourselves. I often wake up and look in the mirror and ask myself a terrifying question, "Had Jesus not saved me, who would I be and what would my life be like?" Had Jesus not saved me and I simply lived out the sinful desires in my fallen nature, I shudder to think of who I would be and what damage I would have done to others. I can with certainty say that I would likely not be a faithful husband to my wife and would be an angry father to my children. I would be a man with a secret life of hidden sexual sin that would grow until it became visible and destroyed most everything in my life. But I have been saved from myself and am continually being saved from myself by my great God and Savior, Jesus Christ. Subsequently, I am also awaiting the great coming of our great God and Savior, Jesus Christ, on the day when the work of his global and total salvation will be completed.[23] Until that day, the saving work of Jesus continues to change the entire course of human history, which is the subject of the next chapter.

ANSWERS TO COMMON QUESTIONS ABOUT JESUS THE SAVIOR

IS JESUS THE ONLY SAVIOR?

It depends on what you need saving from. If you need to be saved from the embarrassment of yet another lonely weekend, Jesus probably won't hook you up with a date. Following Jesus faithfully, however, is an essential step toward having the most satisfying marriage ever. Likewise, Jesus may not get you the interview you desperately want for your dream job. But by living your life with, for, and like Jesus, you will develop the wisdom and character of a fine employee.

If you want to be saved from sin, death, the devil, addiction to your lusts, and God's wrath (along with the other things listed in places such as Ephesians 2:1–3), then Jesus is a great savior. In fact, he's the only one who even claims he saves us from all these things.

IS JESUS REALLY THE ONLY WAY TO SALVATION?

It depends on what you are looking for and where you want to go. If you are looking for money, power, pleasure, or knowledge, Jesus isn't the only way. In fact, in some of these things, he would be something of a hindrance. For example, regarding money, he actually encourages some people to embrace poverty rather than riches by giving their wealth away to others in need. In Luke 16:13 he said, "No servant can serve two masters, for either he will hate the one and love the other, or he will be devoted to the one and despise the other. You cannot serve God and money."

But if you are looking to get connected to the Lord, the God who created the heavens and the earth, the God who loves us enough to come to earth and take the penalty for our sin so that we can one day spend eternity in heaven, then Jesus is the only way.

IS JESUS REALLY THE ONLY WAY TO GOD?

It depends on which god you are looking for. In our age of consumerism, religions are much like salad bars, where people have their own plate and are free to put on it whatever beliefs they find most desirable for themselves. The result is innumerable designer religions that are nothing more than feelings, fantasies, and fancies of people who may have some false sense of comfort but no savior who can forgive sin and connect them to the only real God. People with designer religions and false concepts of god may in fact be participating in the demonic. While there is only one true God who created the heavens and the earth, there are a lot of powerful spiritual beings in the world. The Bible calls them false gods. Many people worship one or several of these demons masquerading as gods. Jesus doesn't serve any of them, nor will he help you get to them because he is the only way to the only God.

HOW MANY GODS ARE THERE?

Lots of them, according to the Bible. It comes as a major surprise to many to learn that the Bible teaches this. I [Gerry] remember my mom getting really upset when she heard us sing the chorus, "For thou, Lord, art high above all the earth: thou art exalted far above all gods." "There's only *one* God," she insisted. "Who wrote that awful stuff?" I had to tell her, "God did, Mom. It's directly from Psalm 97:9." It didn't satisfy her.

The Ten Commandments begin with "You shall have no other gods before me. . . . You shall not bow down to them or serve them, for I the LORD your God am a jealous God."[24] The Lord executes judgment on the gods of Egypt.[25] He warns Israel of the lure of these false gods as they head into the Promised Land. Even a cursory reading of Deuteronomy 32:15–21 reveals a warning about "strange gods" and "new gods" that is very contemporary.

The gods are powerful but created and finite spiritual beings who have revolted against the Lord and have become corrupt, trying to establish their own power base in religions and nations. In a word, they are demons.

Baal, one of the key regional gods of the Canaanites, was typical of these powerful spiritual beings. Baal and his under-spirits controlled business, which in an agrarian society revolved around making land, animals, and people fertile. Apparently Baal was quite the voyeur. If he got turned on by watching the "attendants" in his shrines do kinky things with the worshipers, then he'd grant blessings. If things really got tight, he and the other gods enjoyed human sacrifices, along with all the other horrific practices.[26]

Baal was also the one Elijah humiliated at Mount Carmel.[27] But it didn't last. God's people kept going back. Looking around today, he is still doing a brisk business.

There are many others. Asherah (the mother goddess of Sidon and Tyre), Astarte or Ashtoreth (Baal's sister, a goddess of war, love, storms, the evening star, and the queen of heaven), Chemosh and Molech (infant-loving gods of Moab and Ammon), and Artemis of Ephesus are among those named in the Bible.

We also see the princes of Persia and Greece at spiritual war with the Lord's angels in Daniel 10. It's not a war Daniel was even involved in. Likewise, today there are wars being waged in the heavenly realm between angels and demons that we are unaware of and uninvolved in. But those battles are very real for the angels. The D-day victory has been won by the death and resurrection of Jesus,[28] but the fight goes on as we look with eager anticipation to the final victory in the day of his coming.[29]

There's only one God who created the heavens and the earth, who created every living thing including the other gods. The reminder of Moses in Deuteronomy is still real today and should compel us to cling to the Rock of our salvation.

WHaT aRe THeSe GODS DOING TODaY?

The false gods of our day are doing the same things they always have, from promoting false religions to supporting evil political leaders, encouraging sinful social trends, and empowering godless forms of entertainment.

All the religions of the world worship a god or gods. These gods are not always superstitious figments of imagination (though the designer gods of the Hollywood celebrities sure seem to be). They are created, powerful, spiritual beings who rebelled against the Lord and enticed many people to worship them rather than the Lord.

When you ask devotees of these religions to describe their god, the being they describe doesn't sound anything like the Lord, the Father of Jesus. The religious practices they espouse involve prayer and ritual, but even those basic practices are totally different from the grace-based worship of the Lord.

It is our firm belief that the religions of the world really do worship gods that are not God. In 1 Corinthians 10:20–22, Paul follows the warnings of the Old Testament and reminds us: "What pagans sacrifice they offer to demons and not to God. I do not want you to be participants with demons. You cannot drink the cup of the Lord and the cup of demons. You cannot partake of the table of the Lord and the table of demons. Shall we provoke the Lord to jealousy?" Simply, any religion that does not worship the Trinitarian God of the Bible is worshiping a demon or demons.

HOW CAN YOU BE SO BIGOTED AS TO BELIEVE THERE'S ONLY ONE WAY TO GOD?

Actually we aren't. There are many ways to the many gods. We each choose our god and then choose the appropriate way to get to that god. The Bible verse most often quoted elsewhere in the Bible is Exodus 34:6–7, where God reveals himself as "The LORD, the LORD, a God merciful and gracious, slow to anger, and abounding in steadfast love and faithfulness, keeping steadfast love for thousands, forgiving iniquity and transgression and sin, but who will by no means clear the guilty, visiting the iniquity of the fathers on the children and the children's children, to the third and the fourth generation." The only way to this true God, the creator of the heavens and the earth and not a created being, is the way he lovingly sets out: through his own Son who lovingly gave himself for us. There is only one God and only one way to that God—through Jesus Christ. For those who reject that way, there is only one fate, namely the justice of hell. We say this not to be glib, but rather to be very clear on this incredibly important issue.

CHAPTER ELEVEN

WHAT DIFFERENCE HAS JESUS MADE IN HISTORY?

**All things were created through [Jesus] and for him.
And he is before all things, and in him
all things hold together.**

COLOSSIANS 1:16-17

✝

Considering the humble beginnings of Jesus, it is stunning to see the difference he has made in history. Jesus rises above all of human history in a way that no one else ever has or ever will. Everything from our calendar to our major holidays is in response to his life on the earth.

Entire books have been written to chronicle Jesus' effect on history, such as his place in various centuries[1] and his place in pop culture.[2] When the new millennium was on the horizon, *Newsweek* ran a cover story titled, "2000 Years of Jesus: Holy Wars to Helping Hands—How Christianity Shaped the Modern World." The article said, "By any secular standard, Jesus is also the dominant figure of Western culture. Like the millennium itself, much of what we now think of as Western ideas, inventions, and values finds its source or inspiration in the religion that worships God in his name. Art and science, the self and society, politics and economics, marriage and the family, right and wrong, body and soul—all have been touched and often radically transformed by the Christian influence."[3]

The *Newsweek* issue also included a poll in which Americans were asked, "If there had never been a Jesus, do you think there would be more, less, or about the same amount of war, charity, and happiness?"[4] The results of the poll reveal that Jesus is considered by most Americans to have been a transforming agent of good in history. Regarding war, 48 percent of people thought there would be more, 15 percent thought less, and 24 percent thought it would be the same. Regarding charity, 7 percent thought there would be more, 64 percent thought there would be less, and 18 percent thought it would be the same. Regarding happiness, 9 percent thought there would be more, 57 percent thought there would be less, and 20 percent thought there would be the same had Jesus never lived.

Noted scholar and historian W. E. H. Lecky said in regard to Jesus' impact on history, "The character of Jesus has not only been the highest pattern of virtue, but the strongest incentive in its practice, and has exerted so deep an influence, that it may be truly said that the simple record of three years of active life has done more to regenerate and to soften mankind than all the disquisitions of philosophers and all the exhortations of moralists."[5]

Jesus is both the sum and center of our Christian faith. In a conversation I was privileged to have with noted theologian Dr. David Wells, he made mention of a very insightful fact. Unlike most religions, Christianity has no place, language, race, or culture that serves as a center to hold it together. Christians share no worldwide headquarters, no common language, no common race or ethnic heritage, and no common cultural framework. The only thing that holds all of Christianity together is the risen Lord Jesus Christ who is alive today.

Understanding that the purpose and center of history is Jesus is incredibly important in light of our current purposeless and centerless world. In the movie *Fight Club,* Tyler Durden (played by Brad Pitt) says of this generation, "We are the middle children of history—no purpose or place. We have no great war, no great depression. Our great war is a spiritual war. Our great depression is our lives. We've all been raised on television to believe that one day we'd all be millionaires and movie gods and rock stars. But we won't. We're slowly learning that fact. And we're very, very pissed off."

The lead singer of R.E.M., Michael Stipe, says, "We are floundering more—culturally, politically, spiritually—than I can imagine anyone has been in several centuries. It's hard to imagine that so many people are confused about who they are, what their dreams, hopes, and aspirations and desires are—and who's pulling the strings."[6] Historian Arnold Toynbee has written that of the twenty-one greatest civilizations that have existed on the vast trailer park we call a planet, the modern West is the first that does not have or teach its citizens any answer to the question of why they exist.[7]

Our purpose is to glorify Jesus. Our place is with Jesus. Our fight is for Jesus. Our spirituality is Jesus. Our God is Jesus. Our joy is Jesus.

Many notable people have commented on Jesus' place as the most famous, important, and significant person in history, as the following examples illustrate:

- Stephen Neill (theologian and historian): "He who says 'Jesus' says also 'history.'"

- H. G. Wells: "I am an historian, I am not a believer, but I must confess as a historian that this penniless preacher from Nazareth is irrevocably the very center of history. Jesus Christ is easily the most dominant figure in all history."

- Philip Schaff (historian): "No great life ever passed so swiftly, so quietly, so humbly, so far removed from the noise and commotion of the world; and no great life after its close excited such universal and lasting interest."

- Kenneth Scott Latourette (historian): "As the centuries pass, the evidence is accumulating that, measured by His effect on history, Jesus is the most influential life ever lived on this planet."

- Inscription at the entrance to Rockefeller Center, New York City: "Man's ultimate destiny depends not on whether he can learn new lessons or make new discoveries and conquests, but on the acceptance of the lesson taught him close upon two thousand years ago."

- Napoleon Bonaparte: "I know men and I tell you that Jesus Christ is no mere man. Between Him and every other person in the world there is no possible term of comparison. Alexander, Caesar, Charlemagne, and I have founded empires. But on what did we rest the creation of our genius? Upon force. Jesus Christ founded His empire upon love; and at this hour millions of men would die for Him."

- ⊚ Fidel Castro: "I have always considered Christ to be one of the greatest revolutionaries in the history of humanity."
- ⊚ Charles Haddon Spurgeon: "Christ is the great central fact of the world's history. To him everything looks forward or backward. All the lines of history converge upon him. All the great purposes of God culminate in him. The greatest and most momentous fact which the history of the world records is the fact of his birth."

One book that does a great job in answering the question "What difference has Jesus made in history?" is *What If Jesus Had Never Been Born?* by D. James Kennedy and Jerry Newcombe.[8] In the remainder of this chapter, much of the information I will be sharing to answer that question is taken from their book, which I recommend for further insight into the difference Jesus has made in history.

While the life of Jesus was simple, the legacy of Jesus is stunning. Jesus is not only worshiped as God by one-third of the people on planet earth, but no army or king has wrought as much influence on history as he. To illustrate this point we will briefly examine some of the differences Jesus has made in history.

JESUS AND CHILDREN

Tragically, the plight of children in the ancient world was horrendous. Both child sacrifice and child abandonment were common. Only half of all children lived beyond the age of eight. It was not uncommon for people to discard healthy babies by simply placing them out with the trash to be taken to the dump. It was not uncommon for such children to be taken home by the worst kind of people, who molested the children, sold them into prostitution, or forced them into slavery.

But the coming of Jesus made an enormous difference in the treatment of children. Because Jesus himself had been a child born into poverty to a single mother, he was seen by many children in tragic circumstances as giving them both dignity and hope. By coming as a child, Jesus honored childhood.

Although he himself did not have any children, Jesus loved and cared for children. Jesus taught that God is a loving Father and that we are his children who should treat our children as our Father treats us.[9] In the Gospel of Matthew alone, Jesus healed children,[10] said that God imparts wisdom to children,[11] taught children,[12] said heaven was made for children,[13] said that God would punish anyone who harmed a child,[14] laid his hands on children to pray over them,[15] invited children to himself,[16] cast demons out of tormented children,[17] and was worshiped by children.[18]

Furthermore, Jesus himself was born of a single mother and was adopted by the godly man Joseph. Building on this same metaphor, the New Testament teaches that in our salvation, God acts in much the same way; he is our Father who adopts us into his family, the church.[19] As God's people began seeing themselves as spiritual orphans who had been adopted by God the Father, they not only treated children with great dignity as God's image bearers like Jesus did, but they also began adopting discarded children and telling them about Jesus as a demonstration of the gospel. This practice continues throughout the world today with orphanages, foster care, and adoption, whereby God's people demonstrate the gospel of Jesus Christ to children.

In Mars Hill Church, this includes a long-standing partnership with an orphanage in rural India run by Vision Nationals Ministries. We were privileged to help purchase the land on which the orphanage was built. When I visited, I was very moved to see many children (who would have otherwise been literally scavenging for their survival in the streets) well housed, fed, loved, and taught. Hearing the children sing in their school chapel to Jesus was life changing. In the same ministry there is also a Bible college that trains the boys to become church planters because many rural villages have never heard of Jesus. To think that many of these boys and girls would otherwise be slaves or prostitutes or defiled at the hands of pedophiles makes me exceedingly glad for the difference Jesus has made.

JESUS AND WOMEN

In many ancient cultures, as in many contemporary cultures, women were essentially regarded as the property of their husband. For example, in India, if a woman's husband died, she could be burned alive on her husband's funeral pyre in a ceremony called *suttee*. She essentially had no value or right to live apart from her husband. Likewise, infanticide was commonly practiced for girls in India, along with "child widows," which were little girls raised to be temple prostitutes for the pleasures of men, until the coming of Christian missionaries such as William Carey and Amy Carmichael.

Conversely, the Bible teaches that God made us male and female, and that men and women, though different, are absolutely equal because they both bear the image of God.[20] Furthermore, while not sinning, Jesus did often violate social taboos regarding women and in so doing honored them. Examples include when he befriended the Samaritan woman at the well of Sychar[21] and spoke publicly with the widow of Nain.[22] Jesus often healed and cast demons out of women.[23] Jesus used women as examples of exemplary faith in his teachings.[24] In what was likely quite controversial because women were generally omitted from theological instruction, Jesus did teach women theology.[25] Jesus allowed himself to be anointed by a sinful woman.[26] Two of Jesus' closest friends were women whom he loved like sisters.[27] The funding of Jesus' ministry included generous support from godly women.[28] Lastly, the Bible records that godly women were the first to know that Jesus had risen from death.[29] In summary, Jesus honored, taught, and loved women and even included them in vital positions in his ministry.

Furthermore, historian Rodney Stark says, "In Roman as in Jewish society, women were regarded as inherently inferior to men. Husbands could divorce their wives but wives could not divorce their husbands. In rabbinic circles, only males were allowed to study the Torah. Jesus challenged these arrangements. Although he called only men to be apostles, Jesus readily accepted women into his circle of friends and disciples. . . . Christianity's appeal for women was a major reason that it grew so rapidly in competition with other religions of the Roman Empire. Then, as now, most Christians were women. The new religion offered women not only greater status and influence within the church but also more protection as wives and mothers."[30]

JESUS AND MERCY

One of the innumerable benefits of the gospel of Jesus Christ is the concept of mercy. At the cross, Jesus paid the penalty of justice and then granted us mercy. In so doing, Jesus forever changed the world by paving a way to be merciful without being unjust.

This mercy that Christians enjoy from Jesus compels us to extend that same mercy to others, particularly in deeds of kindness. Such deeds are not done by us as Christians because we have to love our neighbor, but rather because through Jesus we have been loved, given mercy, and enabled to share Jesus' love and mercy with others.

Informally, the extension of Jesus' mercy through Christians is something that happens in countless ways every day. Formally, innumerable Christian churches and mercy-based organizations are hard at work to help everyone in need, from single mothers to the homeless, hungry, sick, elderly, poor, and abused.

Christian relief organizations such as World Vision spend over a billion dollars a year in an effort to provide mercy in its various forms to needy people around the world. Their mercy includes housing, food, water, medical care, and education.

JESUS AND SLAVES

In the days of Jesus, roughly half of the people in the Roman Empire were slaves, and some three-fourths of the population of Athens were slaves. By calling himself a servant or slave, Jesus identified himself with those who were enslaved. Following Jesus' teaching, Paul listed slave trading as among the most heinous of sins, and pleaded for the merciful treatment of a Christian slave named Onesimus.[31] Many years later, the great British statesman William Wilberforce labored to end the slave trade from Africa to the West Indies and was more effective in the fight against slavery than anyone who has ever lived.

In the United States, the fight against slavery was led in large part by Christians. Their number included President Abraham Lincoln, who is widely regarded as perhaps the most important American to fight against slavery.

JESUS AND EDUCATION

As a teacher, Jesus the rabbi has made an unparalleled difference in education. Because Christians are people of the Book, as Christianity has spread, so has language translation, publishing, education, and literacy.

Many of the world's languages were first set to writing by missionaries seeking to translate the Bible into the native language of a people group. They recognize that God loves people from every nation, tribe, and tongue of the earth. This work continues today as the Bible has been translated into roughly three thousand languages. When Christians encounter a people group without a written language, ministries such as Wycliffe actually create a written language for such people prior to translating the Bible into their newly created language.

In the so-called Dark Ages, many of the classics of Western literature were preserved by priests and monks who hand-copied them and started the first European universities in cities like Paris and Bologna. The printing press was invented by the Christian man Johannes Gutenberg (1398–1468). Bibles and other Christian literature were chiefly in his mind when he created the revolutionary device. Soon thereafter, Christianity became the leading force in literacy and education in the Western world.

With the landing of the Christian Puritans in America came this passionate commitment to literacy and education. From 1620 when the pilgrims landed until 1837, virtually all American education was private and Christian. In the nineteenth-century colonies of Massachusetts and Connecticut, for example, the literacy rate among men ranged from 89 percent to 95 percent. The pastors in the colonies were often the most educated men and led both the intellectual and spiritual life of the people. In Puritan New England, the first schools (known as common schools) were founded and were distinctively Christian. Soon, tax monies were raised to support these schools, and the first public schools in the United States were Christian and remained that way for 217 years.

Regarding higher education, nearly every one of the first 123 American colleges and universities founded in the United States was of Christian origins, including Yale, William and Mary, Brown, Princeton, NYU, and Northwestern. Harvard was started by a donation of money and books by Rev. John Harvard. Dartmouth was founded to train missionaries to the Native Americans.

The correlation between literacy, education, and Christianity in America was also common in other nations. By the turn of the twentieth century, largely non-Christian nations such as India and China had a literacy rate ranging from 0 to 20 percent, primarily Catholic nations had a literacy rate ranging from 40 to 60 percent, and largely Protestant nations had a literacy rate ranging from 94 to 99 percent.[32]

The practice of Christian education for all continues in many other nations where Christian schools have been established by missionaries. For example, Nelson Mandela, who has been lauded by many as a hero for his stand against apartheid, graduated from two missionary schools.

JESUS AND AMERICA

At the risk of sounding like I believe that the Declaration of Independence was delivered to our founding fathers on stone tablets after being penned by God himself, our nation was, as a general rule, founded as an experiment in religious freedom by devout Christians. The inauguration of our first president, George Washington, included his getting on his knees to kiss the Bible before leading the Senate and House of Representatives to an Episcopal church for a two-hour worship service. At the very least, the founding fathers were greatly influenced by the Bible, even if they were not all Christians. In fact, 34 percent of all the founding fathers' citations in books, pamphlets, articles, and other works were from the Bible.[33] Furthermore, every president in the history of America has claimed to be a Christian and to worship Jesus as his God.

Among the most practical benefits of the Christian influence on our nation's founding are the rule of law, equality of all citizens under the law, rights granted to us by God our Creator, and individual liberty as the foundational principles undergirding our rule of law. Additionally, the Christian belief of human sinfulness helped to bring about the separation of government into three branches, in an effort to avoid unchecked power in the hands of sinners.

We should not arrogantly argue that our nation is more holy or Christlike than some other nations on the earth. But we should humbly thank God that every day we do enjoy some freedoms that would not have otherwise been granted to us apart from the influence of Jesus and Christianity on the framework of our nation.

JESUS AND SCIENCE

For science to operate there must first exist a worldview that provides a comprehensive understanding of how the world works and our place in it. Because Christianity teaches that behind creation is a God of order who made us to explore his world, scientific exploration and discovery were possible. Scientific inquiry would not have been possible in other

religious worldviews so fatalistic that change is not possible or so ani-
mistic that scientific study would be religiously condemned. Various
Eastern religions see reality as little more than an illusion that is therefore unable to be scientifically explored. This, in part, explains why
Christians such as geneticist Francis Collins (director of the National
Human Genome Research Project and an evangelical Christian) see no
conflict between their faith in Jesus and their work as scientists. Collins,
in fact, explains the relationship between his saving faith in the Creator
and his scientific exploration of creation in his book *The Language of God:
A Scientist Presents Evidence for Belief.*

JESUS AND ECONOMICS

The influence of Jesus and Christianity has also been profound in the world
of economics. For brevity, we will mention only two important factors.

The Bible teaches private property rights, and one of the Ten
Commandments forbids stealing anyone's private property, simply
because it rightfully belongs to its owner. This simple principle is one
of the pillars on which our entire economy is built. In nations where
Christianity has not spread, this principle is not accepted, and, for
example, the government owns people's homes and reserves the right
to seize their property.

The Bible also teaches that all work is sacred if done for the glory
of God. Jesus himself modeled this principle by spending roughly 90
percent of his life working an honest job as a simple carpenter. His
example, along with the teaching of Scripture regarding work, helped
to create the Protestant work ethic.

JESUS AND MEDICINE

In the world of pre-Christian Rome, hospitals were only for soldiers,
gladiators, and slaves. Sadly, laborers and the poor had no medical
options for their care.

This was transformed by Jesus. Jesus was called "the Great
Physician."[34] The Gospel of Luke was written by a Christian doctor and
recorded many of the miraculous healings that Jesus performed on the
bodies of those who were sick and dying. As a result of Jesus, Christian
ministry included concern for the human body as a gift from God. In
A.D. 325 at the Council of Nicaea, it was decreed that hospitals were to

be established wherever there was a Christian church. This tradition continues in our day, as many hospitals have Christian origins, such as Baptist, Presbyterian, and Catholic. Internationally, the Red Cross continues its medical ministry, thanks to the founding of that organization by the Christian Henri Dunant.

JESUS AND ART

With the Bible teaching that God is both Creator and creative and that God created us to be creative like him, it is not surprising to see the great connection between Jesus and many of the greatest artists in the history of the world.

In architecture, cathedrals are widely appreciated as some of the most inspiring places on the earth. In the world of music, the works of Bach, Handel, and Vivaldi, along with the many great hymns of the faith, all flowed out of the fount of inspiration from Jesus. In art, Christians such as Michelangelo, Raphael, and Leonardo da Vinci remain the standard by which all others are measured. In literature, Dante, Chaucer, Shakespeare, Donne, Dostoevsky, Bunyan, Milton, Dickens, Tolstoy, Eliot, Lewis, Tolkien, Sayers, and Solzhenitsyn all wrote out of their faith and were greatly influenced by Christianity.

JESUS AND CHARITY

Jesus was poor and often spoke of his heart for the poor.[35] Additionally, Jesus also cared for the poor in practical ways such as providing food for the hungry.[36]

It is not surprising, therefore, to discover that even the most ardent unbelievers agree that people who worship Jesus tend to be more generous in their charitable giving. Arthur C. Brooks, professor at Syracuse University and director of the Nonprofit Studies Program for the Maxwell School of Citizenship and Public Affairs, has researched the issue and concluded that religious conservatives donate more money to all sorts of charitable causes, regardless of income, than their liberal and secular counterparts.[37] Brooks says, "These are not the sort of conclusions I ever thought I would reach when I started looking at charitable giving in graduate school, 10 years ago. . . . I have to admit I probably would have hated what I have to say in this book."[38] The book goes on to point out that his research confirms that religious people give more than their secular counterparts in every possible way. This includes everything from volunteer hours to donating blood.

JESUS AND ATROCITIES

In fairness, it must also be noted that horrible and wicked evils have been done by people who claim to be serving the cause of Jesus.[39]

In an interview focusing on his sexuality and on gay musicians, British pop idol Elton John said, "From my point of view I would ban religion completely, even though there are some wonderful things about it. I love the idea of the teachings of Jesus Christ and the beautiful stories about it, which I loved in Sunday school and I collected all the little stickers and put them in my book. But the reality is that organised [*sic*] religion doesn't seem to work. It turns people into hateful lemmings and it's not really compassionate."[40]

Echoing his sentiments, radio shock-jock Howard Stern said, "I'm sickened by all religions."

But before we make too many claims, let's look at some startling facts. During the twentieth century alone, some 170 million people were killed by other human beings.[41] Of those, roughly 130 million people died at the hands of those holding an atheistic ideology.[42] For example, Stalin killed forty million people, Hitler killed six million Jews and nine to ten million others (mainly Christians),[43] and Mao killed some seventy million Chinese. In addition to this number could be added the more than one billion people worldwide who were aborted and killed in the wombs of their mothers during the twentieth century alone.

Comparatively, roughly seventeen million people were killed by professing Christians in the name of Christ in twenty total centuries of Christian history. No Christian today lauds them or calls them heroes. Rather, we condemn their misguided zeal. So in all of history, those proclaiming but possibly not professing Christian faith have killed only a tiny fraction of the number of people that atheists and followers of other religions have killed in one century.

Regarding the sins of Christianity, at least three things deserve mention. First, without excusing the sins committed by those who profess to be Christians, statistically it is atheism, which denies God and judgment from God, that has been the source of far more atrocity than any religion, including Christianity. Second, not everyone who claims to be a Christian is in fact a Christian. Jesus himself taught that Christians would be known by the fruit of love in their life.[44] He also said that on the day of judgment many people will be surprised to find that they are not in fact Christians before being sent to hell for their life of sin.[45] Third, if someone is a Christian and they do sin, they are acting against Jesus and doing the very things that he forbids them to do. This kind of hypocrisy is grievous and wrong and is practiced by all Christians, myself included, to varying degrees. We are sinners who sin. Apart from Jesus not only would we not change, we would sin more greatly and more often. But it is Jesus who shows us a new way of life and makes that new life possible, which is why his influence on human history is the most positive and beneficial of anyone who has or will ever live.

Jesus' legacy is truly without peer.

Jesus never wrote a book, but the Library of Congress holds more books about Jesus (seventeen thousand) than about any other historical figure, roughly twice as many as Shakespeare, the runner-up.[46] One University of Chicago scholar has estimated that more has been written about Jesus in the last twenty years than in the previous nineteen centuries combined.[47]

Jesus never ran for a political office, but more people have chosen him to be their leader than anyone else who has ever lived.

Jesus was not formally educated nor did he lecture in a classroom, but he has more students than anyone else ever has or will have.

Jesus was not a therapist, but he has helped more people than all the counselors, therapists, and psychologists combined.

Jesus was not an artist, but more artwork has been commissioned of him than of anyone else who has ever lived.

Truly, the difference Jesus has made in history is staggering. Even more endearing is the difference Jesus makes in our personal history. Billions of people on the earth have their own testimony of the difference Jesus has made in their life. Their stories are absolutely amazing—they are the people Jesus has loved, saved, forgiven, healed, restored, encouraged, empowered, and utterly transformed.

ANSWERS TO COMMON QUESTIONS ABOUT JESUS' PLACE IN HISTORY

ISN'T JESUS JUST A MYTH THAT SCIENCE HAS DISPROVED?

There are a bunch of "scholars" who followed the Enlightenment rules of knowing and decided together that the supernatural and miracles are impossible. Instead, they decided that everything, including what appears supernatural, can be explained by the random application of presently operating laws of nature. As a logical next step, they said the traditional picture of Jesus, the God who miraculously became human, had to be wrong. In their estimation, Jesus could not have been born of a virgin, performed miracles, died as a substitute for anyone's sins, or risen from death. To then explain the records of the life of Jesus, they said the stories had to be legends, superstition, or hallucination. The "scholars" did not arrive at these conclusions because of any investigation of the facts. Rather, they began with biased philosophical assumptions and then proceeded to rewrite history according to their own preferences and expected others to agree simply because they said it was so.

The Jesus Seminar is the latest project of these scholars. They did learn a lot about the cultural and sociological conditions in the first century and so it would be unfair to say that they have contributed nothing helpful to the study of Jesus. Nonetheless, many of their conclusions are simply groundless and reckless. For example, in their great sociological erudition, they found the *Gospel of Thomas* a more reliable testimony to the "real" Jesus than any of the canonical Gospels found in the Bible.

Rather than allowing them, us, or anyone else to tell you what to believe about the real Jesus, we would encourage you to examine the facts for yourself. You can find the research and findings easily enough online. To get you started, let's look at the last saying in the *Gospel of Thomas* 114:

Simon Peter said to them, "Make Mary leave us, for females don't deserve life." Jesus said, "Look, I will guide her to make her male, so that she too may become a living spirit resembling you males. For every female who makes herself male will enter the kingdom of Heaven."

This alleged statement by Jesus sounds nothing like Jesus and is rightfully repugnant.

Another example can be found in the creation story in the recently made famous *Gospel of Judas*. In that book we are told that this world was created by a third-rate god named El that no one cares about. Furthermore, the universe is evil because it's made of physical stuff and no one from our corrupt world will ever amount to anything in the spiritual world. Does this really sound like the lovingly personal Creator God of the Bible?

This kind of tabloid-like garbage has been blowing around since the early days of the church. Wisely, those who knew the real Jesus rejected this Gnostic trash when it started appearing in the middle of the second century. We are wise to learn from their example.

IS THERE ANY CREDIBLE EVIDENCE FOR THE EXISTENCE OF THE SUPERNATURAL JESUS?

Absolutely. When the noted scholar N. T. Wright debated Marcus Borg, one of the leaders of the Jesus Seminar, he used a powerful argument on this point:[48] People are always looking for messiahs, leaders who will save us from our troubles. People get passionately loyal to their messiahs. But what happens when they fail? For example, think of the guy who was the Democratic presidential candidate/messiah in 2000. You have to think a bit to remember his name, don't you? What happened to his followers when he failed? They either gave up their pursuit, or gave up their messiah to search instead for another messiah.

What happened when Jesus got himself killed and "failed"? His closest followers did not simply give up the ministry to get better-paying jobs or go looking for another messiah. They were all the more zealous, claiming that he had risen bodily, and the kingdom of God was inaugurated. They gave their lives to the truth of what they saw and suffered gladly without recanting the truth claim that Jesus was God as evidenced by the miracle of his resurrection.

There are a lot of books that summarize the evidence for the supernatural aspects of Jesus' earthly life. A few good places to begin include Gary Habermas's *The Historical Jesus: Ancient Evidence for the Life of Jesus* and James Edwards's *Is Jesus the Only Savior?* Also helpful is New Testament scholar Ben Witherington's blog (http://benwitherington.blogspot.com).

CHAPTER TWELVE

WHAT WILL JESUS DO UPON HIS RETURN?

Amen. Come, Lord Jesus!

REVELATION 22:20B

✝

In my public high school we had something called the Natural Helpers. The Natural Helpers were students chosen to be peer counselors to other students because, of course, what every teenager needs is the deep insight and wise counsel of another teenager. Anyway, I was chosen to be a Natural Helper and received some very brief training on how to get fellow students to open up about their lives. In retrospect, this was like being trained to cut a sick person open without any idea how to do surgery.

As a non-Christian, I wanted to be able to help people but had no idea what to do when I started hearing that my friends had been raped by their boyfriend, molested by their dad, were doing hard-core drugs, stealing from stores at the mall, or attempting suicide. The more I got to see the pain of sin in the lives of my friends, the more depressed I became. Since I had no idea that Jesus is the only way for sin to be dealt with, I simply got really bummed and found myself listening to stupid songs such as "What a Wonderful World" by jazz great Louis Armstrong over and over like some pagan mantra, just trying to pull myself out of my naturally helpless, Natural Helper funk.

What I learned from the entire fiasco is that some days on the earth stink. The other days on the earth really stink, no matter what stupid songs say. This tethering to reality has proven helpful over the years, which is why if I hear one more perma-grin motivational speaker on television tell me to have positive thoughts, be happy, or stay positive, I swear I will hunt them down and punch them in the throat while reading Lamentations aloud.

I have never had a suicidal thought, but in the darkest seasons of life I do find myself daydreaming about Jesus' return, some people getting loaded into a wood chipper, the curse being lifted, and the never-ending sunshine promised in Revelation so I won't have to put the top back on my Jeep. In the meantime, the feces and the fan are certain to continue interfacing until the day Jesus gets back and cleans up the mess we've all made.

Scripture repeatedly states that Jesus will return to earth suddenly and visibly in his glorified, resurrected body. This is promised by Jesus,[1] two angels,[2] Paul,[3] James,[4] Peter,[5] John,[6] and the author of Hebrews.[7] We are also told that God's people should eagerly long for the return of Jesus and live lives of holiness in the meantime.[8] Furthermore, contrary to the calculations of some people (the type theologian Millard Erickson calls "eschatamaniacs"), we do not know when Jesus will return, even if we have read every one of the 650 million-dollar-grossing *Left Behind* novels and put together our own really cool second coming charts and graphs while watching those television shows co-hosted by a wife wearing so much makeup she looked like she lost a paintball war.[9]

Christians of the "eschatamaniac" variety are not alone in their bizarre speculations. What Jesus will do upon his return has been the subject of some curious speculation in pop culture, including the following conjecture:

- Comedian/moral authority Woody Allen, who married his own daughter: "If Jesus came back and saw what was being done in his name, he wouldn't be able to stop throwing up."
- Thomas Carlyle (British historian): "If Jesus Christ were to come today, people would not crucify him. They would ask him to dinner, hear what he had to say, and make fun of it."
- Bob Hope: "The good news is that Jesus is coming back. The bad news is that he's really pissed off."

- Mike Tyson (boxer/theologian): "All praise is to Allah, I'll fight any man, any animal; if Jesus were here I'd fight him too."
- Carson Daly (MTV veejay): "Everybody stands—that's our policy. If Jesus Christ comes on the show, guess what? It's like, 'Stand right here Jesus, we got Papa Roach coming up at number six.'"
- Mark Twain: "If Christ were here now there is one thing he would not be—a Christian."
- Paul Boutin (contributing editor, *Wired* magazine): "I really think that if Jesus were around today, he would have a blog."
- Puritan Thomas Adams: "[He] that rose from the clods, we expect from the clouds."

While Scripture is not clear regarding when Jesus will return, it is clear about what he will not do upon his return. Jesus will not throw up like a supermodel, be mocked by the late-night talk-show hosts, be knocked out by has-been boxers with freakish tattoos and junior high–girl voices, end up on MTV, protest Christianity, or have a blog on which other bloggers could post their criticisms and disagreements. Furthermore, contrary to what some Mormons say, Jesus will not touch down on the tip of the temple in Independence, Missouri, for it to become the New Jerusalem, because only a bunch of nutty rednecks could possibly mistake Missouri for heaven. The Scriptures do declare what Jesus will do upon his return to this cursed world that is limping along to the White Throne.

JESUS WILL JUDGE EVERYONE WHO HAS EVER LIVED

One of the most painful aspects of pastoral ministry is having a front-row seat for human depravity and its effects. I can still remember the haunting moments when people whom I love and pastor told me their deepest, darkest secret and the source of their greatest shame. The young woman who told me that her father, a church elder, began raping her when she was a very little girl, and began his demonic work by telling her that she needed to take her jammies off and obey her father as the Bible commands, brought forth tears that I could not restrain and sent me into a dark despair that did not lift for days. The young man who told me how his father would force him to perform oral sex on him while he watched porno in the family living room while the rest of the family went about their business, acting as if nothing was happening, nearly made me throw up, and I literally had to swallow the vomit back down my throat rather than let it explode over the front of my shirt. As a pastor of thousands, I could write thousands of similar tragic tales. To mask much of the deep pain caused by pastoral ministry, I make jokes and try to give myself a reprieve from the horror of walking with the wounded people whom I love deeply.

In the depths of my soul is a deep and profound love for righteous judgment and justice. I do not labor under the silly myth that deep down we are all good people and that our sins are simply occasional aberrations. No, we are rebels, lawbreakers, Satan's minions, fools, and evildoers without exception, beginning with the guy I see brushing his teeth in my mirror every morning. That fact is blinded by our own hypocrisy. We are prone to clearly see the sin that others commit against us and the corresponding pain that it causes. Subsequently, when we are sinned against, we tend to complain, yell, or honk our horn because we refuse to sit idly by without demanding justice. Conversely, when we sin, we cry with equal volume, not for justice, but rather for mercy, which is only a further indication of how corrupt and hypocritical we are.

In the gospel of Jesus Christ we see, unlike anywhere else in all creation, both justice and mercy. At the cross, Jesus died in my place for my sins thereby satisfying wonderful, glorious, good, pure, and holy justice. Jesus also gave me mercy by his grace.

Because of my deep love for justice, there are days when I literally have to withdraw for my own emotional well-being. On those days I do not schedule counseling meetings, watch the news, or read the newspaper.

I must confess that as I survey the world and all of its evil I wonder why Jesus has not yet returned. There are days when it feels like God is incredibly tardy, the proverbial old man in the sky who is making his return to earth but whose steps are painfully slow. In such dark moments, I have to lean into my theological convictions to make sense of the world. In 2 Peter 3:9–10, I read:

> The Lord is not slow to fulfill his promise as some count slowness, but
> is patient toward you, not wishing that any should perish, but that all

should reach repentance. But the day of the Lord will come like a thief, and then the heavens will pass away with a roar, and the heavenly bodies will be burned up and dissolved, and the earth and the works that are done on it will be exposed.

I am comforted by the reminder that God is patiently granting us sinners opportunities to repent and be saved before the day of judgment when our works will be exposed. Furthermore, I am glad that God did not run out of patience just before he brought me to repentance in late 1989.

Nonetheless, while God's patience in waiting for the elect to turn to him in repentance and faith is encouraging, I also find comfort in the effects of God's patience on the unrepentant. Regarding this, Romans 2:5 says, "But because of your hard and impenitent heart you are storing up wrath for yourself on the day of wrath when God's righteous judgment will be revealed." Thankfully, no one, not the awful parents, evil spouses, false witnesses, crooked attorneys, or negligent authorities, is ultimately going to get away with anything. Rather, unrepentant sinners are merely "storing up wrath" for themselves. With each act of wickedness they are merely adding another rock to the pile that Jesus will throw at them in the end.

One of the stupidest things we sinners say to other sinners is that no one has the right to judge them because no one else is perfect either. Thankfully, Jesus told us that he is the one who will be doing all of the judging in the end and as such we won't be able to say stupid things about his lack of moral qualification to examine our deeds.[10] A porn star will serve as a good illustration of this point.

Jenna Jameson was born in 1974 in Vegas, of course, and is regarded as the "Queen of Porn." She is the most popular porn starlette in the world, having appeared in more than one hundred porn films. She began stripping at the age of sixteen by lying about her age and taking the braces off her teeth with pliers to make herself look older. Before she graduated from high school, she was making upwards of two thousand dollars a night dancing at strip clubs.[11] She has since gone on to be something of a pop-culture icon, having appeared as herself in the television cartoon show *The Family Guy*, and her voice appears in the popular video game *Grand Theft Auto: Vice City*. In 2004 she published her book *How To Make Love Like a Porn Star*, which spent six weeks on the New York Times Bestseller list.

One day I was flipping through the cable channels and found *VH1 Confessions*, which is a biography show (without nudity if you were wondering) on famous people. They were airing the biography of Jameson. To be honest, it was pretty sad. Her dad was not a great guy; she was repeatedly sexually abused and taken advantage of from a young age and did not seem to have a mom to help raise her.

What I found most curious, however, was her adamant declaration that she is a Roman Catholic Christian. In 2003, she married porn-studio owner Jay Grdina in a Roman Catholic ceremony. The biography included a tour of their 6,700-square-foot Spanish-style palace in Arizona. Lining the walls were numerous Catholic-looking religious icons and artwork. Showing off her religious artwork, she declared herself a devoted Catholic, despite the fact that she is a porn star who has done films called *Hell on Heels* and *Jenna Depraved*.

The most peculiar quote she gave in the entire biography was her attempt to defend how she could be a porn-again Christian: "No one can judge me but God." Technically she is correct, and according to Jesus he alone is the God she will stand before in judgment at the end of time. I pray she and others who share her peculiar illogic repent of their sin before facing his otherwise-certain hellish justice. But if they fail to, I will worship God just the same because justice either came for us on Jesus at the cross or comes on us from Jesus in the end, but either way justice must be served.

It is Jesus who will determine who is assigned to heaven and hell. The themes of heaven and hell are woven throughout our culture. In music, songs named "Heaven" are sung by hundreds of artists, including Lionel Richie, Cheap Trick, Talking Heads, Queen, Patsy Cline, Warrant, Jamie Foxx, The Rolling Stones, The Psychedelic Furs, and Led Zeppelin. Songs with the word *heaven* in the title are sung by Blind Melon, Foo Fighters, James Brown, Run DMC, Slayer, Judas Priest, Hank Williams Jr., Kiss, Alice Cooper, Carrie Underwood, and Black Sabbath. The full-length academy award–winning documentary on the life of a legendary rapper was curiously titled *Tupac: Resurrection*. In the world of video games there are titles such as *Dark Resurrection*, *Alien Resurrection*, and *Doom 3: Resurrection of Evil*.

On the matter of heaven and hell, there are numerous curious perspectives:

- Days before dying, hall-of-famer Mickey Mantle said, "I am trusting Christ's death for me to take me to heaven."
- Friedrich Nietzsche: "In heaven all the interesting people are missing."
- Isaac Asimov: "I don't believe in an afterlife, so I don't have to spend my whole life fearing hell, or fearing heaven even more. For whatever the tortures of hell, I think the boredom of heaven would be even worse."
- Mark Twain: "Go to Heaven for the climate, Hell for the company."
- Peter Jennings: "I was raised with the notion that it was okay to ask questions, and it was okay to say, 'I'm not sure.' I believe, but I'm not quite so certain about the resurrection."
- Johnny Cash: "How well I have learned that there is no fence to sit on between heaven and hell. There is a deep, wide, gulf, a chasm, and in that chasm is no place for any man."
- Jimi Hendrix: "Craziness is like heaven."
- Oprah Winfrey: "My idea of heaven is a great big baked potato and someone to share it with."
- Jerry Lee Lewis: "If I'm going to hell, I'm going there playing the piano."
- Puritan Thomas Adams: "Heaven begins where sin ends."

JESUS WILL PUNISH NON-CHRISTIANS IN HELL ACCORDING TO THEIR WICKEDNESS

Not only will Jesus judge with perfect justice, he will also sentence the unrepentant to perfectly suited punishment in hell for their sins.[12] Some who wince at the doctrine and find it incompatible with the loving nature of Jesus may be surprised to discover that Jesus spoke of hell more than anyone in Scripture.[13] In fact, British philosopher Bertrand Russell said, "There is one very serious defect to my mind in Christ's moral character, and that is that He believed in hell."[14] Tragically, unless he turned to Jesus before his death, Russell came to agree with Jesus, discovering in the most painful way that Jesus rules even in hell, over Satan, demons, and unrepentant sinners.[15]

Today there are some notable Christian leaders who have sought to redefine the hellishness of hell. Perhaps the most prominent is

Brian McLaren in his book *The Last Word and the Word after That*.[16] On September 2, 2006, the issue of eternal punishment in hell made the front page of the *Los Angeles Times* in a lengthy article.[17] It explained a falling-out of sorts between notable pastor Chuck Smith Sr., leader of the Calvary Chapel movement with some one thousand churches in the United States alone, and his son and namesake, Chuck Smith Jr., over a number of theological issues. On the issue of hell, the article said, "For years, Smith Jr. said, he had preached about hell uncomfortably, half-apologetically, because he couldn't understand why a loving God would consign his children to eternal flames. It felt like blackmail for a pastor to threaten people with hell-scapes from the Middle Ages to induce piety. Now, he came to believe that the biblical images used to depict hell's torments—such as the 'lake of fire' and the 'worm that does not die'—were intended to evoke a feeling rather than a literal place."[18]

God is literally holy, we are literally sinful, Jesus literally died to forgive our sin, and if we fail to receive his forgiveness, we will literally stand before him for judgment and be sentenced to a literal hell as an act of literal justice. To be honest, the doctrine of hell does not bother me. It makes perfect sense that guilty people would be sentenced and punished for their evil. What has always bothered me is heaven. How could a holy God allow any sinner to enter heaven? Furthermore, how could a loving God allow evil to continue without stopping it forever and bringing justice to all of the victims before wiping all their tears? Indeed, the joys of heaven and not the pains of hell are more difficult for me to reconcile with the character of a good God. The cold, hard truth is that for those who do not love Jesus, this life is as close to heaven as they will ever get. Hell awaits them.

JESUS WILL REWARD CHRISTIANS IN HEAVEN ACCORDING TO THEIR RIGHTEOUSNESS

An episode of the television news show *Dateline* reported that "94 percent of American adults believe in God, 89 percent in heaven and 73 percent in hell."[19] It went on to say, "Fully three-quarters of survey participants felt pretty sure they will be going to heaven when they die, while just 2 percent expected they would wind up in hell." Apparently hell is for the other guy—the terrorist, the relief pitcher who gives up a lot of walks, and anyone who wears a suit and works in Washington DC.

According to Jesus, no one is getting to heaven except through him.[20] While we are saved by grace and faith in Jesus alone,[21] we are also saved to a life of good works that God has appointed for us to do.[22] Practically, this means that the conversion of a Christian is in fact a conversion to both Jesus and Jesus' mission. Not only are we to be converted from worship of people and things other than Jesus to the worship of Jesus, but that worship includes a conversion to Jesus' mission above every other mission in our life. The result of the first aspect of our conversion is that we are connected to the living God. The result of the second aspect of our conversion is that we are commissioned to serve him on the earth and bear what Jesus called good, lasting fruit as branches on his vine. It is true that we are not saved by our works, but instead by the works of Jesus' sinless life, substitutionary death, and bodily resurrection. But it is also true that we are saved to do good works by the empowering grace of God and indwelling Holy Spirit.

Sadly, what I have commonly seen is that many Christians are familiar only with the first aspect of their conversion. They wrongly believe that once they have trusted in Jesus they are free to have their own mission for their life, such as success or wealth, and they expect Jesus to serve their mission. That kind of thinking is completely inverted.

Every Christian will face a day of judgment before Jesus. The judgment of a Christian is not the judgment for salvation, because that judgment was rendered at the cross of Jesus and applied when we trusted in Jesus' finished work for us. The judgment of a Christian is a judgment of our works and how well we lived and labored for Jesus' mission. Sadly, I find it very rare that a Christian really understands this doctrine. The effects are profound. People do not understand the importance of our life and works on the earth and that they will determine our eternal rewards.

Scripture has much to say about eternal rewards for Christians.[23] In sum, every Christian will stand before Jesus and be judged for the degree in which they lived their life in faithfulness to Jesus. Furthermore, because Jesus is just, he will distribute varying degrees of rewards for each Christian in correlation to their faithfulness, just as he will punish non-Christians in varying degrees according to the wickedness they have committed.[24]

Practically, this means that there should be a sense of urgency and priority for God's people to do the good works assigned to them by Jesus—at their job, with their friends and family, in their local culture, and for their church. Furthermore, the doctrine of eternal rewards is a great comfort for those who do faithfully serve God quietly and without recognition, because what awaits them is a day when Jesus, with a smile in his eyes and a hand on their shoulder, tells them, "Well done, good and faithful servant."[25] He will give them eternal rewards in his kingdom that are commensurate with the good deeds they performed by the power of the Holy Spirit and the enabling grace of God. The warm, soft truth is that for those who do love Jesus, this life is as close to hell as they will ever get. Heaven awaits them.

JESUS WILL LIFT THE CURSE AND ITS EFFECTS

The effects of the entrance of sin into the world through our first parents in Genesis 3 are many. We are separated from God, which is the root cause of all problems. We are separated from a humble willingness to accept truth, causing theological problems. We are separated from our created purpose, causing psychological problems. We are separated from each other, causing social/relational problems. We are separated from creation, causing ecological problems.

Additionally, both physical and spiritual death were unleashed along with God's curse upon both men and women. Eve and all her daughters now experience great pain in childbirth and a desire to rule over their husband as sin ruled over Cain in Genesis 4. God is not merely punishing women, but graciously permitting them to feel the effects of their sin so that they see the world as God does. Jesus, like a mother who experiences great pain in childbirth, also experienced great pain on the cross to give us new birth. Like a birthing mother, his blood was shed to bring forth new life. Furthermore, God is a parent who made us and does the hard work of raising us disobedient spiritual children. Every time a mother has to correct her child, she is reminded that God constantly has to correct her. As a woman struggles to be a submissive and helpful wife, she is reminded that she often treats her husband in the same way that Jesus' bride, the church, treats him. This is all because sin entered the world.

Additionally, Adam and all his sons now find that their work is frustrating. Why? Because the ground and all else that is supposed to be under a man's dominion and obedient to him now treats the man the same way that the man treats God. This shows the man how deeply sinful he truly is. Subsequently, no matter what job a man has, how organized he is, how hard he works, how often he delegates, or how meticulously he approaches his work, he will invariably find himself throwing his hands in the air in frustration. By God's grace, the man should then pause to worship God with those same hands. He should realize that he is as difficult for God to work through as the cell phone that works every time except the time you really need it, the vehicle that always breaks down no matter how much money is spent on repairs, the car keys that like Enoch and Elijah were simply taken up to heaven never to be seen again, the computer that is more unstable than the demons Jesus encountered, and the curious fact that only one tool is misplaced at any given time and it just so happens to be the one tool you really need.

In Ecclesiastes, the word "toil" is often used to explain what life is like for men and women on the earth. Subsequently, life on the earth feels like a frantic and exhausting goose chase where there is no goose. This is because we are cursed. The curse serves to remind us that we are sinners and that we need our sin to be forgiven through the first coming of Jesus, and we also need the curse to be lifted at the second coming of Jesus. Ecclesiastes 7:13 rightly asks, "Consider the work of God: who can make straight what he has made crooked?" Indeed, the world is a crooked place and we crooked people cannot straighten out all that God himself has made crooked. Thankfully, Jesus is coming, and when he does he will straighten us and everything else out by lifting the curse: "No longer will there be anything accursed."[26]

JESUS WILL GIVE CHRISTIANS GLORIFIED, RESURRECTED BODIES

The Scriptures are clear that sin leads to death.[27] We feel this impending end practically with every ache, pain, cold, ailment, and injury and each corresponding pill, surgery, or other medical treatment. We are also reminded of our impending death each time we pick up an obituary or attend a funeral.

The first death that touched my life was the passing of my Grandpa George when I was ten. He was a short, stocky, super-funny man about whom I have nothing but joyous memories. We would watch wrestling on television, eat caramel apples, and make stuff with the tools in his woodshop. He died of a sudden heart attack, which devastated me because I loved him so dearly.

My Grandpa George's funeral was one of the worst days in my childhood. As I walked up to his open casket and saw his dead body, I just felt angry that he died. I reached into the coffin but felt nothing but the hard, cold shell of my best friend. When the priest later got up to speak, my anger intensified because he tried to explain that death is a natural thing and part of the cycle of life that we should learn to embrace. I was no theologian, but the priest sounded stupid to me and was no help at all. It was on that day that I decided religion had nothing to offer me, and I basically turned my back on God until he saved me some years later in college.

Part of what led me to become a Christian at the age of nineteen was reading in the Bible that we are all sinners, that sin leads to death in the same way that unplugging something from its power source turns it off, that sin is our enemy and not our friend, and that Jesus defeated sin and death for us to give us eternal life. In reading that death was an enemy, the anger I felt at Grandpa George's funeral finally made sense. I was given hope and joy when I read about Jesus' victory over death.

The fifteenth chapter of 1 Corinthians contains the most extended treatment of the resurrection in all of Scripture. The chapter begins by investigating the resurrection of Jesus and then moves on to explain how his resurrection is prototypical for all whose faith is in him. Paul responds to two questions the Corinthian church and most churches since have asked about the resurrection body of Christians: how are the dead raised, and with what kind of body do they come?[28] Curiously, this longing for a supernatural, immortal new body is also a major theme in most comics, where a mere mortal in some sense experiences death and then emerges with supernatural powers and invincibility as a superhero. It seems God has placed a desire for a glorified body deep within us.

The second question is answered in verses 36–49. Paul uses an agricultural metaphor to explain what will happen to a Christian's body upon death.[29] Much like a seed that is buried in the ground dies and then springs forth as something more glorious than could have ever been imagined, when a Christian dies they too are buried but will likewise spring forth with a glorified resurrection body. Paul then assures us that if God could create the sun, moon, stars, planets, animal life, plant life, and human life, he can certainly take our dead bodies and resurrect us in glorified new bodies.

Paul then seeks to explain the nature of our glorified resurrection bodies in greater detail.[30] First, while our body is mortal and subject to sin and death in this life, the glorified body is not. Second, while our mortal body dies in dishonor, it will be raised in honor. All of this is because our body is in some ways like clothing that covers our immaterial spirit. God will, in essence, exchange our current physical covering for a new and more glorious eternal body.

Quoting Genesis 2:7, Paul then says that just as our mortal body is patterned after Adam's death, our glorified body will be patterned after Jesus' resurrection.[31] Subsequently, our glorified body is made possible because our eternal God Jesus came down from heaven to save us through his death and bodily resurrection. He secured for us the forgiveness of sin and gifted us with resurrection bodies patterned after his own.

The first question is then answered in verses 50–57. Paul begins by stating that our mortal bodies marked by sin and death are not fit for God's perfect and sinless eternal kingdom.[32] Therefore, God must change our bodies to make them fit for his kingdom.

Paul then says that because of our sin, we die.[33] Jesus came to conquer our sin through his death and conquer our death through his resurrection. Therefore, only through faith in Jesus can sin and death be defeated so that we might live forever in new bodies amidst a new world without the pains of sin and death. This transformation of our bodies will not happen gradually but rather in an instant upon Jesus' second coming. Upon Jesus' arrival, those Christians who are alive will see their mortal bodies transformed into glorified bodies in an instant. Simultaneously, those Christians who have died in faith will be resurrected like Jesus was in glorified bodies fit for God's kingdom.

Jesus' resurrection and ascension into heaven as the prototype for what awaits Christians on the other side of the grave utterly transforms our fear of death. For example, a *Newsweek* article reported, "Because Christianity's influence is so pervasive throughout much of the world, it is easy to forget how radical its beliefs once were. Jesus' resurrection forever changed Christians' view of death. Rodney Stark, sociologist at the University of Washington, points out that when a major plague hit the ancient Roman Empire, Christians had surprisingly high survival rates. Why? Most Roman citizens would banish any plague-stricken person from their household. But because Christians had no fear of death, they nursed their sick instead of throwing them out on the streets, not fearing death because of their certainty in eternal life. Therefore, many Christians survived the plague."[34]

JESUS WILL BRING SHALOM

God created the world in a perfect and harmonious beauty that the Hebrews summarize with the word *shalom*. God created the first man and woman in his image and likeness and placed them in shalom to enjoy him and all that he had created.

Deep down all human beings know that something has gone terribly wrong with both themselves and their world and they desperately long for shalom. The only problem is that no matter how many wars we fight, dollars we spend, or discoveries we make, the stone-cold truth is that there can be no shalom until the return of Jesus Christ, whom Isaiah calls the Prince of Shalom.[35]

Isaiah also has a great deal to say about the coming shalom. In shalom, Jesus will sit on a throne to rule over all nations and teach people about living in his ways of perfect harmony with the world as he intended it to be.[36] Shalom will satisfy every person who reads books and attends seminars about the practical matters of life in an effort to balance their checkbook, eat a well-balanced diet, stay married, birth a child, and be happy.

In shalom, the best young men will no longer bleed out on the battlefield because the weapons of war and mass destruction will be melted down and used instead for farming, and Jesus will ensure peace among all peoples.[37] Shalom will be gladly received by everyone who has buried a loved one who died for their country, and every veteran who has lived with the horror of war constantly in mind.

In shalom, Jesus will ensure that the oppressed will receive justice, the poor will be cared for, the wicked will be punished, animals will live at peace with each other and humans, the entire earth will be filled with the knowledge of the one true God alone, jealousy will cease, weather will be made glorious, and all nations will sing in harmonious joy.[38] Shalom alone can satisfy those who feed the hungry, fight injustice, love their pet, think summer is the best season of the year, paint the walls of their home shades of yellow, red, and orange to remind them of the sun, and loudly sing off-key when alone in their car.

In shalom, Jesus will rule with justice, the blind will see, the deaf will hear, the stammering will speak, the fool will be unmasked, the scoundrel will be dishonored, the hungry will eat, the thirsty will drink, the poor will be cared for, the desert will spring up as fertile land, peace will endure, and the honest work of all peoples will find success.[39] Shalom will satisfy those who care for disabled loved ones they pray would be healed, distrust those in power because of corruption, have friends over to dinner, stop to savor the blossoms of spring, love the ocean and rivers because they remind them of God, snore all night as an act of faith, eat and drink until they need to take a nap, and work hard at their job because they work unto the Lord.

In shalom, God blesses his people by gathering us together as one nation under his benevolent rule where joy is unending, wealth is unprecedented, enemies are unwelcome, violence is unheard of, and the shining glory of God's presence surpasses the sun and moon.[40] Shalom will satisfy those who see beauty in all cultures, long for the day when summits and peace negotiations are needless, know the critical importance of timing in telling a good joke, value a dollar, refuse to seek vengeance, and are happy when the sun rises or sets because they get to see it explode into colors and shadows without buying a ticket and without its defilement by some stupid corporate logo.

Upon the return of the Prince of Shalom, weeping and crying will cease, children will not taste death, the elderly will live with unending health, our homes and cars will no longer need locks, our tables will be filled with choice food, our labor will be a fruitful joy, our children and their descendants will share in our abundance, our prayers will be answered before we even utter them, all of creation will live in harmony and peace, and harm and destruction will end forever.[41] Shalom will satisfy those who are weary of weeping, have seen the horror of a tiny coffin, been ripped off, raped, abused, abandoned, betrayed, broke, hungry, unemployed, cheated on, lied to, gossiped about, or drawn into a scuffle.

In shalom, God will lavish choice food and wine upon his people, the lost years of our life will be repaid to us, our shame will be lifted, God will be known, and our joy will burst out of us in song.[42] Shalom will satisfy those who eat and drink as an act of worship, those who wish they could go back and alter a few life-changing decisions they made, those who still blush, those who read their Bible, and those who just need to dance once in a while so they can practice for that day when their mourning turns to song.

Ultimately, our hope is not that pills, politicians, pickets, protests, pouting, or progress will bring shalom. We and everyone and everything else desperately need the return of our Lord Jesus Christ, the Prince of the Kingdom of Shalom.

The practical question remains: how should we live until Jesus returns? President Jimmy Carter once said, "We should live our lives as though Christ was coming this afternoon." Paul wrestled with this same question; he was torn between his desire to exchange this sinful, cursed, fallen world for heaven, and the work that God had given him to do on the earth.[43] Paul's solution was to live as a citizen of heaven while on the earth, bringing some of the joy and healing of the kingdom to the earth.[44] In this way, Paul was not just awaiting his eternal life but rather celebrating that eternal life as both a quality and a duration of life that begins the moment Jesus saves us here on earth and continues forever in his kingdom. By living with our heart and mind heavenward and our hands and feet thrust deep into the earth, we can walk with God so closely that, like Enoch, our transition from this world to the next is as simple as taking another step on a journey.[45] Therefore, in the meantime, as citizens of the kingdom and ambassadors of King Jesus on the earth, we practice for the return of Jesus by throwing the occasional big party where everyone wears white like the huge bashes featured on MTV by P. Diddy a.k.a. Sean Jean a.k.a. Puff Daddy to practice for the grand bash in shalom hosted by the Prince of Shalom for his ragtag bunch of grace-getters.[46]

Now you can put this book down, call your friends, put on something white, eat something tasty, drink something fruity, listen to something funky, and laugh from your belly, just like the early church, as an act of faith that one day you will see Jesus face-to-face.[47]

Shalom.

ANSWERS TO COMMON QUESTIONS ABOUT JESUS' RETURN

IS HEAVEN REALLY JUST SITTING AROUND ON CLOUDS PLAYING HARPS LIKE YOU SEE IN THE CARTOONS?

No. The Bible makes it clear that God will join us on a new earth akin to the one in Eden: "Behold, the dwelling place of God is with man. He will dwell with them, and they will be his people, and God himself will be with them as their God."[48] We surely don't know all the stuff we'll be doing there, but it absolutely won't be boring. We'll be partnered with the King who runs the whole universe and lives in perfect community. He designed us and knows what will make us totally happy there in shalom. Perhaps the best way to envision heaven is as a world without sin but with all of the enjoyments that God gives us. My children have asked me, for example, if we can play catch, go for walks, swim, and climb trees in heaven, and I tell them that I would assume so because all that is forbidden in heaven is sin, not fun.

HOW IS IT FAIR THAT GOD CAN PUT BOTH MY REALLY NICE NEIGHBOR AND ADOLF HITLER SIDE BY SIDE IN HELL?

It is and it isn't. The fundamental problem with a nice neighbor and Hitler is that they both blow off the grace of God to live their own life by their own rule as their own god. As a result, they will both be separated from the love of God. But the Bible also states that there is fair justice in that the punishment will fit the crime perfectly. There are variations in the severity of God's judgments. For example, Jesus said that because they directly rejected the miracles of Jesus, it will be worse on the day of judgment for Capernaum than for Sodom.[49] The Bible gives us little information on hell. But these statements plus the continual affirmation of God's justice make us totally confident that God will deal rightly with everyone in hell.

HOW CAN A LOVING GOD SEND PEOPLE TO HELL?

Actually, he didn't initiate the idea. We are the ones who don't want to be with him.

He made a beautiful garden for humans to live in and to enjoy hanging and working with him. Eve and Adam told God they'd rather depend on their own discernment than trust him. Instead of destroying them, God gave the promise of the Messiah. He invited them and everyone to come back to him, wounded and broken, so he could heal them. First Timothy 2:3–4 says, "This is good, and it is pleasing in the sight of God our Savior, who desires all people to be saved and to come to the knowledge of the truth."

People who reject his grace persist in choosing the way of Adam and Eve. We want to rule our own life and do our own thing as our own god. Then some of us have the audacity to demand that the real God be okay with our self-centeredness, which only proves how messed up we truly are in the first place.

It is fundamentalist preachers, not God, who seem gleeful when they speak of sinners going to hell. God says, "Have I any pleasure in the death of the wicked, declares the Lord God, and not rather that he should turn from his way and live?"[50]

Anyone who wants to accept God's free gift of full membership in his family can do so very simply. Jesus died and rose again so that all who repent of being their own God and trust in the real God will have full forgiveness of sin and new life in God's family. Jesus—there never has been and never will be anyone equal to him.

notes

CHAPTER ONE: IS JESUS THE ONLY GOD?

1. "Celebrity Poker Showdown," produced by Marcia Mule and Bryan Scott, Bravo and Picture This Television (2003), http://imdb.com/title/tto389591/quotes.
2. Steve Rushin, "Too True to Be Good," Air and Space, *Sports Illustrated* (December 23, 2005), http://sportsillustrated.cnn.com/2005/writers/steve_rushin/12/23/air.space/index.html.
3. *The Jesus Christ Show*, http://neilsaavedra.com/Jesuscontents.html.
4. Watch Tower Bible and Tract Society of Pennsylvania, "The Truth about Angels," *What Can Angels Do for You?* Watchtower Society online ed. (November 1, 1995), http://www.watchtower.org/ library/w/1995/11/1/ article_02.htm.
5. "Who Was Jesus?" *Larry King Live*. First broadcast December 24, 2004, CNN, http://transcripts.cnn.com/ TRANSCRIPTS/ 0412/24/lkl.01.html.
6. Ron Rhodes, *The Challenge of the Cults and New Religions* (Grand Rapids, MI: Zondervan, 2001), 276.
7. Levi Dowling, *The Aquarian Gospel of Jesus the Christ* (Santa Fe, NM: New Antlantean Press, 2004), 87.
8. Philip Swihart, *Reincarnation, Edgar Cayce, and the Bible* (Downers Grove, IL: InterVarsity, 1978), 18.
9. Victoria Smithee, "Speaker Discusses Role of Christ in Islam," *The North Texas Daily* (September 14, 2006), http://www.ntdaily.com/media/storage/paper877/news/2006/09/14/ news/2006/09/14/News/Speaker.Discusses.Role.Of.Christ.In.Islam-2271697.shtml.
10. Dalai Lama, "The Karma of the Gospel," *Newsweek*, March 27, 2000.
11. Mahatma Gandhi, *Harijan* (March 6, 1937): 25.
12. John 10:19–21
13. Mark 1:24
14. Kevin Williams, "NDEs of the Rich and Famous: Hollywood Sees the Light," Near-Death Experiences and the Afterlife, http://www.near-death.com/famous.html.
15. John 6:38
16. John 6:41–66
17. John 1:15; 3:13; 8:58; 13:13; 17:15, 24; 1 Cor. 8:6; 15:47; 2 Tim. 1:9; Heb. 5:5–6; 13:8; 1 Pet. 1:20; Rev. 1:8; 13:8
18. Gen. 32
19. Josh. 5:13–14
20. Isa. 6:1–8; John 12:38–41
21. Dan. 3:25
22. Thich Nhat Hanh, *Living Buddha, Living Christ* (New York: Riverhead, 1995), xxi.
23. John 5:18
24. Billy Graham, "God's Hand on My Life," *Newsweek*, March 29, 1999, 65.
25. Matt. 24:30; 26:64; Mark 13:26; 14:62–64; Luke 21:27; 22:69; Acts 1:9–11; 1 Thess. 4:17; Rev. 1:7; 14:14
26. John A. Buehrens and Forrest Church, *A Chosen Faith: An Introduction to Unitarian Universalism* (Boston: Beacon, 1998), 7.
27. Matt. 12:24; 27:42; John 11:47
28. *Sanhedrin* 43a.
29. Origen, *Contra Celsum* 1.38.
30. Flavius Josephus, "Jewish Antiquities" in *The New Complete Works of Josephus*, trans. William Whiston (Grand Rapids, MI: Kregel, 1999), 18.63.
31. Acts 8:7; 9:37–41

32. Pss. 33:7; 65:7; 89:9; 104:7–9; 107:28–30; 135:7; Job 26:12; 38:8; Jonah 1:4, 15
33. John 20:30–31
34. Watch Tower Bible and Tract Society of Pennsylvania, "Is God Always Superior to Jesus?" *Should You Believe in the Trinity?* Watchtower Society online ed., http://www.watchtower.org/e/ti/index.htm?article=article_06.htm.
35. Quoted in Charles Edmund Deland, *The Mis-Trials of Jesus* (Boston, MA: Richard G. Badger, 1914), 118–19.
36. Matt. 26:63–65; John 5:17–23; 8:58–59; 10:30–39; 19:7
37. For example, Luke 4.
38. Mark 14:55–56
39. George Barna, "Beliefs: Trinity, Satan," *Barna by Topic* (2007), http://www.barna.org/FlexPage.aspx?Page=Topic&TopicID=6.
40. George Barna, "Teenagers' Beliefs Moving Farther from Biblical Perspectives," *The Barna Update* (October 23, 2000), http://www.barna.org/FlexPage.aspx?Page=BarnaUpdate&BarnaUpdateID=74.
41. John 8:46
42. Acts 3:14; 1 Pet. 1:19; 2:22; 3:18
43. John said that anyone who claims to be without sin is a liar (1 John 1:8) and also said that Jesus was without sin (1 John 3:5).
44. James 5:6
45. 2 Cor. 5:21
46. Matt. 27:3–4
47. Luke 23:22
48. Luke 23:47
49. Luke 23:41
50. Ps. 51:4
51. Jer. 31:34; Ps. 130:4
52. John 14:13–14; 15:16; 16:24
53. Acts 7:59–60
54. Matt. 15:25
55. Matt. 7:13–14
56. Jeff Chu, "10 Questions for Katharine Jefferts Schori," *Time* (July 10, 2006), http://www.time.com/time/ magazine/article/0,9171,1211587-2,00.html.
57. C. S. Lewis, *Mere Christianity* (New York: Macmillan, 1952), 40–41.
58. Kenneth Samples, *Prophets of the Apocalypse: David Koresh and Other American Messiahs* (Grand Rapids, MI: Baker, 1994), 15, 59–60, 69–70.
59. Ibid., 70.
60. Ex. 20:1–6
61. John 9:38
62. Mark 5:6
63. John 20:28
64. Isa. 6:1–5; cf. John 12:41; Rev. 1:17–18
65. Matt. 14:33; 28:17
66. Matt. 28:8–9
67. Matt. 20:20
68. Heb. 1:6
69. 1 Cor. 1:2
70. Acts 1:14
71. James; Jude
72. Matt. 21:14–16 cf. Ps. 8:2
73. Rom. 9:5; Col. 1:15; 2:9; Titus 2:13
74. Matt. 16:15
75. Matt. 4:7; 28:9; Luke 4:12; John 1:1–4, 14; 5:17–18; 8:58; 10:30–33; 12:37–41 cf. Isa. 6:9–11; 20:28–29; Acts 20:28; Rom. 9:5; Col. 1:16–17; 2:8–9, Phil. 2:10–11; 1 Cor. 2:8; 4:4; 8:4–6; 1 Tim. 6:15; Titus 2:13; 1 John 5:20; Heb. 1:8; 2 Pet. 1:1; Rev. 1:8, 17–18; 17:14; 19:16; 22:13–16
76. Isa. 41:4; 44:6; 48:12 cf. Rev. 1:17; 2:8; 22:13
77. Ps. 27:1 cf. John 1:9
78. Pss. 18:2; 95:1 cf. 1 Cor. 10:4; 1 Pet. 2:6–8
79. Hos. 2:16; Isa. 62:5 cf. Eph. 5:28–33; Rev. 21:2

80. Ps. 23:1 cf. Heb. 13:20
81. Hos.13:14; Ps. 130:7 cf. Titus 2:14; Rev. 5:9
82. Isa. 43:3 cf. John 4:42
83. Isa. 42:8 cf. 1 Cor. 2:8
84. Watch Tower Bible and Tract Society of Pennsylvania, "The Truth about Angels."
85. Phil. 2:7
86. John 1:18; 3:16; 6:46; 17:3
87. John 5:19–30; 8:28; 12:49
88. For example, see Gary R. Habermas's *The Historical Jesus: Ancient Evidence for the Life of Christ* (Joplin, MO: College Press, 1996).

CHAPTER TWO: HOW HUMAN WAS JESUS?

1. Mark 6:3
2. Num. 6
3. 1 Cor. 11:14–15a
4. *The Passion: Religion and the Movies*, A&E Television and The History Channel.
5. Stephen Prothero, *American Jesus: How the Son of God Became a National Icon* (New York: Farrar, Straus & Giroux, 2003), 85.
6. Ibid., 65.
7. Ibid., 98.
8. Ibid., 89.
9. Mike Fillon, "The Real Face of Jesus," *Popular Mechanics* (December 2002), http://www.popularmechanics.com/ science/research/1282186.html.
10. Isa. 53:2
11. Gal. 4:4
12. Luke 24:39
13. Luke 2:52
14. Matt. 13:54–58; Mark 6:3; 1 Cor. 9:5
15. Luke 2:51
16. Luke 4:16
17. Mark 1:35; 6:46
18. Mark 6:3
19. Matt. 4:2; 21:18
20. John 4:7; 19:28
21. Mark 9:16–21; John 11:34; 18:34
22. John 13:21
23. Mark 6:6; Luke 7:9
24. Luke 10:21–24; John 15:11; 17:13; Heb. 12:2, 22
25. Matt. 7:6; 23:24; Mark 4:21
26. Mark 1:41; Luke 7:13
27. John 11:3–5
28. Mark 12:41–44
29. Matt. 19:13–15
30. Luke 2:41
31. Matt. 11:19
32. John 19:26–27
33. For more technical insights on this, read Millard Erickson's *The Word Became Flesh: A Contemporary Incarnational Christology* (Grand Rapids, MI: Baker Books, 1996).
34. Creflo Dollar, *Changing Your World*, TBN, December 8, 2002, quoted in Bob Hunter, "Christianity Still in Crisis: A Word of Faith Update," *Christian Research Journal*, 30, no. 3 (2007): 16.
35. Watch the video clips of Dollar's sermon "Jesus' Growth into Sonship" (December 8, 15, 2002) on YouTube: http://www.youtube.com/watch?v=Kq3y1Bw5Y6Q and http://www.youtube.com/watch?v=JONZ4BVcFo8 (emphasis added).
36. Watch Tower Bible and Tract Society of Pennsylvania, "The Truth About Angels," *What Can Angels Do for You?* Watchtower Society online edition, November 1, 1995, http://www.watchtower.org/library/w/1995/11/1/ article_02.htm.

37. For example, Matt. 4:1–10; Mark 1:12–13; Luke 4:1–13; Heb. 2:18; 4:15.
38. 1 Tim. 2:5
39. Dietrich Bonhoeffer, *Christ the Center* (New York: Harper, 1978), 92.
40. Quoted in G. C. Berkouwer, *The Person of Christ*, trans. John Vriend (Grand Rapids, MI: Eerdmans, 1954), 94.
41. Gen. 1:27; 2 Cor. 4:4
42. Mark 2:1–7
43. Ps. 139:7–12; Matt. 28:20
44. Isa. 37:16; 44:24; John 1:3; Col. 1:16; Heb. 1:2
45. Joel 2:32; Rom. 10:9–13
46. Isa. 45:21b–23; Phil. 2:10–11
47. Luke 1–2
48. Luke 3:16
49. Luke 3:21–22
50. Luke 4:1–2
51. Luke 4:14
52. Luke 4:18 cf. Isa. 61:1
53. Luke 10:21
54. Luke 11:13
55. Luke 12:12
56. Acts 1
57. Acts 2
58. Matt. 1:23
59. Donald Bloesch, *Jesus Christ: Savior and Lord* (Downers Grove, IL: InterVarsity, 1997), 56.
60. G. K. Chesterton, *Orthodoxy: The Romance of Faith* (New York: Doubleday, 1990), 160.
61. Quoted in Elton Trueblood, *The Humor of Christ* (New York: Harper & Row, 1964), 15.
62. For example, Elton Trueblood's *The Humor of Christ* and Douglas Wilson's *A Serrated Edge*.
63. Elton Trueblood, *The Humor of Christ*, 10.
64. Ibid., 15.
65. Matt. 19:23–24; Mark 10:25; Luke 18:25
66. Leland Ryken, James C. Wilhoit, and Tremper Longman III, eds. *Dictionary of Biblical Imagery* (Downers Grove, IL: InterVarsity, 1998), s.v. "Humor—Jesus as Humorist," 410.
67. Matt. 16:16–18
68. Matt. 23:33
69. John 8:44
70. Luke 11:42
71. Matt. 6:5
72. Matt. 6:16
73. See Isa. 42:3.
74. For more on this, read Philip Yancey's *The Jesus I Never Knew* (Grand Rapids, MI: Zondervan, 1995).
75. For more, read Mark Galli's *Jesus Mean and Wild: The Unexpected Love of an Untamable God* (Grand Rapids, MI: Baker, 2006).
76. For more, read Stephen Prothero's *American Jesus*.
77. Stephen Prothero, *American Jesus*, 94.
78. Matt. 4:1–10
79. 2 Cor. 8:9
80. John 12:6
81. Matt. 17:27
82. Matt. 8:20
83. Matt. 26:57–60
84. Matt. 26:67–68
85. Matt. 27:27–31
86. Matt. 9:11, 34; 12:2, 14, 38; 16:1
87. Mark 14:32–34; 15:34
88. Matt. 26:37
89. Matt. 8:24
90. Luke 19:41; John 11:35

91. Matt. 26:36–46
92. Matt. 26:47–50
93. Matt. 26:69–75
94. Mark 3:21; John 7:5
95. Matt. 26:42
96. Luke 22:44; John 19:34
97. Luke 23:46
98. Luke 23:34
99. See Robert S. Birchard, *Cecil B. DeMille's Hollywood* (Lexington, KY: University Press of Kentucky, 2004).
100. John 1:14; Phil. 2:5–6; Col. 2:9; 1 John 4:2
101. Douglas LeBlanc, "Falling Apart," *Christianity Today* (August 2006), http://www.christianitytoday.com/ct/2006/ august/6.51.html.
102. Isa. 53:9; John 8:46; 2 Cor. 5:21; Heb. 4:15; 7:26; 1 Pet. 1:19; 1 John 3:5
103. Luke 23:47
104. Matt. 4:1–10; Heb. 4:15
105. Heb. 5:9
106. Mark 1:21–27
107. John 2:14–17
108. Matt. 9:11
109. Mark 7:1–23

CHAPTER THREE: HOW DID PEOPLE KNOW JESUS WAS COMING?

1. Matt. 5:17–18
2. John 5:36–40
3. John 5:39–47
4. Luke 24:27, 44–45
5. Wilbur M. Smith, in Josh McDowell, *Evidence That Demands a Verdict*, vol. 1 (San Bernardino, CA: Here's Life, 1992), 22.
6. J. Dwight Pentecost, *Prophecy for Today* (Grand Rapids, MI: Zondervan, 1971), 14–15.
7. Josh McDowell, *Evidence That Demands a Verdict*, 141.
8. Blaise Pascal, *Pensées*, trans. A. J. Krailsheimer (London: Penguin, 1966), 129.
9. Thomas Paine, "Examination of the Prophecies," in William M. Van der Weyde, ed., *The Life and Works of Thomas Paine*, vol. 9 (New Rochelle, NY: Thomas Paine National Historical Association, 1925), 206.
10. Jer. 31:15–17, in 722 B.C.
11. Acts 1:5

CHAPTER FOUR: WHY DID JESUS COME TO EARTH?

1. John 3:34; 4:34; 5:23, 24, 30, 36, 37, 38; 6:29, 38, 39, 44, 57; 7:16, 28, 29, 33; 8:16, 18, 26, 29, 42; 9:4; 10:36; 11:42; 12:44, 45, 49; 13:20; 14:24; 15:21; 16:5; 17:3, 8, 18, 21, 23, 25; 20:21
2. Deut. 18:15–18
3. Acts 3:22–24
4. Matt. 5:22
5. Mark 1:22
6. John 1:1, 14
7. Mark 1:36–42
8. Heb. 3:1; 4:14
9. 1 Tim. 2:5
10. Heb. 9:26
11. Heb. 7:25
12. Matt. 20:28
13. Abraham Kuyper, *Abraham Kuyper: A Centennial Reader*, ed. James D. Bratt (Grand Rapids, MI: Eerdmans, 1998), 488.
14. Luke 11:19–21
15. Isa. 53:4

16. Ps. 22:6
17. Mark 9:12
18. 2 Cor. 5:21
19. Matt. 26:37; John 11:33; 12:27; 13:21
20. Eph. 2:8–9
21. Eph. 2:10

CHAPTER FIVE: WHY DID JESUS' MOM NEED TO BE A VIRGIN?

1. For example, Genesis 5 and 11.
2. Gal. 4:4
3. Isa. 7:14
4. Isa. 7:10–14
5. Isa. 9:6–7
6. Gen. 24:16
7. Gen. 24:43
8. Micah 5:2–3
9. Gen. 2:24
10. 1 Cor. 7:3–5
11. Matt. 12:46–50; 13:55–57; Mark 3:31–35; 6:3–4; Luke 8:19–21; John 2:12; 7:3, 5, 10; Acts 1:14; 1 Cor. 9:5; Gal. 1:19
12. Rom. 5:12–21
13. Ps. 51:5
14. Rom. 3:23
15. Luke 1:46–47
16. Luke 2:22–24 cf. Lev. 12:6–8
17. 2 Cor. 5:21; Heb. 4:15
18. Albert Mohler, "Can a Christian Deny the Virgin Birth?" http://www.albertmohler. com/ commentary_read.php?cdate=2006-12-25.
19. Rob Bell, *Velvet Elvis: Repainting the Christian Faith* (Grand Rapids, MI: Zondervan, 2006), 26.
20. Matt. 13:55; Mark 6:3; John 8:41
21. Robert Funk, *Honest to Jesus: Jesus for a New Millennium* (New York: HarperCollins, 1996), 313.
22. Acts 1:14
23. J. Gresham Machen, *The Virgin Birth of Christ* (New York: Harper & Brothers, 1930), 382.
24. Ibid., 383.
25. James Orr, *The Virgin Birth of Christ* (New York: Charles Scribner's Sons, 1907), 138.
26. *The Apology of Aristides*, trans. and ed. Rendel Harris (London: Cambridge University Press, 1893), 25.
27. William A. Jurgens, *Faith of the Early Fathers* (Collegeville, MI: Liturgical Press, 1998), ß42.
28. Machen, *The Virgin Birth of Christ*, 269.
29. Quoted in Mohler, "Can a Christian Deny the Virgin Birth?"
30. Luke 1:38
31. Acts 1:13–14
32. Donald Bloesch, *Jesus Christ: Savior and Lord* (Downers Grove, IL: InterVarsity, 1997), 86.
33. Heb. 11:17
34. John 1:14, 18; 3:16, 18
35. John 1:14, 18; 3:16, 18
36. John 1:14; 1 John 4:2–3; 2 John 1:17
37. Rom. 16:20; Rev. 12:9
38. Gordon Wenham, *Genesis 1–15*, Word Biblical Commentary (Dallas: Word, 1987), 1:80.
39. Max Wilcox, "The Promise of the 'Seed' in the New Testament and Targumim," *Journal for the Study of the New Testament* 2, no. 5 (1979): 2–20.
40. Gen. 4:25
41. Gen. 9:9
42. Gen. 12:7; 17:7; 22:17–18; 24:7; 26:4; 28:13–14; 35:12; Deut. 34:4; Ps. 105:9–11; Neh. 9:8
43. Rom. 16:20; Heb. 2:14; Rev. 12
44. Gal. 3:16

CHAPTER SIX: WHAT DID JESUS ACCOMPLISH ON THE CROSS?

1. Josephus, *Jewish War* 7.203.
2. Cicero, *Pro Rabirio* 5.16.
3. Isa. 52:14
4. Matt. 27:29
5. John 19:19
6. Isa. 53:3–4
7. "Al Qaeda Threat over Pope Speech," *CNN.com* (September 18, 2006), http://www.cnn.com/2006/WORLD/ europe/09/17/ pope.islam/index.html.
8. "NBC Cuts Madonna 'Crucifixion,'" *BBC News* (October 20, 2006), http://news.bbc.co.uk/2/hi/entertainment/ 6069260.stm.
9. Lev. 19:2; Isa. 6:3; 1 John 1:5
10. Gen. 1:31; Eccles. 7:29a
11. Gen. 2:16–17; Rom. 6:23; Eph. 2:1; Col. 2:13
12. John 8:46; Heb. 4:15; 7:26; 1 Pet. 2:22
13. Ps. 53:3, 6; Isa. 64:6; Rom. 3:23; 1 John 1:8
14. 2 Cor. 5:21
15. John 10:18; Phil. 2:8; Heb. 12:2
16. Quoted in Rhodes, *The Challenge of the Cults*, 239.
17. Isa. 53:10
18. John 15:12–13
19. Lev. 16:15
20. Hebrews; John 1:29
21. Rom. 3:23–25; 5:9; 1 Thess. 1:9–10; Heb. 2:17; 1 John 2:2; 4:10
22. For example, see Psalm 106:39; Proverbs 30:11–12; Mark 7:20.
23. Lev. 16:30; Jer. 33:8; Zech. 13:1; 1 John 1:7–9
24. Titus 2:14; Heb. 9:14
25. 2 Chron. 5:12; Eccles. 9:8; Acts 1:10; Rev. 3:4–5; 6:11; 7:9–14; 15:6; 19:8
26. John 10:17–18
27. Rev. 5:5
28. Eccles. 3:11
29. 1 Cor. 1:18; Gal. 5:11
30. Mark 8:34–35
31. Quoted in Philip Yancey, *The Jesus I Never Knew* (Grand Rapids, MI: Zondervan, 1995), 226.
32. Lev. 17:11; 1 Cor. 15:3–4; 2 Cor. 11:3–4; Gal. 1:6–9, 11–12, 15–17
33. Rom. 3:25–26
34. John 12:20–28; 13:30–32; 17:1
35. Isa. 53:10; Eph. 1:3–14; Heb. 2:2
36. Rom. 11:33–36; 1 Cor. 1:7–2:5
37. Lev. 4:13–20; 16; 17:11; Deut. 29:22–29; Matt. 26:26–29; Mark 14:22–25; Luke 22:19–20; John 1:29, 36; Rom. 3:23–25; 5:8–10; 1 Cor. 11:23–25; Eph. 5:2; Heb. 7:9; 9:11–28; 10:10, 12; 1 Pet. 1:18–19; 1 John 1:5–8; Rev. 1:5
38. Pss. 32:1–5; 130; Luke 7:47; 18:9–14; Acts 10:43; Rom. 3:24; 4:5, 23; 5:16; 10:8; 1 John 1:7–22
39. Ex. 6:2–8; 15:1–18; Deut. 7:8; 15:15; 2 Sam. 7:23; 1 Chron. 17:21; Neh. 1:10; Ps. 74:2; 77:15; Isa. 43:11; Jer. 31:11; Titus 2:14; Heb. 2:14–15; 9:12; 1 Pet. 1:18–19; Rev. 1:5
40. Rom. 5:18; 6:6; 8:1–4; 1 Pet. 2:24
41. Rom. 8:1
42. Gal. 3:13
43. Rom. 7:1–5; 1 Cor. 9:20–24; Eph. 2:15; Col. 2:14–23
44. Col. 1:13–17; 2:13–15
45. Isa. 59:2; Hos. 5:6; Rom. 5:10–11; 2 Cor. 5:18–21; Eph. 2:16; Col. 1:22; 1 Pet. 3:18
46. Ps. 110:1; Luke 4:1–13; John 12:31; 16:11; Acts 26:18; Rom. 6:14; 7:4; 8:2, 20–23, 37–39; Col. 1:13; Heb. 2:14–15
47. Mark 10:45; 1 Tim. 2:5–6
48. Rom. 4:5–6; 5:17–19; 10:4; 1 Cor. 1:30; 2 Cor. 5:21; Phil. 3:9; 1 Pet. 2:24; 3:18
49. Matt. 16:24–25; 2 Cor. 5:14–21; Phil. 2:5–8; 1 Pet. 2:19–25; 1 John 3:16; 4:9–11

50. John Calvin, "Commentary on John 13:31," in *The Gospel According to St. John*, ed. David and Thomas Torrance, trans. T. H. L. Parker (Grand Rapids, MI: Eerdmans, 1959), 68.
51. John 19:30
52. 2 Cor. 5:21; Col. 2:13–15
53. Luke 23:43
54. Luke 16:22
55. Luke 24:46–47; Acts 2:23–47; 13:26–39; Rom. 4:24–25; 1 Cor. 15:1–4
56. 2 Cor. 5:14–21

CHAPTER SEVEN: DID JESUS RISE FROM DEATH?

1. *Playboy* interview (January 2000), http://www.celebatheists.com/index.php?title=Hugh_Hefner.
2. Isa. 53:8–12
3. Matt. 12:38–40; Mark 8:31; 9:31; 10:33–34; John 2:18–22
4. Mary Baker Eddy, *Science and Health with Key to the Scripture* (Boston: First Church of Christ, 1934), 46.
5. John 19:34–35
6. Isa. 53:9
7. Matt. 27:57–60
8. Matt. 28:9
9. John 20:17
10. John 20:20–28
11. Luke 24:36–43
12. William Lane Craig, "Did Jesus Rise from the Dead?" in *Jesus Under Fire*, ed. J. P. Moreland and Michael J. Wilkins (Grand Rapids, MI: Zondervan, 1996).
13. Mark 14:53, 54, 60, 61, 63
14. J. P. Moreland, *Scaling the Secular City* (Grand Rapids, MI: Baker, 1987), 172.
15. Quoted in Richard N. Ostling, "Who Was Jesus?" *Time*, August 15, 1988, 41.
16. John 7:5
17. 1 Cor. 15:7
18. James 1:1
19. Acts 12:17; 15:12–21; 21:18; Gal. 2:9
20. Acts 1:14
21. Acts 1:14; Jude 1
22. Phil. 3:4–6; Acts 7:54–60
23. Acts 9
24. John 20:19
25. Simon Greenleaf, *The Testimony of the Evangelists: The Gospels Examined by the Rules of Evidence Administered in Courts of Justice* (Grand Rapids, MI: Kregel, 1995), 32.
26. Acts 20:7; 1 Cor. 16:1–2
27. Pliny, *Letters*, trans. William Melmoth (Cambridge: Harvard University Press 1935), 2:10.96.
28. Lucian, "The Death of Peregrine," in *The Works of Lucian of Samosata*, trans. H. W. Fowler and F. G. Fowler (Oxford: Clarendon, 1949), 4:11–13.
29. Mark 15:40, 47; 16:1
30. Murray J. Harris, *Raised Immortal: Resurrection and Immortality in the New Testament* (Grand Rapids, MI: Eerdmans, 1985), 40.
31. Edwin Yamauchi, "Easter: Myth, Hallucination, or History? Part One," *Christianity Today* 18, no. 12, March 15, 1974, 4–7.
32. James D. G. Dunn, *The Christ and the Spirit* (Grand Rapids, MI: Eerdmans, 1998), 67–68.
33. Acts 4:27
34. Flavius Josephus, "Jewish Antiquities," in *The New Complete Works of Josephus*, trans. William Whiston (Grand Rapids, MI: Kregel, 1999), 18.63–64 (emphasis added).
35. Suetonius, *Vita Nero* 16.11–13
36. Pliny the Younger, *Letters* 10.96.1–7
37. Matt. 28:13–15
38. Kenneth L. Woodward, "2000 Years of Jesus," *Newsweek*, March 29, 1999, 54.

39. John 5:16–30
40. John Stott, *Basic Christianity* (Grand Rapids, MI: InterVarsity, 1971), 49.
41. C. Truman Davis, "The Crucifixion of Jesus: The Passion of Christ from a Medical Point of View," *Arizona Medicine* (March 1965): 183–87.
42. Matt. 28:11–15
43. John 20:24–28
44. Edwin Yamauchi, "Easter: Myth, Hallucination, or History?" *Christianity Today* 18, nos. 12 and 13, March 15, 1974, and March 29, 1974, 4–7 and 12–16.
45. Richard N. Ostling, "Jesus Christ, Plain and Simple," *Time*, January 10, 1994, 32–33.
46. 1 Cor. 15:1–6
47. For example, Dan. 12:2.
48. William Lane Craig, "Did Jesus Rise from the Dead?" in *Jesus Under Fire*, 159–60.

CHAPTER EIGHT: WHERE IS JESUS TODAY?

1. Philip Yancey, *The Jesus I Never Knew* (Grand Rapids, MI: Zondervan, 1995), 230.
2. Quoted in Prothero, *American Jesus*, 28.
3. Robert W. Funk, Roy W. Hoover, and The Jesus Seminar, *The Five Gospels: What Did Jesus Really Say?* (New York: HarperCollins, 1993), 5.
4. John 6:62; 14:2, 12; 16:5, 10, 28; 20:17
5. John Dominic Crossan, *Jesus: A Revolutionary Biography* (New York: HarperCollins, 1994), 198.
6. Isa. 6:1b–5
7. John 12:41
8. Yancey, *The Jesus I Never Knew*, 226.
9. Rev. 1:1
10. 1 Cor. 15:3–8; Acts 1:1–3
11. Acts 1:9–11
12. John 16:28
13. Luke 16:19–31; Rev. 20:13–14
14. Gen. 14:22; Ezek. 17:18; Dan. 12:7
15. Gen. 48:17–20
16. Ps. 48:10
17. Pss. 80:15–16; 89:13
18. 1 Kings 2:19; Ps. 45:9
19. Acts 2:33–36; Eph. 1:20–22; Heb. 1:3; 10:12; 12:1–2; 1 Pet. 3:22
20. Matt. 26:64
21. Matt. 11:27; John 3:35; Acts 10:36; Eph. 1:22; Col. 1:17–18
22. 1 Cor. 6:3
23. Eph. 6:10–13; James 4:7; 1 Pet. 5:8
24. 2 Cor. 5:1–8
25. 1 Cor. 15
26. John 14:2–3
27. Ps. 19:1; Rom. 1:20
28. Rom. 8:19–21
29. Isa. 65:17; 66:22; 2 Pet. 3:12–13
30. Rev. 21:1–2
31. I want to thank Dr. Tim Keller for many conversations over meals throughout the past years in which he has really helped me to understand God's urban vision for his people.
32. For example, see his books *The Victory of Reason*, *Cities of God*, and *The Rise of Christianity*.
33. For example, see his book *The First Urban Christians*.
34. Matt. 28:18–20
35. For example, see Acts 13:33 or Hebrews 5:5.
36. Phil. 3:20; Eph. 2:12
37. John 16:33
38. Amos 5:24
39. Titus 2:12–14

40. Col. 1:12–14
41. Eph. 1:19–22
42. Acts 1:8, 22; 26:16; Rom. 1:9
43. F. F. Bruce, *The Epistle to the Hebrews* (Grand Rapids, MI: Eerdmans, 1990), 333.

CHAPTER NINE: WHY SHOULD WE WORSHIP JESUS?

1. Eph. 5:19–20; Col. 3:16
2. A. W. Tozer, *The Tozer Pulpit* (Camp Hill, PA: Christian Publications, 1994), 1:51.
3. Ex. 20:1–6
4. Peter Kreeft, *Christianity for Modern Pagans* (San Francisco: Ignatius Press, 1993), 50.
5. Rom. 1:21–25
6. Eric Schlosser, "The Business of Pornography," *US News and World Report,* February 10, 1997, http://www.usnews.com/usnews/biztech/articles/970210/archive_006163_10.htm.
7. "American Porn: Corporate America Is Profiting from Porn—Quietly," *ABC News,* May 27, 2004.
8. Ralph Frammolino and P. J. Huffstutter, "The Actress, the Producer and Their Porn Revolution," *Los Angeles Times,* January 6, 2002.
9. "American Porn: Corporate America Is Profiting from Porn—Quietly," *ABC News*; Ralph Frammolino and P. J. Huffstutter, "The Actress, the Producer and Their Porn Revolution."
10. "American Porn: Corporate America is Profiting from Porn—Quietly," *ABC News.*
11. Candi Dushman, "Stop Pretending" *World Magazine,* August 5, 2000.
12. "Alexa Research Finds 'Sex' Popular on the Web," *Business Wire,* February 14, 2001.
13. Eric Retzlaff, "Pornography's Grip Tightens by Way of Internet," *National Catholic Register,* June 13–19, 2000.
14. For example, see "Putting Flesh on Phones," *Wired,* Daniel Terdiman, April 8, 2005, http://www.wired.com/gadgets/wireless/news/2005/04/67165.
15. Alvin Cooper, Dana E. Putnam, Lynn A. Planchon, and Sylvain C. Boies, "Online Sexual Compulsivity: Getting Tangled in the Net," *Sexual Addiction and Compulsivity,* 6 (2): 79–104.
16. American Academy of Pediatrics, Committee on Public Education, "Sexuality, Contraception, and the Media," *Pediatrics* 107, no. 1 (January 2001): 191–94, http://www.aap.org/policy/re0038.html.
17. Ibid.
18. Ibid.
19. Ibid.
20. Ibid.
21. Gen. 3:5
22. John 17:5, 24
23. 1 Cor. 10:31; see also 1 Cor. 6:20
24. Bruce McConkie, "Our Relationship with the Lord," speech at Brigham Young University (March 2, 1982), http://speeches.byu.edu/reader/reader.php?id=6843.
25. Isa. 6:1–3
26. John 12:41
27. Matt. 2:11
28. John 9:38
29. Mark 5:6
30. John 20:28
31. Isa. 6:1–5 cf. John 12:41; Rev. 1:17–18
32. Matt. 14:33; 28:17
33. Matt. 28:8–9
34. Matt. 20:20
35. Heb. 1:6
36. 1 Cor. 1:2
37. Acts 1:14
38. Acts 1:14; James; Jude
39. Matt. 21:14–16 cf. Ps. 8:2

40. Rom. 9:5; Col. 1:15; 2:9; Titus 2:13
41. Kenneth L. Woodward, "2000 Years of Jesus," *Newsweek*, March 29, 1999, 54.
42. Rev. 21:22–23
43. Matt. 5:17. The book of Hebrews is most helpful in explaining this in great detail.
44. John 1:14
45. John 2:19–22; Rev. 21:22
46. Heb. 3:1
47. John 1:29
48. Ps. 95:6
49. Ps. 47:1
50. Neh. 8:6; Pss. 28:2; 63:4; 134:2; 141:2; 143:6; Lam. 2:19; 3:41; 1 Tim. 2:8
51. Isa. 1:16–17
52. Gen. 1:26–28
53. Ex. 20:3–5. See Cornelius Plantinga, "Not As They Seem," *Perspectives*, January 6, 1991, 7–9.

CHAPTER TEN: WHAT MAKES JESUS SUPERIOR TO OTHER SAVIORS?

1. Emily Smith, "Cruise 'Is Christ' of Scientology," *The Sun Online* (January 23, 2007), http://www.thesun.co.uk/article/0,,4-2007030603,00.html.
2. Matt. 1:21
3. Luke 2:11
4. Luke 2:28–30
5. Acts 5:30–31
6. Eph. 5:23
7. 1 John 4:14
8. Luke 19:10
9. 1 Tim. 1:15–17
10. Rom. 10:13
11. Quoted in John Fritscher, "Straight from the Witch's Mouth," in Arthur C. Lehmann and James E. Meyers, eds., *Magic, Witchcraft, and Religion*, 4th ed. (Mountainview, CA: Mayfield, 1996), 389.
12. Matt. 1:21
13. 2 Tim. 1:10
14. 2 Thess. 2:6–10
15. Rom. 5:9
16. Rom. 5:9–10
17. Rom. 2:5; 3:5; 5:9; Eph. 5:6; Col. 3:6; 1 Thess. 1:10
18. Acts 4:12
19. Matt. 7:13–14
20. Luke 13:23–25
21. John 14:6
22. David Powlison's resources, some of which include these questions, are available at http://www.ccef.org.
23. Phil. 3:20; Titus 2:11–14
24. Ex. 20:3–5
25. Ex. 12:12
26. For example, Deut. 12:31; Ps. 106:36–40; 2 Kings 21:1–9.
27. 1 Kings 18
28. Matt. 12:22–30; Eph. 1:18–23; Col. 2:13–15
29. Rev. 20:1–3

CHAPTER ELEVEN: WHAT DIFFERENCE HAS JESUS MADE IN HISTORY?

1. Jaroslav Pelikan, *Jesus through the Centuries: His Place in the History of Culture* (New Haven, CT: Yale University Press, 1999).
2. Stephen Prothero, *American Jesus: How the Son of God Became a National Icon* (New York: Farrar, Straus & Giroux, 2003).
3. Kenneth L. Woodward, "2000 Years of Jesus," *Newsweek*, March 29, 1999, 54.

4. Ibid., 63.
5. Quoted in F. F. Bruce, *Jesus: Lord and Savior* (Downers Grove, IL: InterVarsity, 1986), 15.
6. Michael Stipe, quoted in *Rolling Stone*, January 6, 2000, in Dick Staub, *The Culturally Savvy Christian* (San Francisco: Jossey-Bass, 2007), xii.
7. Quoted in Peter Kreeft, *Three Philosophies of Life* (San Francisco: Ignatius, 1989), 20.
8. D. James Kennedy and Jerry Newcombe, *What If Jesus Had Never Been Born?* (Nashville: Thomas Nelson, 2005).
9. Matt. 7:11
10. Matt. 9:23–25
11. Matt. 11:25
12. Matt. 14:21
13. Matt. 18:3; 19:14
14. Matt. 18:5–6
15. Matt. 19:13
16. Matt. 19:14
17. Matt. 17:14–18
18. Matt. 21:15
19. Rom. 8:12–23; Gal. 4:1–7; Eph. 1:5
20. Gen. 1:26–27
21. John 4:7–26
22. Luke 7:12–13
23. Matt. 9:20–22; Luke 8:40–56; 13:10–17
24. Matt. 25:1–10; Luke 4:26; 18:1–5; 21:1–4
25. Luke 10:38–42; 23:27–31; John 20:10–18
26. Luke 7:36–50
27. Luke 10:38–39
28. Luke 8:1–3
29. Matt. 28:1–10
30. Quoted in Woodward, "2000 Years of Jesus," *Newsweek*, 57–58.
31. Philem. 10–19
32. Kennedy and Newcombe, *What if Jesus Had Never Been Born?* 46.
33. Ibid., 70.
34. Luke 4:23; 5:31
35. Matt. 11:5; 19:21; Luke 4:18; 6:20
36. Matt. 14:14–21; 15:32–38
37. Arthur C. Brooks, *Who Really Cares: The Surprising Truth about Compassionate Conservatism* (New York: Basic Books, 2006).
38. Quoted in Frank Brieaddy, "Philanthropy Expert: Conservatives Are More Generous," *Beliefnet.com*, (2006), http://www.beliefnet.com/story/204/story_20419_1.html.
39. For further study of this issue, the book *Christianity on Trial: Arguments against Anti-Religious Bigotry* by Vincent Carrol and David Shiflett is most helpful.
40. "When Elton Met Jake," *Observer Music Monthly* (November 12, 2006), http://observer.guardian.co.uk/omm/ story/0,,1942193,00.html.
41. D. James Kennedy and Jerry Newcombe, *What if Jesus Had Never Been Born?* 225.
42. Ibid.
43. D. James Kennedy and Jerry Newcombe, *What if Jesus Had Never Been Born?* 235.
44. Matt. 5:43–46; 22:37–39; John 13:34–35
45. Matt. 25:31–46
46. Prothero, *American Jesus*, 11.
47. Philip Yancey, *The Jesus I Never Knew* (Grand Rapids, MI: Zondervan, 1995), 20.
48. Debate at Trinity Episcopal Cathedral's Center for Spiritual Development, Portland, OR (http://www.center-for-spiritual-development.org), based on material in Marcus J. Borg and N. T. Wright, *Meaning of Jesus: Two Visions* (San Francisco: Harper, 2000). Wright's arguments are presented in greater depth in *The Resurrection of the Son of God* (Minneapolis, MN: Augsburg Fortress, 2003).

CHAPTER TWELVE: WHAT WILL JESUS DO UPON HIS RETURN?

1. Matt. 24:44; John 14:3
2. Acts 1:11
3. 1 Thess. 4:16
4. James 5:8
5. 2 Pet. 3:10
6. 1 John 3:2; Rev. 1:7; 22:20
7. Heb. 9:28
8. Matt. 24:44; Titus 2:12–13; Rev. 22:20
9. Matt. 24:44; 25:13; Luke 12:40
10. John 5:19–29; Acts 10:42; 2 Tim. 4:1
11. This information is largely summarized from *VH1 News Presents: Jenna Jameson's Confessions,* http://www.vh1.com/shows/dyn/vh1_news_presents/85657/episode_about.jhtml.
12. Eccles. 12:14; Matt. 12:36; Luke 12:2–3, 47–48; 20:47; Rom. 2:5–7; Rev. 20:12–13
13. Matt. 8:11–12, 29; 13:40–42; 18:8–9; 22:13; 24:50–51; 25:30, 41, 46; Mark 9:43–48; Luke 12:46–48; 16:19–31
14. Bertrand Russell, *Why I Am Not a Christian* (New York: Simon & Schuster, 1957), 17.
15. Rev. 14:9–11
16. Brian D. McLaren, *The Last Word and the Word after That* (San Francisco: Jossey-Bass, 2005).
17. Christopher Goffard, "Father, Son and Holy Rift," *Los Angeles Times,* September 2, 2006.
18. Ibid.
19. Keith Morrison, "Hell, You Say?" *MSNBC Dateline* (August 10, 2006), http://www.msnbc.msn.com/id /14274572/.
20. John 11:25; 14:6
21. Eph. 2:8–9
22. Eph. 2:10
23. Matt. 25:31–46; Luke 19:17–19; Rom. 2:6–11; 8:1; 14:10–12; 1 Cor. 4:5; 2 Cor. 5:9–10; Col. 3:25; Rev. 11:18
24. Rev. 20:12–15
25. Matt. 25:21, 23; Luke 19:17
26. Rev. 22:3
27. Gen. 2:16–17; Rom. 6:23
28. 1 Cor. 15:35–58
29. 1 Cor. 15:36–41
30. 1 Cor. 15:42–44
31. 1 Cor. 15:45–49
32. 1 Cor. 15:50
33. 1 Cor. 15:51–57
34. Kenneth L. Woodward, "2000 Years of Jesus," *Newsweek,* March 29, 1999, 55.
35. Isa. 9:6
36. Isa. 2:1–3
37. Isa. 2:4
38. Isa. 11:1–12:6
39. Isa. 32:1–8, 15–20
40. Isa. 60:1–22
41. Isa. 65:17–25
42. Joel 2:24–27
43. Phil. 1:20–25
44. Phil. 3:20
45. Gen. 5:24; Heb. 11:5
46. Rev. 19:6–9
47. Acts 2:42–47
48. Rev. 21:3
49. Matt. 11:24
50. Ezek. 18:23

SUBJECT INDEX

addictions, 175–76
advertising, 189
agnosticism, 188
America, Christian influences upon, 207
angel, Jesus as, 28–29
Apostles' Creed, 38, 123
Arians, 95
art, 199, 209
atheism, 188
atonement, 112, 114–15, 118–19
atrocities, 210–11
Augustine, 36, 96, 113
authority, in Jesus' name, 156

Baal, 195–96
Bahá'ís, 14, 148
baptism, 124, 138
Barna, George, 83
Barton, Bruce, 32
Bell, Rob, 97–98
blasphemy, 21, 22, 23
blessed hope, 160
Bloesch, Donald, 38
blood, 116
Bonhoeffer, Dietrich, 36
boredom, in worship, 177
Borg, Marcus, 213
Brooks, Arthur C., 209
Brown, Dan, 30, 50
Bruce, Lenny, 112
Buddha, 18, 22, 188
Buddhism, 14–15, 21, 183

Caiaphas, 133
Campus Crusade for Christ, 48
Carter, Jimmy, 230
cell phone, 169
Celsus, 20
charity, 209–10
Chesterton, G. K., 39
children, 2023
Chopra, Deepak, 14
Christ (title), 11
Christian (name), 120
Christian Science, 21, 131
Christlikeness, 86
Christmas, 73, 89
Christology, 150
christophanies, 18
Chronicles of Narnia, 118
church, 139, 185
city, 157–58
colleges and universities, 206
Collins, Francis, 208
Confucianism, 183
consumerism, 195
conversion, 223
Council of Chalcedon, 36, 45, 50
Council of Nicaea, 208
creeds, of the church, 134
cross, 111–12, 115, 119–20, 121
Crossan, John Dominic, 146, 149
crucifixion, 107–10, 117–18, 121, 143
cults, 14, 27
culture, 158
curse, 161, 224–25

Dalai Lama, 15, 18–19
Da Vinci Code (book and film), 12, 30, 34, 50, 149
Day of Atonement, 116
day of judgment, 223
death, 113, 187, 224, 225–26
DeMille, Cecil B., 46
demons, 16, 20
designer religions, 195
disciples, 135–36, 146
diversity, 188
Dollar, Creflo, 35
Douglas, Lloyd, 46
Dunant, Henri, 209
Dunn, James D. G., 139

earth, age of, 70
Ebionites, 98
economics, 199, 208
Eddy, Mary Baker, 21, 131
education, 205–7

Edwards, James, 214
emotions, 44
empty tomb, 138, 144
eternal punishment, 222
evangelicalism, 82–83
evolution, 70

fact and faith, 130
false gods, 195–97
false saviors, 189–92
false worship, 167–71
films, about Jesus, 45–49
flesh, 50
forgiveness, 25, 124
Freemasonry, 14
fundamentalism, 82, 124
Funk, Robert, 97

Gandhi, Mahatma, 15, 22, 24
Gibson, Mel, 48
glorification, 156, 225–27
glory, 166, 171
Gnostics, 98
God, as alone savior, 183–84; holiness of, 113; love of, 122, 125–26
Godspell (film), 47
good works, 86–87, 224
gospel, 111
Gospel According to Matthew, The (film), 47
Gospel of Judas, 213
Gospel of Thomas, 212–13
grace, 86, 232–33
Graham, Billy, 19, 24
Greeks, 103, 151
Greenleaf, Simon, 135

Habermas, Gary, 214
happiness, 174
heaven, 151, 155, 189–92, 220–21, 223
heavenly citizenship, 160
Hefner, Hugh, 129–30
hell, 122–23, 189–92, 220–23, 232–33
Hinduism, 15, 18, 103, 164, 183, 188
Hitler, Adolf, 108, 232
Holy Spirit, 37–38
homosexuals, 13
Human Genome Project, 208
humor, 39–41
hypostatic union, 36

idolatry, 167–71
image of God, 36, 42, 113, 119
Immanuel, 38
incarnation, 149–50
Irenaeus, 95
Islam, 15, 183

James (Jesus' half-brother), 134
Jameson, Jenna, 219–20
Jefferson, Thomas, 148
Jehovah's Witnesses, 14, 21, 28–29, 34, 95, 132, 148
Jesus, ascension of, 151–61, 228; authority of, 153, 155, 158–59; became our sin, 114; birth of, 11–12; burial of, 132–33; death of, 29, 107–12, 114–16, 121–22, 123–24; descent into hell, 122–23; divinity of, 18–19, 21–23, 28–30, 33–37, 45, 95; effect on history, 65–66, 199–214; fulfillment of prophecies, 71–72; humanity of, 31–54; humility of, 78; humor of, 39–41; incarnation of, 17–18, 30, 37, 50; intercession of, 154–55; as King, 78–79, 81, 160; learned obedience, 52, 53; name of, 11; as object of worship, 137; as passionate, 41–44; as person, 50–51; as priest, 76–78, 81; as prophet, 74–75, 81; public ministry of, 11–12; resurrection of, 123–24, 129–46, 228; return of, 72, 142, 160, 216–17, 229, 232–33; as savior, 184–93, 194–97; sinlessness of, 23–24, 85–86, 113; suffering of, 44–45, 52; temptations of, 36, 54
Jesus Christ Superstar (film), 47
Jesus Film, The, 48
Jesus of Nazareth (film), 47
Jesus Seminar, 97, 146, 148, 212–13
Jews, 141–42, 185
John, Elton, 210
Josephus, 108, 140
Judaism, 183
Jude (Jesus' half-brother), 134
justice, 218, 222
justification, 86, 124

Kennedy, D. James, 202
Koresh, David, 27
Kreeft, Peter, 167
Krishna, 22
Kuyper, Abraham, 78–79

Last Temptation of Christ, The (film), 48
LaVey, Anton, 186
law, observances of, 138
Lecky, W. E. H., 200
legalism, 82
Lennon, John, 13
Lewis, C. S., 26
liar, lunatic, or Lord, 26–27
liberalism, 83–84, 124
Lincoln, Abraham, 205
Lucian of Samosata, 137
Luther, Martin, 100, 167

Machen, J. Gresham, 98
Madonna, 112
Mandela, Nelson, 207
Marcion, 42
marketing, 189
marriage, 94–95
Mary, 93–95, 96, 97–100, 102, 134
McDowell, Josh, 67
McLaren, Brian, 222
mediation, of Jesus, 154–55
medicine, 208–9
Meeks, Wayne, 157
Mencia, Carlos, 39–40
mercy, 204–5, 218
Messiah, 59, 71–72, 103–5
millennial kingdom, 160
miracles, 20–21
Miscavige, David, 183
misery, 175
Mohler, Al, 97
Monty Python, 48
moralism, 82
Mormonism, 14, 34, 96, 102, 149, 172, 217
Mother Teresa, 24
Muhammad, 17, 22, 24
music, 165
Muslims, 144, 149

naturalism, 20
Nazirite vow, 31
near-death experiences, 17
New Agers, 35, 183
Newcombe, Jerry, 202
new creation, 156, 232
Nicene Creed, 123
Nietzsche, Friedrich, 39

obedience, 179
occult, 14
Old Testament, 56–69, 73, 90–93, 138, 177
only begotten Son, 101

pagans, 121, 157
Paglia, Camille, 40
Paine, Thomas, 68, 148
paradise, 156–58
Pascal, Blaise, 67
Pasolini, Pier Paolo, 47
Passion of Christ, The (film), 12, 48
Paul, 135, 168, 185–86
penal substitutionary atonement, 114–15, 118–19, 122
Pentecost, J. Dwight, 67
persecution, 160
pets, 169
pictures of Jesus, 32
Plantinga, Cornelius, 179
Pliny the Younger, 137, 141
politics, 199
Pol Pot, 108
poor, 209
popular culture, on Jesus, 12–13, 147–48, 199
pornography, 169–70, 219–20
Powlison, David, 192
prayer, to Jesus, 25
pride, 113
priests, 76–78
promise and fulfillment, 56–65, 71, 73–74
property rights, 208
prophets, 74–75
propitiation, 117, 122
protoevangelium, 104

purgatory, 152
Puritans, 206

Rad, Gerhard von, 74
Rana, Fazale, 70
reconciliation, 126
Red Cross, 209
regeneration, 123
repentance, 219
resurrection, 145, 151, 225–27
rewards, 223–24
right hand of God, 152
Rodgers, John, 133
Ross, Hugh, 70
Russell, Bertrand, 221

Sabbath, 136–37
sacrifice, 166–67
Sallman, Warner, 32
salvation, 86–87
Satan, 187
savior, in pop culture, 181–83
scapegoat, 117
Schaberg, Jane, 99
science, 130, 199, 207–8
Scientology, 14, 183
Scorsese, Martin, 48
Seattle, 120, 169
Second Council of Constantinople, 94
Septuagint, 104
sexual addiction, 170
sexual intimacy, 94–95
shalom, 228–31
sin, 23–25, 113–14, 116–17, 125–26, 186, 224–25, 227
singing, 178
sins, of Christianity, 210–11
slaves, 205
Smith, Chuck, 222
Son of Man, 19
Stark, Rodney, 157, 204, 228
Stern, Howard, 210
Stevens, George, 46–47
Stipe, Michael, 201
Stott, John, 143
substitution. *See* penal substitutionary atonement
Suentonius, 140
Sunday, 136
Sunday, Billy, 42
swoon theory, 143–44

Talmud, 20
technology, 169
temptation, 54
Ten Commandments, 195, 208
Tertullian, 95, 111
theology of the cross, 119
throne, of Jesus, 153
toll, 225
tolerance, 188
Toynbee, Arnold, 201
Tozer, A. W., 166
Trinity, 102, 171
Trueblood, Elton, 40

Unitarian Universalism, 14, 20,115

virgin birth, 89–101, 103
Vision Nationals Ministries, 203
Vulgate, 104

war, 200
Wells, David, 200
Wilberforce, William, 205
Wink, Walter, 120
Witherington, Ben, 214
witness, 161
women, 203–4
World Vision, 205
worship, 165–67, 171–79
wrath of God, 114, 187
Wright, N. T., 213
Wycliffe, John, 206

Yancey, Philip, 147

SCRIPTURE INDEX

Genesis

Book of	92, 148
1:1	28
1:26–27	246n11:20
1:26–28	245n9:52
1:27	238n2:41
1:31	241n6:10
2:7	227
2:16–17	241n6:11, 247n12:27
2:24	240n5:9
3	224
3:5	244n9:21
3:15	57, 90, 103, 104, 105
4	224
4:25	240n5:40
5	70, 240n5:1
5:24	247n12:45
9:9	240n5:41
11	70, 240n5:1
12:3	57
12:7	240n5:42
14:22	243n8:14
17:7	240n5:42
17:19	57
22:17–18	240n5:42
24:7	240n5:42
24:16	240n5:6
24:43	240n5:7
26:4	240n5:42
28:13–14	240n5:42
32	235n1:18
35:12	240n5:42
48:17–20	243n8:15
49:10	58

Exodus

6:2–8	241n6:39
12:12	245n10:25
12:46	63
15:1–18	241n6:39
20:1–6	236n1:60, 244n9:3
20:3–5	245n9:53, n10:24
34:6	125
34:6–7	197

Leviticus

Book of	116
4:13–20	241n6:37
12:6–8	240n5:16
16	241n6:37
16:15	241n6:19
16:30	241n6:23
17:11	241n6:32, n6:37
19:2	241n6:9

Numbers

6	237n2:2
24:17	58

Deuteronomy

7:8	241n6:39
12:31	245n10:26
15:15	241n6:39
18:15–18	239n4:2
21:22–23	107
22:14–22	91
29:22–29	241n6:37
32:15–21	195
34:4	240n5:42

Joshua

5:13–14	235n1:19

1 Samuel

16	160

2 Samuel

7:23	241n6:39

1 Kings

2:19	243n8:18
18	245n10:27

2 Kings

21:1–9	245n10:26

1 Chronicles

17:21	241n6:39

2 Chronicles

5:12	241n6:25

Nehemiah

1:10	241n6:39
8:6	245n9:50
9:8	240n5:42

Job

9:8	28
26:12	236n1:32
38:8	236n1:32

Psalms

Book of	183
8:2	236n1:72, 244n9:39
16:10	64
18:2	236n1:78
19:1	243n8:27
22:1	63
22:6	240n4:16
22:16	62
22:18	61
23:1	237n1:80
27:1	236n1:77
28:2	245n9:50
32:1–5	241n6:38
33:7	236n1:32
34:20	63
41:9	61
45:9	243n8:18
47:1	245n9:49
48:10	243n8:16
51:4	236n1:50
51:5	240n5:13
53:3, 6	241n6:13
63:4	245n9:50
65:7	236n1:32
68:18	64
74:2	241n6:39
77:15	241n6:39
80:15–16	243n8:17
9:9	236n1:32
89:13	243n8:17
95:1	236n1:78
95:6	245n9:48
97:9	195
104:7–9	236n1:32
105:9–11	240n5:42
106:36–40	245n10:26
106:39	241n6:22
107:28–30	236n1:32
110	19
110:1	64, 152, 241n6:46
130	122, 241n6:38
130:4	236n1:51

130:7 — 237n1:81
134:2 — 245n9:50
135:7 — 236n11:32
139:7–12 — 238n2:43
141:2 — 245n9:50
143:6 — 245n9:50

Proverbs
30:11–12 — 241n6:22

Ecclesiastes
Book of — 225
3:4 — 39
3:11 — 241n6:28
7:13 — 225
7:29a — 241n6:10
9:8 — 241n6:25
12:14 — 247n12:12

Song of Solomon
Book of — 95

Isaiah
Book of — 38, 100, 183
1 — 178
1:16–17 — 245n9:51
2:1–3 — 247n12:36
2:4 — 247n12:37
6:1–3 — 244n9:25
6:1–5 — 236n1:64, 244n9:31
6:1–8 — 235n1:20
6:3 — 241n6:9
6:9–11 — 236n1:75
7:10–14 — 240n5:4
7:14 — 58, 89, 91, 92, 95, 98, 103, 240n5:3
9:6 — 247n12:35
9:6–7 — 240n5:5
11:1–12:6 — 247n12:38
20:28–29 — 236n1:75
32:1–8, 15–20 — 247n12:39
35:5–6 — 60
37:16 — 238n2:44
40:3 — 60
41:4 — 236n1:76
41:21–24 — 65
42:3 — 238n2:73
42:8 — 237n1:83
43:3 — 237n1:82
43:11 — 183, 241n6:39
44:6 — 236n1:76
44:24 — 28, 238n2:44
45:21 — 183–84
45:21b — 238n2:46
48:12 — 236n1:76
50:6 — 61
52:14 — 241n6:3
53:2 — 237n2:10
53:3 — 44, 62
53:3–4 — 241n6:6
53:4 — 239n4:15
53:5 — 115
53:6 — 114
53:7 — 62
53:8b — 63
53:8–12 — 242n7:2
53:9 — 59, 63, 239n2:102, 242n7:6
53:10 — 241n6:17, n6:35
53:10–11 — 64
53:12 — 62, 115
59:2 — 241n6:45
60:1–22 — 247n12:40
61:1 — 238n2:52
6:1b–5 — 243n8:6
62:5 — 236n1:79
62:11 — 184

64:6 — 241n6:13
65:17 — 243n8:29
65:17–25 — 247n12:41
66:22 — 243n8:29

Jeremiah
31:11 — 241n6:39
31:15–17 — 239n3:10
31:34 — 236n1:51
33:8 — 241n6:23

Lamentations
Book of — 39, 216
2:19 — 245n9:50
3:41 — 245n9:50

Ezekiel
17:18 — 243n8:14
18:23 — 247n12:50
36 — 72
36:24–38 — 72

Daniel
Book of — 19
3:25 — 235n1:21
10 — 196
12:2 — 243n7:47
12:7 — 243n8:14

Hosea
Book of — 71
2:16 — 236n1:79
5:6 — 241n6:45
11:1 — 59
13:14 — 237n1:81

Joel
2:24–27 — 247n12:42
2:32 — 238n2:45

Amos
5:24 — 243n8:38

Jonah
1:4, 15 — 236n1:32

Micah
5:2 — 58
5:2–3 — 240n5:8
5:3 — 94

Zechariah
9:9 — 60
11:12–13 — 61
13:1 — 241n6:23

Malachi
3:1 — 59

Matthew
Gospel of — 103
1 — 70
1:1–2 — 58
1:18–23 — 58
1:18–25 — 92
1:21 — 245n10:2
1:21 — 245n10:12
1:23 — 31, 238n2:58
1:25 — 94–95
2:11 — 244n9:27
2:13–15 — 59
3:1–3 — 60
4:1–10 — 238n2:37, n2:78, 239n2:104
4:2 — 237n2:19
4:7 — 236n1:75

5:17 — 245n9:43
5:17–18 — 73, 239n3:1
5:22 — 239n4:4
5:43–46 — 246n11:44
6:5 — 238n2:71
6:16 — 238n2:72
7:6 — 237n2:25
7:11 — 246n11:9
7:13–14 — 236n1:55, 245n10:19
8:11–12, 29 — 247n12:13
8:20 — 238n2:82
8:24 — 238n2:89
9:9–13 — 77
9:11 — 239n2:108
9:11, 34 — 238n2:86
9:20–22 — 246n11:23
9:23–25 — 246n11:10
11:2–5 — 60
11:5 — 246n11:35
11:19 — 237n2:31
11:24 — 247n12:49
11:25 — 246n11:11
11:27 — 243n8:21
12:2, 14, 38 — 238n2:86
12:22–30 — 245n10:28
12:24 — 235n1:27
12:36 — 247n12:12
12:38–40 — 242n7:3
12:46–50 — 240n5:11
13:40–42 — 247n12:13
13:54–58 — 237n2:14
13:55 — 240n5:20
13:55–57 — 240n5:11
14:14–21 — 246n11:36
14:21 — 246n11:12
14:33 — 236n1:65, 244n9:32
15:25 — 236n1:54
15:32–38 — 246n11:36
16:1 — 238n2:86
16:15 — 236n1:74
16:16–18 — 238n2:67
16:24–25 — 241n6:49
17:14–18 — 246n11:17
17:27 — 238n2:81
18:3 — 246n11:13
18:5–6 — 246n11:14
18:8–9 — 247n12:13
19:13 — 246n11:15
19:13–15 — 237n2:29
19:14 — 246n11:13, n11:16
19:21 — 246n11:35
19:23–24 — 238n2:65
20:20 — 236n1:67, 244n9:34
20:28 — 239n4:12
21:14–16 — 236n1:72, 244n9:39
21:15 — 246n11:18
21:18 — 237n2:19
22:13 — 247n12:13
22:37–39 — 246n11:44
23:24 — 237n2:25
23:33 — 238n2:68
24:30 — 235n1:25
24:44 — 247n12:1, n12:8, n12:9
24:50–51 — 247n12:13
25:1–10 — 246n11:24
25:13 — 247n12:9
25:21, 23 — 247n12:25
25:30, 41, 46 — 247n12:13
25:31–46 — 246n11:45, 247n12:23
26:14–15 — 61
26:26–29 — 241n6:37
26:36–46 — 239n2:91
26:37 — 238n2:88, 240n4:19
26:42 — 239n2:95
26:47–50 — 239n2:92
26:49–50 — 61

26:57–60 — 238n2:83
26:63–65 — 23, 236n1:36
26:64 — 235n1:25, 243n8:20
26:67 — 61
26:67–68 — 238n2:84
26:69–75 — 239n2:93
27:3–4 — 236n1:46
27:5–7 — 61
27:12 — 62
27:27–31 — 238n2:85
27:29 — 241n6:4
27:38 — 62
27:39–44 — 62
27:42 — 235n1:27
27:46 — 63
27:57–60 — 63, 242n7:7
28:1–10 — 246n11:29
28:8–9 — 236n1:66, 244n9:33
28:9 — 236n1:75, 242n7:8
28:11–15 — 243n7:42
28:13–15 — 242n7:37
28:17 — 236n1:65, 244n9:32
28:18–20 — 243n8:34
28:20 — 238n2:43

Mark

Gospel of — 16, 20, 42–44, 148
1:12–13 — 238n2:37
1:21–27 — 239n2:106
1:22 — 239n4:5
1:24 — 235n1:13
1:33–34 — 16
1:35 — 237n2:17
1:36–42 — 239n4:7
1:41 — 237n2:26
2:1–7 — 238n2:42
3:21 — 239n2:94
3:31–35 — 240n5:11
4:21 — 237n2:25
4:41 — 21
5:6 — 236n1:62, 244n9:29
6:3 — 237n2:1, n2:14, n2:18, 240n5:20
6:3–4 — 240n5:11
6:6 — 237n2:23
6:46 — 237n2:17
7:1–23 — 239n2:109
7:20 — 241n6:22
8:31 — 242n7:3
8:34–35 — 241n6:30
9:12 — 240n4:17
9:16–21 — 237n2:21
9:31 — 242n7:3
9:43–48 — 247n12:13
10:17–18 — 19
10:25 — 238n2:65
10:33–34 — 242n7:3
10:45 — 241n6:47
12:41–44 — 237n2:28
13:26 — 235n1:25
14:22–25 — 241n6:37
14:32–34 — 238n2:87
14:53, 54, 60, 61, 63 — 242n7:13
14:55–56 — 236n1:38
14:61–64 — 21
14:62–64 — 235n1:25
15:40 — 238n2:87
15:40, 47 — 242n7:29
16:1 — 242n7:29

Luke

Gospel of — 37, 48, 85, 100, 103, 208
1–2 — 238n2:47
1:26–38 — 92
1:38 — 240n5:30
1:46–47 — 240n5:15

Reference	Pages
2:1–7	59
2:11	181, 245n10:3
2:22–24	240n5:16
2:25–27	60
2:28–30	245n10:4
2:41	237n2:30
2:51	237n2:15
2:52	237n2:13
3	70
3:16	238n2:48
3:21–22	238n2:49
4	236n1:37
4:1–2	238n2:50
4:1–13	238n2:37, 241n6:46
4:12	236n1:75
4:14	238n2:51
4:16	237n2:16
4:18	238n2:52, 246n11:35
4:23	246n11:34
4:26	246n11:24
4:33–34	16
4:40–41	16
5:20–21	25
5:31	246n11:34
6:20	246n11:35
7:9	237n2:23
7:12–13	246n11:22
7:13	237n2:26
7:36–50	246n11:26
7:47	241n6:38
7:48	25
8:1–3	246n11:28
8:19–21	240n5:11
8:40–56	246n11:23
10:21	238n2:53
10:21–24	237n2:24
10:38–39	246n11:27
10:38–42	246n11:25
11:13	238n2:54
11:19–21	239n4:14
11:42	238n2:70
12:2–3, 47–48	247n12:12
12:12	238n2:55
12:40	247n12:9
12:46–48	247n12:13
13:10–17	246n11:23
13:23–25	245n10:20
16:13	194
16:19–31	123, 152, 243n8:13, 247n12:13
16:22	242n6:54
18:1–5	246n11:24
18:9–14	241n6:38
18:25	238n2:65
19:10	77, 245n10:8
19:11–27	72
19:17	247n12:25
19:17–19	247n12:23
19:28, 35–38	60
19:41	238n2:90
20:47	247n12:12
21:1–4	246n11:24
21:27	235n1:25
22:19–20	241n6:37
22:44	239n2:96
22:69	235n1:25
23:22	236n1:47
23:27–31	246n11:25
23:33	62
23:34	239n2:98
23:41	236n1:49
23:43	242n6:53
23:46	63, 239n2:97
23:47	236n1:48, 239n2:103
24:27, 44–45	239n3:4
24:36–43	242n7:11
24:39	237n2:12
24:44	55
24:46–47	242n6:55

John

Reference	Pages
Gospel of	73, 75
1:1	28
1:1, 14	239n4:6
1:1–4, 14	236n1:75
1:3	28
1:3	238n2:44
1:9	236n1:77
1:14	50, 172, 239n2:100, 240n5:36, 245n9:44
1:14, 18	240n5:34, 240n5:35
1:15	235n1:17
1:18	237n1:86
1:29	241n6:20, 245n9:47
1:29, 36	241n6:37
2:12	240n5:11
2:14–17	239n2:107
2:18–22	242n7:3
2:19–22	245n9:45
3:13	235n1:17
3:16	102m 115, 237n1:86
3:16, 18	240n5:34, n5:35
3:34	239n4:1
3:35	243n8:21
4	166
4:7	237n2:20
4:7–26	246n11:21
4:34	239n4:1
4:42	237n1:82
5:16–30	243n7:39
5:17–18	236n1:75
5:17–23	236n1:36
5:18	235n1:23
5:19–29	247n12:10
5:19–30	237n1:87
5:23, 24, 30, 36, 37, 38	239n4:1
5:36–40	239n3:2
5:39–47	239n3:3
6:29, 38, 39, 44, 57	239n4:1
6:38	73, 235n1:15
6:41–66	235n1:16
6:46	237n1:86
6:62	243n8:4
7:3, 5, 10	240n5:11
7:5	239n2:94, 242n7:16
7:16, 28, 29, 33	239n4:1
8:16, 18, 28, 29, 42	239n4:1
8:28	237n1:87
8:41	240n5:20
8:44	238n2:69
8:46	236n1:41, 239n2:102, 241n6:12
8:58	235n1:17, 236n1:75
8:58–59	22, 236n1:36
9:4	239n4:1
9:38	236n1:61, 244n9:28
10:17–18	241n6:26
10:18	241n6:15
10:19–21	235n1:12
10:30–33	22, 236n1:75
10:30–39	236n1:36
10:33	11
10:36	239n4:1
10:36b–39	20
11	128
11:3–5	237n2:27
11:25	127, 247n12:20
11:33	240n4:19
11:34	237n2:21
11:35	238n2:90
11:42	239n4:1
11:47	235n1:27
12:6	238n2:80
12:20–28	241n6:34

12:27 240n4:19
12:27–28 107
12:31 241n6:46
12:37–41 236n1:75
12:38–41 235n1:20
12:41 236n1:64, 243n8:7, 244n9:26, n9:31
12:44, 45, 49 239n4:1
12:49 237n1:87
13:13 235n1:17
13:20 239n4:1
13:21 237n2:22, 240n4:19
13:30–32 241n6:34
13:34–35 246n11:44
14:2–3 243n8:26
14:2, 12 243n8:4
14:3 247n12:1
14:6 26, 154, 245n10:21, 247n12:20
14:13–14 236n1:52
14:24 239n4:1
15:11 237n2:24
15:12–13 241n6:18
15:16 236n1:52
15:21 239n4:1
16:5 239n4:1
16:5, 10, 28 243n8:4
16:11 241n6:46
16:24 236n1:52
16:28 147, 243n8:12
16:33 243n8:37
17:1 241n6:34
17:3 237n1:86
17:3, 8, 18, 21, 23, 25 239n4:1
17:5, 24 244n9:22
17:13 237n2:24
17:15, 24 235n1:17
18:34 237n2:21
18:36–37 78
19:7 236n1:36
19:19 241n6:5
19:23–24 62
19:26–27 237n2:32
19:28 237n2:20
19:30 242n6:51
19:32–36 63
19:34 239n2:96
19:34–35 144, 242n7:5
20:10–18 246n11:25
20:17 242n7:9, 243n8:4
20:19 242n7:24
20:20–28 242n7:10
20:21 239n4:1
20:24–28 243n7:43
20:28 236n1:63, 244n9:30
20:30–31 236n1:33

Acts
Book of 37, 38, 139, 157
1 238n2:56
1:1–3 243n8:10
1:5 239n3:11
1:8, 22 244n8:42
1:9–11 235n1:25, 243n8:11
1:10 241n6:25
1:11 151, 247n12:2
1:13–14 240n5:31
1:14 236n1:70, 240n5:11, n5:22, 242n7:20, n7:21, 244n9:37, n9:38
2 238n2:57
2:23–47 242n6:55
2:25–32 64
2:33–36 243n8:19
2:42–47 247n12:47
3:14 236n1:42
3:22–24 239n4:3

4:12 245n10:18
4:27 242n7:33
5:30–31 245n10:5
7:54–60 242n7:22
7:59 25
7:59–60 236n1:53
8:7 235n1:31
9 242n7:23
9:37–41 235n1:31
10:36 243n8:21
10:42 247n12:10
10:43 241n6:38
12:17 242n7:19
13:26–39 242n6:55
13:33 243n8:35
15:12–21 242n7:19
20:7 242n7:26
20:28 236n1:75
21:18 242n7:19
26:16 244n8:42
26:18 241n6:46

Romans
Epistle to 30
1:9 244n8:42
1:20 243n8:27
1:21–25 244n9:5
2:5 219, 245n10:17
2:5–7 247n12:12
2:6–11 247n12:23
3:5 245n10:17
3:23 240n5:14, 241n6:13
3:23–25 241n6:21, n6:37
3:24 241n6:38
3:25–26 241n6:33
4:5, 23 241n6:38
4:5–6 241n6:48
4:24–25 242n6:55
4:25 115
5:8 115
5:8–10 241n6:37
5:9 241n6:21, 245n10:17, n10:15
5:9–10 245n10:16
5:10–11 241n6:45
5:12–21 240n5:12
5:16 241n6:38
5:17–19 241n6:48
5:18 241n6:40
6:4 171
6:6 241n6:40
6:14 241n6:46
6:23 241n6:11, 247n12:27
7:1–5 241n6:43
7:4 241n6:46
8:1 241n6:41, 247n12:23
8:1–4 241n6:40
8:2, 20–23, 37–39 241n6:46
8:3 51
8:12–23 246n11:19
8:19–21 243n8:28
9:5 30, 236n1:73, n1:75, 245n9:40
10:4 241n6:48
10:8 241n6:38
10:9–13 238n2:45
10:13 245n10:10
11:33–36 241n6:36
11:36–12:1 166
12:1 178
14:1–12 247n12:23
16:20 240n5:37, n5:43

1 Corinthians
1:2 236n1:69, 244n9:36
1:7–2:5 241n6:36
1:18 241n6:29
1:30 241n6:48

2:8	236n1:75, 237n1:83
4:4	236n1:75
4:5	247n12:23
6:3	243n8:22
6:20	244n9:23
7:3–5	240n5:10
8:4–6	236n1:75
8:6	30, 235n1:17
9:5	237n2:14, 240n5:11
9:20–24	241n6:43
10:4	236n1:78
10:20–22	197
10:31	244n9:23
11:14–15a	237n2:3
11:23–25	241n6:37
15	131, 151, 226, 243n8:25
15:1–4	242n6:55
15:1–6	243n7:46
15:3	115
15:3–4	134, 241n6:32
15:3–8	243n8:10
15:7	242n7:17
15:35–58	247n12:28
15:36–41	247n12:29
15:42–44	247n12:30
15:45–49	247n12:31
15:47	235n1:17
15:50	247n12:32
15:51–57	247n12:33
16:1–2	242n7:26

2 Corinthians

4:4	238n2:41
8:9	238n2:79
5:1–8	243n8:24
5:9–10	247n12:23
5:14–21	241n6:49, 242n6:56
5:18–21	241n6:45
5:21	236n1:45, 239n2:102, 240n4:18, n5:17, 241n6:14, n6:48, 242n6:52
11:3–4	12, 241n6:32

Galatians

1:6–9, 11–12, 15–17	241n6:32
1:19	240n5:11
2:9	242n7:19
3:13	115, 241n6:42
3:16	240n5:44
4:1–7	246n11:19
4:4	57, 103, 237n2:11, 240n5:2
5:11	241n6:29

Ephesians

1:3–14	241n6:35
1:5	246n11:19
1:18–23	245n10:28
1:19–22	244n8:41
1:20–22	243n8:19
1:22	243n8:21
2:1	241n6:11
2:1–3	194
2:6	155
2:8–9	240n4:20, 247n12:21
2:10	240n4:21, 247n12:22
2:12	243n8:36
2:15	241n6:43
2:16	241n6:45
4:7–10	64
4:8	152
4:8–10	123
5:2	241n6:37
5:6	245n10:17
5:19–20	244n9:1
5:23	245n10:6
5:28–33	236n1:79

6:10–13	243n8:23

Philippians

Epistle to	38, 178
1:20–25	247n12:43
2:5–6	239n2:100
2:5–8	241n6:49
2:5–11	37
2:6	29
2:7	237n1:85
2:8	241n6:15
2:10–11	236n1:75, 238n2:46
3:4–6	242n7:22
3:9	241n6:48
3:20	243n8:36, 245n10:23, 247n12:44

Colossians

1:12–14	244n8:40
1:13	241n6:46
1:13–17	241n6:44
1:15	236n1:73, 245n9:40
1:16	238n2:44
1:16–17	28, 199, 236n1:75
1:17–18	243n8:21
1:22	241n6:45
2:8–9	236n1:75
2:9	236n1:73, 239n2:100, 245n9:40
2:13	241n6:11
2:13–15	241n6:44, 242n6:52, 245n10:28
2:14–23	241n6:43
3:6	245n10:17
3:16	244n9:1
3:25	247n12:23

1 Thessalonians

1:9–10	241n6:21
1:10	245n10:17
4:16	247n12:3
4:17	235n1:25

2 Thessalonians

2:6–10	245n10:14

1 Timothy

1:15–17	245n10:9
1:17	29, 37
2:3–4	233
2:5	154, 238n2:38, 239n4:9
2:5–6	241n6:47
2:8	245n9:50
6:15	236n1:75

2 Timothy

1:9	235n1:17
1:10	245n10:13
4:1	247n12:10

Titus

2:11–14	245n10:23
2:12–13	247n12:8
2:12–14	243n8:39
2:13	184, 236n1:73, n1:75, 245n9:40
2:14	237n1:81, 241n6:24, n6:39

Philemon

10–19	246n11:31

Hebrews

Epistle to	76, 241n6:20, 245n9:43
1:2	238n2:44
1:3	65, 243n8:19
1:6	236n1:68, 244n9:35

1:8	236n1:75
2:2	241n6:35
2:10	52, 171
2:14	240n5:43
2:14–15	241n6:39, n6:46
2:17	29, 51
2:18	238n2:37
3:1	239n4:8, 245n9:46
4:14	239n4:8
4:15	51, 238n2:37, 239n2:102,
	n2:104, 240n5:17, 241n6:12
4:15–16	78
5:5	243n8:35
5:5–6	235n1:17
5:7–9	53
5:8–9	52
5:9	53, 239n2:105
7:9	241n6:37
7:25	154, 239n4:11
7:26	239n2:102, 241n6:12
7:26–27	51
9:11–28	241n6:37
9:12	241n6:39
9:14	241n6:24
9:26	239n4:10
9:28	247n12:7
10:10, 12	241n6:37
10:12	243n8:19
10:14	52
11:5	247n12:45
11:17	240n5:33
12:1	161
12:1–2	243n8:19
12:2	241n6:15
12:2, 22	237n2:24
2:17	241n6:21
13:8	235n1:17
13:20	237n1:80

James
Epistle of	236n1:71, 244n9:38
1:1	242n7:18
1:13	36
1:14	54
4:7	243n8:23
5:6	236n1:44
5:8	247n12:4

1 Peter
1:18–19	241n6:37, n6:39
1:19	236n1:42, 239n2:102
1:20	235n1:17
2:6–8	236n1:78
2:19–25	241n6:49
2:21–22	59
2:22	236n1:42, 241n6:12
2:24	107, 241n6:40, n6:48
3:18	115, 236n1:42, 241n6:45,
	n6:48
3:22	243n8:19
5:8	243n8:23

2 Peter
1:1	236n1:75
3:9–10	218–19
3:10	247n12:5
3:12–13	243n8:29

1 John
Epistle of	32
1:5	241n6:9
1:5–8	241n6:37
1:7–9	241n6:23
1:7–22	241n6:38
1:8	236n1:43, 241n6:13
2:2	115, 241n6:21

3:2	247n12:6
3:5	236n1:43, 239n2:102
3:16	241n6:49
4:2	239n2:100
4:2–3	240n5:36
4:9–10	116
4:9–11	241n6:49
4:10	241n6:21
4:14	245n10:7
5:20	236n1:75

2 John
1:17	240n5:36

Jude
Epistle of	134, 236n1:71, 244n9:38
1	242n7:21

Revelation
Book of	150, 153, 173, 177, 216
1:1	243n8:9
1:5	241n6:37, n6:39
1:7	235n1:25, 247n12:6
1:8	235n1:17
1:8, 17–18	236n1:75
1:17	236n1:76
1:17–18	236n1:64, 244n9:31
2:8	236n1:76
3:4–5	241n6:25
4	153
4:10–11	173
5	173
5:5	241n6:27
5:9	185, 237n1:81
5:11–13	173
5:12	163
6:11	241n6:25
7:9–14	241n6:25
7:11–12	174
11:18	247n12:23
12	240n5:43
12:9	240n5:37
13:8	235n1:17
14:9–11	247n12:15
14:10	123
14:14	235n1:25
15:2–4	174
15:6	241n6:25
17:14	236n1:75
19:1	174
19:6–9	247n12:46
19:8	241n6:25
19:11–16	150
19:16	236n1:75
20:1–3	245n10:29
20:10	123
20:11–15	123
20:12–13	247n12:12
20:12–15	247n12:24
20:13–14	243n8:13
21:1–2	243n8:30
21:2	236n1:79
21:3	247n12:48
21:22	245n9:45
21:22–23	245n9:42
22:3	247n12:26
22:13	236n1:76
22:13–16	236n1:75
22:20	247n12:6, n12:8
22:20b	215